Jazz Diplomacy

Jazz Diplomacy

Promoting America in the Cold War Era

Lisa E. Davenport

UNIVERSITY PRESS OF MISSISSIPPI   JACKSON

www.upress.state.ms.us

The University Press of Mississippi is a member
of the Association of American University Presses.

First printing 2009

Library of Congress Cataloging-in-Publication Data

Davenport, Lisa E.
    Jazz diplomacy : promoting America in the Cold War era / Lisa E.
Davenport.
        p. cm. — (American made music series)
        Includes bibliographical references and index.
        ISBN 978-1-60473-268-9 (cloth : alk. paper) 1. Jazz—Political
aspects—United States—History—20th century. 2. Cold War—Social
aspects—United States. 3. United States—Foreign relations—20th
century. I. Title.
        ML3918.J39D38 2009
        781.650973'0947—dc22   2009005135

British Library Cataloging-in-Publication Data available

Contents

Abbreviations

ANTA	American National Theater Academy
CU	Bureau of Educational and Cultural Affairs
CPP	Cultural Presentations Program
NARA	National Archives and Records Administration
USIS	United States Information Service
USIA	United States Information Agency

Jazz Diplomacy

Introduction

In January 1965 Jazz Night at the Blue Bird Youth Café in Moscow was in full swing. Soviet club managers closely monitored the club's clientele, and audiences were carefully selected by Soviet cultural authorities. Those attending included U.S. cultural attaché Ernest G. Weiner, who had visited Jazz Night with a select group of people at the invitation of a Soviet friend. Weiner characterized the café as though it had a mystical aura. He commented that it was ensconced "on a narrow and dimly lit street" and gave "practically no outward indication of its existence." It was especially alluring "at night" when "the small white globe light over the entranceway d[id] not even illuminate a perfunctory 'Kafe' sign nearby on the wall of the building."[1]

Inside, however, Western influence abounded. A young Russian trumpeter played with an "upturned bell a la Gillespie." Such developments attested to the enduring impact of American jazz on Soviet culture and society. Jazz imbued the Soviet bloc with unique and bold American values, and in the 1960s several American officials reported on the ubiquitous presence of jazz in many Soviet bloc cities.[2] Ultimately, the proliferation of jazz in the Soviet Union and Eastern Europe helped determine the course of the Cold War cultural rivalry between the superpowers. Benny Goodman's State Department tour to the Soviet Union in 1962 was critical in shaping this rivalry and emerged as a global symbol of the U.S.-Soviet cultural thaw that briefly came about in the early 1960s.

Such American cultural tours first became possible in 1954—a watershed year in U.S. domestic and foreign affairs. In July 1954 President Dwight D. Eisenhower, seeing it as a Cold War imperative, called for the creation of a worldwide cultural exchange program for the performing arts to improve the world's perception of American cultural and political life. As Nicholas Cull has deftly shown, cultural diplomacy became part of an expansive American effort to invest the P factor—the "psychological dimension of power"—to wage the Cold War.[3] Cull's pivotal work offers an authoritative history of the USIA, its informational and cultural initiatives, and its vital impact on the course of Cold War diplomacy. Cull explains in the preface that public diplomacy—"an international actor's attempt to conduct its foreign policy by engaging with foreign publics" involved five "core practices—listening, advocacy, cultural diplomacy, exchange diplomacy, and international broadcasting."[4] At the same time, with *Brown v. Board of Education*, the United States ended its legally sanctioned system of racial segregation, the culmination of legal efforts to end segregation since the end of Reconstruction in 1877. *Brown* symbolized the flourishing of liberal ideas with regard to race. Thereafter, hundreds of performing artists traveled around the globe as representatives of the U.S. government. At this critical moment in Cold War history, jazz diplomacy profoundly helped reshape perceptions of the American identity throughout the world.[5]

This book explores how American jazz as an instrument of global diplomacy dramatically transformed superpower relations in the Cold War era as jazz reshaped the American image worldwide. It tells the story of jazz diplomacy with the Soviet Union and other regions of the world from 1954 to 1968, revealing that these years represent a critical arc in the superpowers' cultural rivalry. Like Nicholas Cull's *The Cold War and USIA*, it underscores the centrality of Western cultural forces in diminishing the credibility and appeal of Soviet Communism in the Eastern bloc through the use of public diplomacy, especially after the Geneva Summit in 1955. Like Walter Hixson's *Parting the Curtain*, it presents a cultural approach to diplomacy. This study also exemplifies how jazz diplomacy dramatically influenced perceptions of the United States as a democracy as it eased U.S.-Soviet political tensions in the midst of critical Cold War events: the Little Rock crisis, the dispute over the Berlin Wall, the Cuban missile crisis, the Vietnam War, and the Soviet invasion of Czechoslovakia. In addition, like Penny Von Eschen's *Satchmo Blows Up the World*, it portrays jazz as a pivotal Cold War trope and emphasizes that jazz diplomacy reflects the United States' symbolic acknowledgment that the dual problems of race and culture had to be addressed in a global context.[6]

But unlike Von Eschen, it argues that ultimately the problem of culture and jazz diplomacy in American foreign policy had to be addressed apart from worldwide economic and military exigencies that had arisen during this era. Even in the midst of critical Cold War disputes, jazz diplomacy existed in a realm that often transcended economic and strategic priorities. Jazz often became the subject of heated debates about aesthetic agency and cultural property. Moreover, the goal of containing Communism remained paramount in shaping the course of jazz diplomacy and prevailed over America's policy of redefining relations with emerging new nations in Africa, Asia, and Latin

America. The United States addressed the issues of race and jazz in a global context only to align its cultural policies with its anti-Communist agenda—to win the Cold war, counter Soviet cultural propaganda, and defeat Communism.

Jazz diplomacy thus remained steeped in both America's cultural realism and its cultural idealism. It became a unique and enigmatic instrument of ideological and intellectual warfare. In the midst of cultural tours that included high culture, science, technology, athletic groups, and many other American cultural products, jazz held a unique place in American cultural policy. As the United States propelled jazz into new international arenas, jazz diplomacy transformed relations between nations and created a bold Cold War paradox: the cultural expression of one of the nation's most oppressed minorities came to symbolize the cultural superiority of American democracy.

The American Image Abroad

As jazz diplomacy played a pivotal role in recontextualizing the U.S.-Soviet cultural rivalry, jazz tours reflected aspects of the cultural and political revolution occurring in the United States of which jazz musicians took part.[7] During the "Americanized Century," the world increasingly scrutinized the American image as the nation wrestled to redefine its racial and cultural identity. As white Americans celebrated freedoms conceded by postwar prosperity, black Americans still lived under a system of legal apartheid; and the idea of race, always central to the American character, arose as a controversial dimension of Cold War diplomacy. This phenomenon resulted from what W. E. B. DuBois, a premier black activist and intellectual, identified as "the problem of the twentieth century"—the "color line."[8] The United States could not ignore the paradox of race on the world stage because it undermined its ability to counter Soviet cultural initiatives and promote cultural understanding between nations.

Concepts of race and culture throughout the centuries deeply influenced perceptions of the American character at home and abroad. In this vein, the idea of white racial superiority has defined American history and culture since European explorers first encountered the shores of North America. Importantly, the direction of domestic and international affairs frequently changed, and, as Allison Blakely has deftly shown, by the seventeenth-century colonial era in North America, the "stigmatization of blackness" had become a central tenet of Western tradition and thought. Slavery defined the American moral character and became a reflection of its core belief system. Such historians as John Hope Franklin have illuminated that "two worlds of race" began to emerge. Even as the American Revolution surged, the fledgling United States briefly embarked on "international image making" to justify its policies to the world.[9] Race in this context did not compel American leaders to alter domestic or international policies because they did not recognize blacks as American citizens.[10]

At home and abroad, views of American society became redefined in the era of nineteenth-century abolitionism. With the rise of England's predominance in world affairs and shared Anglo-Saxon ideals, the United States further justified maintaining a legalized system of slavery and racial apartheid. Only the United States and Spain had not outlawed slavery by the middle of the century. It was not until the age of the Civil War and Reconstruction and its aftermath that many white Americans endorsed legally sanctioning black citizenship and equality as a national imperative.[11]

In the late nineteenth and early twentieth centuries, as social Darwinism provided the theoretical foundations for Western expansion, an American empire began to emerge. After the tumultuous culmination of two world wars, and amid the rising tide of independence movements and black freedom struggles, many American leaders grappled with the question of how to reconcile the celebration of democratic values and political and civil liberties with entrenched ideas of white racial superiority. As the civil rights movement began, the United States reexamined its legal obligation to enforce and protect the rights granted to black Americans by the Thirteenth, Fourteenth, and Fifteenth amendments to the Constitution. With the decision in *Brown v. Board of Education* in 1954 and the passage of the Civil Rights Act of 1964 and the Voting Rights Act of 1965, this obligation became vigorously tested. Racial violence and oppression persisted, and the world assessed the American image at home and abroad by how well the United States upheld and enforced civil rights for African American citizens.[12] The enforcement of racial justice consequently became a benchmark by which the Soviet Union and the world measured America's wealth, potential, and power.

Thus the American image during the Cold War differed from its image in previous eras in significant ways. First, in the midst of the rise of the superpower rivalry, the United States became the world's dominant political, economic, and cultural power and in part sought to maintain its global supremacy through cultural means. Most significant, it aimed to thwart Soviet power and to defeat international Communism, which, in American eyes, represented a threat to the survival of all free peoples. Second, it was the era of nuclear weapons—of "hard power." Appreciably, the world of ideas—"soft power"—held significance in ways it had not in the past. Third, as civil rights and black liberation movements burgeoned at home, rapid decolonization in Africa and Asia drastically changed geopolitical realities between the superpowers. These developments changed the contours of international relations in the twentieth century. At no other time had the United States confronted both Communism and the "color line" in this complex international context.[13]

As the United States grappled to devise policies to keep neutral countries from "going Communist," Cold War competition necessitated conveying sympathy, not disdain, for the very same values the United States often subverted at home: healthy race relations and the sanctity of civil liberties. Moreover, America had to buttress its racial and cultural image to maintain credibility among the declining colonial powers of Britain, France, Spain, Portugal, Belgium, and the Netherlands.[14]

Toward this end, and to foster the idea that America had a robust and resilient culture despite prevalent racial conflicts, the United States began to appropriate black cultural products, most notably jazz, in cultural tours. Policy makers argued that American democracy made such creativity possible and that jazz, a uniquely American art form, was a critical reflection of America's cultural exuberance. In building upon the cultural dynamics of the Cold War struggle, and by employing jazz to exemplify U.S. race relations as a positive feature of American life, American Cold Warriors redefined the global policy of cultural containment. Jazz became another instrument in the effort to "contain" criticism about America's cultural and racial identity. Yet as jazz also symbolized integration and the country's emergence from colony to nationhood, the paradigm of race and culture shifted during the Cold War. Blacks once seen as "separate but equal" began to signify the ideal of American nationhood. Theoretically, racial equality and integration became emblematic of American democracy. As Ingrid Monson points out, this dynamic reflected the arch of modernity in Western thought that embraced "transcendence, universality, freedom, autonomy, subjectivity, and progress." Modernity broadly refers to "the expansive sense of Western thought since the Enlightenment."

In the realm of civil rights, this meant "political democracy, equality before the law, and individual freedom." At the same time, aesthetic modernism incorporated a set of "ideas about form and content, abstraction, individuality, iconoclasm, rebellion, the autonomy of art, authenticity, progress, and genius."[15]

Jazz diplomacy also became significant to many U.S. officials who remained increasingly aware that black leaders and intellectuals helped transform worldwide perceptions of American society. Most notably, DuBois, whom biographer David Levering Lewis characterizes as an intellectual powerhouse, galvanized some of the most prominent black intellectuals who critiqued race relations. Henry Louis Gates Jr. has discussed how these intellectuals represented those whom DuBois would call the "Talented Tenth."[16]

Although modernist ideals abounded in theory, in practice, these ideals had not yet been realized for African Americans. Not surprisingly, DuBois and other black intellectuals denounced Western imperialism, and numerous black artists and musicians supported their cause. In 1949 Paul Robeson, another pivotal African American intellectual—who was also an accomplished singer—wrote an article in the Soviet journal *Sovetskaia Muzyka* in which he expressed the view that black American spirituals played a significant role in invigorating both Soviet and world cultures.[17] Robeson was one of the most celebrated African American artists in the Soviet Union. Revered by the Soviet people, he and other black activists periodically traveled to the Soviet Union and identified with many aspects of Soviet culture and life.

Beginning in the 1930s, and throughout World War II, African American activists like Robeson and such notable cultural figures as boxer Joe Louis avidly championed the cause of black liberation at home and abroad, especially after the Italian invasion of Ethiopia in 1935. Elliot P. Skinner has pointed out that they especially recognized that "African peoples intend to bring their own brick to the construction of a universal civilization."[18]

With the onset of McCarthyism and the intensification of the U.S.-Soviet Cold War rivalry, however, new Cold War exigencies, beginning in 1947 with the enunciation of the Truman Doctrine and the Marshall Plan, transformed the American approach to Communism and the color line. After 1947, in the name of anti-Communism, black activists had to adopt an anti-Communist tone and denounce countries and causes that they had previously supported. The robust and vocal protests against discrimination at home and abroad underwent attack and curtailment, and as the Cold War intensified in the early 1950s, many white Americans abundantly decried Robeson and DuBois. By the mid-1950s, to voice appropriate political protest, activists had to forego criticism of race and anti-Communism. Ideas of social advancement, ideological supremacy, and the exceptionalism of American democratic traditions became the only suitable themes for public debate. Moreover, the American Cold War establishment increasingly defined the American race problem as an anomalous, unusual dynamic in American society. Race officially became interpreted as an arcane national issue rather than the impetus for international change.[19]

Black intellectuals, nevertheless, dramatically redefined the idea of race in a global context during the postwar years. In 1948 DuBois illuminated his idea of race when he declared: "I came then to advocate, not pride of biological race, but pride in a cultural group, integrated and expanded by cultural ideals."[20] Years earlier, in 1911, black intellectual Alain Locke had described how the idea of race shaped political thinking in the United States. Seeking to refute social Darwinism and biological theories of white racial superiority put forth by such racial theorists as Arthur Comte de Goubineau in *The Inequality of Human Races*, Locke asserted that "any true [theory] of race must be a sociological theory of race."[21] Such a theory must describe the different stages of a nation's or a people's social and cultural development by applying uniform philosophical criteria to different groups when analyzing their evolution. Employing similar criteria precluded the perpetuation of cultural biases that might lead to an assessment of the cultural superiority or inferiority of one group of people in relation to another.[22]

Locke presented the idea of race as a cultural and historical construct. The idea of race, he asserted, emerged when a particular group's external biological differences led them to have a common historical experience. Such experiences gave rise to what he called a "sense of kin." In this way, Locke implied that the idea of race actually represented a common historical experience among a social or ethnic group, and he claimed that racial difference based on biological attributes was a fallacy. Race actually constituted a social experience that "parade[d] itself as biological inheritance."[23] Locke, also a professor of philosophy at Howard University during the Harlem Renaissance, emphatically defined race in terms of culture and nationhood. Foreshadowing DuBois, he asserted that culture illuminated an "unconscious set of rules, reflexes, and attitudes" that determined "the social etiquette of race relations." For him, America's diverse culture in particular reflected "the promise of American democracy. Race becomes a tool for understanding the highest aspirations and potentials of the American character. Race is a constitutive force of American identity."[24]

Similarly, a variety of scholars helped inaugurate a philosophical shift in national racial attitudes between the wars. As political prejudice in Europe escalated, culminating in the emergence of nazism, scientific racism was discredited by scholars in the natural and social sciences. Yet racism toward blacks persisted in the United States. In 1944, near the end of World War II, as European empires crumbled, Swedish sociologist Gunnar Myrdal succinctly expounded upon the problem of race in America and elaborated on the prospect of forging black equality in the American context. In his pivotal study, *An American Dilemma*, in which he thoroughly documented political, economic, and social discrimination against black Americans, he concisely argued that white Americans would eventually embrace the idea of racial equality. His work repudiated America's racial ideology as irrational and gave significant impetus to efforts to dismantle segregation in the United States.[25] International acceptance of ideas of racial equality and black citizenship gained momentum during the Cold War, and desegregation in America progressed further. As various theories emerged to illustrate that race was a social and cultural construct, black intellectuals reexamined the ways in which race remained an integral component of American culture, and new "racial" experiences played a critical role in influencing black American cultural activities abroad.

Culture, Internationalism, and the American Ethos

The "worldview" of Americans and their conception of "self" and of society remained critical for American officials in their efforts to reconstruct the image of America's cultural and racial life. With the intensification of the superpower rivalry, the U.S. government hoped that redefining the nation's identity abroad—by depicting positive images of America in cultural tours—would highlight analogous developments in American society. In the 1970s anthropologist Clifford Geertz characterized a nation's and a people's ethos as the tone, character, and quality of . . . life, its moral and aesthetic style and mood; . . . the underlying attitude toward themselves and their world that life reflects. Their world view is their picture of the way things in sheer reality actually are, their concept of nature, of self, of society. It contains their most comprehensive ideas of order. . . . The world is made emotionally acceptable by being presented as an image of an actual state of affairs of which such a way of life is an authentic expression.[26]

Jazz was often presented abroad as an "authentic expression" of American life. This effort to use culture to portray the country's changing Cold War ethos represented a form of cultural internationalism—one of the most pivotal elements of the Cold War cultural struggle. Cultural internationalism occurred when "[i]ndividuals and groups of people from different lands . . . sought to develop an alternative community of nations and peoples on the basis of their cultural interchanges. . . . [T]heir efforts have significantly altered the world community and immeasurably enriched our understanding of international affairs. [Cultural internationalism is] [t]he inspiration behind these endeavors and the sum of their achievements."[27] In this international context, official person-to-person contacts between nations strikingly redefined the American ethos.[28]

Jazz and "Cultural Containment"

Containing the criticism of America that emanated from the jarring, trenchant propaganda that the Soviet Union disseminated throughout the world became central to American cultural efforts. Although Soviet elites held complex views of the United States, ranging from cultural reverence, envy, curiosity, and admiration to boldfaced ideological mistrust, the fear and anxiety created by U.S. actions against Japan at the end of World War II, along with the onset of tensions that gave rise to the Cold War, gave impetus to strident anti-Americanism in Soviet foreign policy. Soviet imperial ambitions distinctly shaped these international efforts. The Soviet Union characterized Americans as racist and segregationist and criticized American culture as decadent, amoral, materialist, and individualistic. By 1950 the Soviet Union had initiated a "Hate America" campaign.[29] Soviet propaganda highlighted the fact that the United States protected democratic rights for whites, while it violently denied those rights to African Americans. Thus racial discrimination in the United States pointedly damaged the

American position in the global struggle against Communism. As cultural policy makers devised jazz policy through the paradigm of the U.S.-Soviet cultural rivalry, racialist thinking in jazz diplomacy unavoidably arose. For example, after the independence of French West Africa in 1960, when Africa became a more critical focal point of the Cold War cultural struggle, race conflicts in the United States complicated American cultural efforts to counter the Soviet Union's worldwide cultural offensive, even in Eastern Europe.

Additionally, Soviet cultural initiatives were far-flung. The Soviets reportedly sponsored three times as many cultural exchanges around the world as the United States did in the 1950s and 1960s; it also signed cultural agreements with countries in every geographic region of the world, including the United States in 1958. Through cultural relations, the Soviet Union attempted to engender in other peoples sympathy for Communist politics and ideology. Through the mass media, the performing arts, education, science, and technology, the Soviet Union aspired to portray appealing aspects of Soviet socialism to sway independent nations to support Communist regimes—targeting decolonizing nations in Africa, Asia, and the Middle East. In Soviet ideology, colonial revolution symbolized the weakening of capitalist imperialism and the imminent demise of the West. And some outspoken Soviets viewed jazz as the music of the class struggle—through jazz, subjugated black lower classes struggled for self-expression and autonomy from capitalist oppressors.[30]

In the midst of this vast Soviet effort, McCarthyism, a xenophobic effort to fight the Communist enemy within by restructuring American culture and society, exacerbated the struggle for racial equality in the United States. McCarthyism bred fears of Communist subversion in America, sweeping away common sense and subverting principles of democracy for the sake of Cold War competition. America's phobic reaction to Communism permeated every arena of American life, from religious worship to Hollywood movies, from the mass media to fiction writing. Americans feared World War III and massive nuclear destruction by the Soviet Union. Such fears, so eloquently outlined by Paul Boyer in *By the Bomb's Early Light*, transformed the American mind, altered the American character, and permeated the country's cultural ethos in cartoons, songs, books, movies, and music. Americanism—an ideology of affluence, patriotism, and free enterprise, accompanied by a belief in authority that would preserve traditional

American values—likewise dominated the minds of white Americans.[31]

Working through such forums as the House Un-American Activities Committee (HUAC), McCarthyism denounced all criticism of legal, social, and economic inequalities in the United States. Paradoxically, sympathy for civil rights signified Communist subversion and threatened the stability the United States had worked so hard to achieve. HUAC deemed almost every form of social and cultural activism a product of Bolshevik instigation. Moreover, the Federal Bureau of Investigation (FBI) characterized the entire civil rights movement as Communist inspired. Such sentiments led to the complete suppression of cultural and political norms.[32]

It was in this atmosphere that the American government began to persecute such black artists and intellectuals as Paul Robeson, W. E. B. DuBois, and Josephine Baker—those whom it considered political firebrands. These intellectuals spoke out loudly against McCarthyism and increasingly showed sympathy for the ideals of the Soviet Union. DuBois's evolution toward Communism grew significantly during these years.[33]

How did such developments impinge upon Cold War cultural affairs? In the international arena, culture explicitly became an instrument of the Cold War competition. Yet in the first half of the twentieth century, American cultural relations had reflected a reliance on the concept of "liberal developmentalism." Liberal developmentalism "merged 19th century liberal tenets with the historical experience of America's own development, elevating the beliefs and experiences of America's unique historical time and circumstance into developmental laws thought to be applicable everywhere."[34] Furthermore, it supported the view that others should imitate America's historical experience—the experience of a chosen people. Proponents of liberal developmentalism also advocated free enterprise and the free exchange of cultural products by means of government-sponsored programs and activities.[35]

Thus this approach to cultural affairs changed drastically during the Cold War era. Upon the defeat of the Axis powers, as the U.S. State Department debated how it would conduct diplomacy in the midst of anti-Communist fervor from 1945 to 1954, conflicts between "culturalists" and "informationalists" intensified—these two groups had clashed upon the inception of government-sponsored cultural programs and the establishment of the Division of Cultural Relations in 1938. "Culturalists" discouraged the use of culture for political purposes. They urged that cultural internationalism remain separate from politics. They supported the power of ideas to facilitate understanding among different cultures that were thought to belong to a common "intellectual and moral" universe and which shared common values. Culture served as a unifying influence among people.[36] Contrarily, "informationalists" urged using culture solely as an instrument of Cold War competition—as "kulturpolitik."[37]

In 1947, when the American containment policy began to typify American political thought, the "distinction between politics and ideas" disappeared in American cultural policy. Congress also passed the Smith-Mundt Act of 1948, calling for cultural exchange to oppose the Soviet's Cold War activities. Additionally, American Cold War policy began to target Europe and Asia, the main theaters of cultural competition in the 1940s and early 1950s. By 1950, with the onset of the Korean War, the enunciation of National Security Council (NSC) Paper #68, and the "loss" of China, the United States formalized the "use of idea[s]" to fight the Cold War—to further the goals of the realpolitik.[38] This resulted from pervasive anti-Communism in the American establishment, which thwarted the liberal tradition of internationalism. The United Nations Educational, Scientific, and Cultural Organization (UNESCO) was viewed as an instrument of ideological warfare to help thwart Communist expansion. New cultural rhetoric aspired to mask American realities. This activity culminated with the creation of the United States Information Agency (USIA) in 1953, formed explicitly for the purpose of conducting propaganda activities throughout the world during peacetime. Nonetheless, as Cull points out, the USIA did not seek to adopt an explicitly propagandistic tone when promoting its activities abroad.[39]

Thus in the early 1950s American cultural policy changed in significant ways. First, the State Department expanded cultural activities to a greater number of geographic regions: the Division of Cultural Relations had been created in 1938 specifically to increase cultural contacts with Latin America and to insulate the region culturally from the rising specter of fascism—Hitler, Mussolini, and Japan. Second, the State Department shifted its priorities from cultural to explicitly propaganda purposes with the creation of the USIA. Soviet cultural activities, along with Cold War exigencies in Greece, Turkey, and Korea, prompted by George Kennan's Long Telegram (1946), his X article "Sources of Soviet Conduct" (1947), the Truman Doctrine, and NSC #68, pointed to the use of culture to thwart Communist expansion. Kennan had argued that the United States could use nonmilitary means to contain Soviet expansion, while NSC #68 urged employing "means short of war" toward this end. Culture thus became an explicit component of the American containment policy. Third, the State Department called for the exchange of persons—blacks and whites—in cultural programs, in addition to books, literature, and the media. Cultural programs initially did not include African Americans. This development became central to the evolution of postwar global diplomacy.[40] Fourth, cultural exchanges, which had been sponsored mostly by the private sector, were increasingly sponsored by the U.S. government.

As cultural containment expanded, the influence of McCarthyism—though it lingered in the minds of Americans well into the 1960s—declined when President Dwight D. Eisenhower denounced Senator Joseph McCarthy in 1954. America's Cold War cultural rhetoric simultaneously changed as the course of the Cold War shifted in its focus, scope, and intensity. Frequent racial incidents in the 1950s and the 1960s caused considerable embarrassment for the country and altered official views toward kulturpolitik. Black nationalism worldwide also caused American policy makers to view new black nations with caution and sometimes fear.[41] Never before had American policy makers faced this political paradox: ultimately, race relations reflected a contradiction in American democracy that undermined the nation's ability to implement the policy of cultural containment, inside and outside the world of people of color.

As jazz musicians traveled abroad, the U.S. government, as stated earlier, actively curtailed and censured the activities of some black intellectuals in the domestic and international arena. Significantly, as race, culture, jazz, and global diplomacy became interconnected, American global influence grew increasingly enigmatic. Although internationalist ideals gave impetus to cultural diplomacy, informationalists often prevailed in the State Department's Bureau of Educational and Cultural Affairs (CU) because anti-Communism played the most significant role in forging America's worldwide cultural agenda. The causes of art, jazz, and internationalism did not merge in cultural policy until the late 1960s, when the Soviet Union increasingly showed signs of its impending disunity.

Jazz in the Cold War

Jazz diplomacy poignantly illuminated America's cultural and racial paradoxes on the world stage. Jazz often symbolized black Americans' alienation from American society. Yet, at the same time, it also emerged as a unique symbol of the artistic and cultural dynamism of American democracy. It exposed how "[i]n a culture that lauds whiteness there is yet an attraction and an energy to blackness."[42] Through jazz, the world recognized that what DuBois has called "spiritual strivings" thrived in the midst of white oppression.[43] As American society rendered blacks invisible, jazz men and women carved out their own cultural space, acknowledging that they were not fully accepted as equals in American life. In the words of Ralph Ellison, Louis Armstrong has "made poetry out of being invisible."[44]

As a minority resisting a dominant power through cultural means, some jazz musicians—and often practitioners of rhythm and blues and rock and roll—sometimes played with the principles of cultural nationalism in mind. Others embraced revolutionary nationalism. In short, revolutionary nationalists followed the tenets of Marxism, while cultural nationalists rejected Marxism and "favored African socialism." Both emphasized autonomy and black cultural identity.[45] Jazz's polyrhythms, syncopation, collective improvisation, and melodic lines often emerged in opposition to what musicologist Gunther Schuller calls the "democratization of rhythmic values."[46] Race relations became axiomatic, accentuating a moral tension: jazz challenged its practitioners either to affirm their heritage by struggling against racial oppression or to seek acceptance into white society.[47] This tension in part gave rise to the clearer assertion of a unique black aesthetic in jazz, sometimes resulting in racial unity, and at other times, disunity. It also epitomized the moral dilemma that DuBois put forth in 1903 in *The Souls of Black Folk*, that

> the Negro is a sort of seventh son, born with a veil, and gifted with second-sight in this American world, a world which yields him no true self-consciousness, but only lets him see himself through the revelation of the other world. It is a peculiar sensation, this double-consciousness, this sense of always looking at one's self through the eyes of others, of measuring one's soul by the tape of a world that looks on with amused contempt and pity. One ever feels his twoness—an American, a Negro; two souls, two thoughts, two unreconciled strivings; two warring ideals in one

dark body whose dogged strength alone keeps it from being torn asunder. . . . He simply wishes to make it possible for a man to be both a Negro and an American . . . without having the doors of Opportunity closed roughly in his face. . . . This, then, is the end of his striving: to be a co-worker in the kingdom of culture.[48]

As Monson has shown, the "story of jazz" in the 1950s and 1960s— the "golden age of jazz"—became a story of cultural experimentation and unprecedented aesthetic innovation, set against the backdrop of political and social limits that redefined the country's cultural milieu. Jazz music took on a "set of symbolic meanings" that defined the jazz genre well into the twenty-first century.[49]

Donning the Mask

The revolutionary changes in jazz music paralleled the rise and fall of the American civil rights movement. In the era of civil rights, "the intractable conflicts that emerged over race, leadership, strategy, and policy goals were similar in many respects to the arguments over race, power, aesthetics, and economics that took place in jazz. . . . The civil rights movement and jazz musicians drew from a common set of discourses (or ideas) that shaped the way disputes were conceived and the way in which various constituencies chose to put ideas into practice."[50] A potent symbol of resistance, jazz music "in many ways" became the "sonic alter ego" of the American struggle for racial equality.[51] As American values shifted, many jazz performers saw their music as a means to bring about "social change" and assert "cultural self-determination."[52] Such jazz theorists as Amiri Baraka saw that the political implications of jazz were unavoidable. The musicians themselves asked: Did they hold a place in the postwar world that set them apart? Did the civil rights movement promise them a more secure place in American society?[53] Thus the intermingling of jazz expression and political activism, which characterized jazz's controversial evolution in the twentieth century, reached a critical juncture in the Cold War years.

In the 1920s, after World War I challenged prevalent ideas of the superiority of Western civilization, this struggle for identity and cultural autonomy became fully enunciated in African American art and thought. Black culture, in all of its expressiveness, from literature to music, from dance to drama, from sculpture to the movies, burgeoned into a provocative social movement: the Harlem Renaissance. The Harlem Renaissance saw African Americans embarking upon political, social, and artistic activities with an intensity never before seen, expressions that provided impetus for the musical and artistic activism of the 1950s and 1960s. This was a distinctly modernist tendency indicative of black artists' evolution toward self-redefinition as they pioneered an "imaginative transformation" that transcended international borders.[54] They defined their cause: to be a "public Negro, not merely an [artist], but a credit to his race."[55] Locke himself never believed in art for propaganda's sake. In the 1920s a "Negro artist in the United States live[d] in a peculiar province—a spiritual geography. His art is self-consciously national, while at the same time, special, ethnically, regionally. It attempts to speak with two voices, one from the stage of national culture and the other from the soul of ethnic experience."[56]

Even in the context of segregation in the 1920s, as in the 1950s and 1960s, significant artistic and interracial collaborations took place. But because segregation became entrenched in the American social landscape, the black artist "had to defy whites' eyes, which were too often his eyes as well."[57] As intellectuals, African American artists grappled with the notion of whether art should provide a "moral center" to define themselves. Thus many blacks struggled with the concept of "racial dualism."[58] Trying to overcome racial barriers involved a process of "becoming." For writer Langston Hughes, jazz represented the powerful, expressive art of the black lower classes. Yet a dilemma arose in that some intellectuals believed that in order to "become" American, blacks had to adopt a new culture—a white culture—and leave African American culture behind. They were cut off from their own past and told that they could not partake in the American dream. For Hughes, however, to deny the social distinctions between blacks and whites was to deny the significance of a distinct black experience in the United States rooted in slavery. Blacks continually confronted this tension between race and culture in America, and, in the words of George Hutchinson, they were "mediating race and nation."[59]

In the 1930s, in the aftermath of the Great Depression, black oppression in the United States led to increasingly "revolutionary" tendencies among black artists.[60] During these years—it was the big band era, when swing music overtook the musical landscape at home and abroad—jazz musicians and black artists embraced the idea of "self-determination," a central tenet of the new American Commu-

nist Party.[61] In the 1930s black culture became infused with Communist ideals, making African American culture diverse and profoundly
innovative. Inspired by the Russian Revolution of 1917, some blacks,
including Paul Robeson, traveled to the Soviet Union and embraced
broader international causes. By engaging in cultural activities abroad,
moreover, and in joining the Popular Front against the rising scepter
of fascism, especially in Spain, some black radicals also became active
in the cause of black cultural internationalism.[62] Such activities gave
rise to a nascent "black Marxism" as the "transnational contours of
black expression between the wars . . . was molded through attempts
to center the 'destinies of mankind.'"[63] Such black cultural figures as
the poet and writer Zora Neale Hurston reflected this new black voice
in America's national culture.[64]

As DuBois's and Locke's notion of racial duality became redefined
in the jazz art form itself, jazz criticism emerged with such publications as *Down Beat* and *Metronome*. In the 1930s the foundations of
the formal jazz establishment were laid.[65] In the 1940s World War II
significantly changed the relationship of jazz musicians to American
cultural life as the be-boppers emerged onto Fifty-second Street in
New York City, the heart of the jazz world. The 1920s music of Louis
Armstrong, although still popular, became overshadowed by the new
sounds of such jazz greats as Charlie Parker, Dizzy Gillespie, and Billy
Eckstine.[66]

During the war, be-boppers created new cultural identities with the
zoot suit and the "conk," inspiring a fashionable "hipster culture" that
brought fresh life to the American cultural scene. They were quickly "condemned" for their frivolity and drug use by many in the jazz
establishment and criticized by conservative reactionaries—"moldy
figs"—just as free jazz was later criticized in the 1960s.[67] The war itself
nevertheless helped popularize jazz throughout the world. Swing and
be-bop bands performed abroad, significantly increasing troops' mo-
rale. As they galvanized the war effort at home, swing bands thrived,
and the market for jazz bands surged. Jazz remained a poignant political symbol of America's fight for freedom at home and abroad.[68]

In the 1950s, however, jazz musicians necessarily adjusted to the new
demands of Cold War culture. They strove to appeal to the emerging,
affluent white American suburban middle class in order to popularize
their music as postwar American mores changed. Thus jazz musicians
found themselves struggling to redefine the contours of their art form
as they attempted to appeal to rapidly shifting American values. While

some jazz musicians became ardent political activists, others wrestled with the new Cold War politics and chose to conform.[69] Amid the emerging liberal, anti-Communist consensus that guided the jazz establishment, jazz musicians often abandoned the more radical ideas of the 1930s and embraced forms of the music that reflected America's new ethos—many jazz musicians closed ranks to help fight the Cold War, consciously adopting a color blind approach to jazz. The consequent emerging jazz "mainstream" articulated by such outspoken white jazz critics as Marshall Stearns and Nat Hentoff consisted of most forms of modern jazz music from the 1930s and 1940s and led to the emergence of "stylistic unity" among many jazz artists.[70] The resulting jazz canon became embraced by American policy makers who determined the direction of jazz diplomacy. By the 1960s jazz musicians redefined their art in new and old global venues—festivals, magazines, recordings, radio shows, and universities. Jazz had particular appeal among the youth.

In this period of redefinition, a plethora of new musicians and styles appeared on the jazz scene in New York, Chicago, New Orleans, and other thriving urban centers. Some jazz theorists and activists, like Amiri Baraka, expressed the view that even for the new generation of musicians, "at the expense of the most beautiful elements of the Afro-American musical tradition, to be successful and rich one had to be white." Benny Goodman, not Duke Ellington or Count Basie, remained the "King of Swing," he asserted.[71] Nevertheless, the younger generation of jazz musicians, in their early twenties and thirties, roused the jazz world. Thelonious Monk revolutionized piano styles and influenced an entire generation of pianists that included Randy Weston, Herbie Nichols, Oscar Peterson, Dave Brubeck, Amhad Jamal, and Bill Evans.[72] Simultaneously, such musicians as drummer Mel Lewis spearheaded Third Stream jazz by incorporating classical techniques, chord progressions, and formal practices into jazz music. Echoing the East Coast in the 1950s, the West Coast emerged as a center for new jazz styles. Here, cool jazz became a potent "alternative" to bop and reflected many of the modern tendencies of white Americans. The Modern Jazz Quartet became a leading proponent of cool jazz. Significantly, many of the cool jazz musicians were white, including Gerry Mulligan, Jimmy Giuffre, Shelly Manne, Shorty Rogers, and Dave Brubeck. With octets and nonets, they created counterpoints to formal musical composition, and jazz styles fragmented further. Their music—less strident—appealed to the more conservative white Americans even though some of the musicians echoed the sentiments of earlier be-boppers who shunned conformity. The musical and aesthetic battles between be-bop, or "hot jazz," and cool jazz intensified.[73]

Other emerging styles of jazz included hard-bop, post-bop, and soul-jazz.[74] Max Roach became the preeminent hard-bop drummer of the day. He also emerged as a vocal jazz activist who wrote *We Insist! Freedom Now Suite*—the most politically explicit jazz piece of the era.[75] Charles Mingus, one of the foremost innovators of hard-bop, admired such composers as Beethoven, Bach, and Debussy. He became one of the most outspoken musicians in the jazz world as he used all styles of jazz to create his own rebellious, powerful musical style. "Mingus was the closest jazz has come to having its own Ezra Pound," jazz scholar Ted Gioia has professed.[76] Yet Mingus often felt "persecuted by the white man and the black man" as he became an ardent "spokesperson" for linking jazz with the movement for social equality.[77] Eminent jazz drummer Cozy Cole likewise lamented the elitist attitudes that arose toward jazz both inside and outside the musical establishment. He declared that not all jazz musicians received the respect that they desired in many of the venues in which they played, especially in the context of segregation. White musicians held most of the jobs. Some observers, he asserted, "just figured every jazz musician they saw was a junkie or just nothing." Cole recognized that jazz was regarded as a "put down" art form in the eyes of many outsiders.[78]

Unlike many mainstream artists, the musicians who spearheaded the new form of jazz in the 1960s—free jazz—often defined their own national culture through national struggle, echoing yet not completely mimicking Africans taking up arms against colonial rule. Thus the intermingling of jazz expression, aesthetic self-determination, and political activism that characterized jazz's controversial evolution in the twentieth century reached a critical juncture. During this era, a shift in ideology occurred in the jazz community. Rather than advocate the idea of color-blind race relations in jazz, musicians and supporters of the music asserted a renewed black consciousness in which the idea of universality centered on black musical values. The musicians used their instruments as arms to fight creative monotony, conformity, and oppression. They capitalized on the music's "revolutionary potential."[79] Free jazz performers were often maligned in the press for their outspokenness.[80] Excluded from performing in the clubs, they created an underground movement, performing instead in alluring cafés. Some embraced cultural nationalism and Leopold Senghor's concept of negritude: a black culture separate from that of the national culture. Like the native intellectuals in Franz Fanon's *The Wretched of the Earth*, free jazz musicians,

> [s]ince they could not stand wonderstruck before the history of today's barbarity, decide to back further and to delve deeper down; and let us make no mistake, it was with the greatest delight that they discovered that there was nothing to be ashamed of in the past, but rather dignity, glory, and solemnity. . . . The claims of the native intellectual are not a luxury but a necessity in any coherent program. The native intellectual who takes up arms to defend his nation's legitimacy and who wanted to bring proofs to bear out that legitimacy, who is willing to strip himself naked to study the history of his body, is obliged to dissect the heart of his people.[81]

Amid this cultural depth and complexity in the 1960s, the more vocal assertion of jazz modernism and the expansion of the jazz intelligentsia occurred along with the globalization of jazz in the twentieth century. The international popularity of jazz reflected the diffusion of a uniquely American cultural ethos. Such cities as New York embodied this multifaceted ethos, which became revered internationally. In his memoirs, premiere bandleader Duke Ellington alluded to this dynamic in cultural and political terms when he professed that in Harlem:

> It is Sunday morning. We are strolling from 110th Street up Seventh Avenue, heading north through the Spanish and West Indian neighborhood toward the 125th Street business area. . . . Everybody is in a friendly mood. Greetings are polite and pleasant, and on the opposite side of the street, standing under a street lamp, is a real hip chick. She, too, is in a friendly mood. You may hear a parade go by, or a funeral, or you may recognize the passage of those who are making our Civil Rights demands. . . . Harlem has its heroes, too. . . . Jackie Robinson, Ray Robinson, Chief Justice Thurgood Marshall, Countee Cullen, Langston Hughes, Bill Robinson.[82]

Ellington did not believe that black jazz musicians would have to abandon their own culture to become members of the American mainstream, and he focused more on artistic achievement than political activism to work toward this goal.[83]

Black jazz was nurtured by the boorish yet alluring entertainment and nightclub world that thrived in such cities as Chicago, St. Louis,

New Orleans, and especially the Upper West Side of New York. Although the color line kept jazz musicians from performing in many venues, musicians honed skills in smoky bars and dimly lit rooms, and the jazz club became a rueful place. Often frequented by white audiences, such clubs as Birdland and Café Society became popular gathering spots. People came to dance, to listen, to learn, and to endure, as

> [u]nder the ceiling light . . . they believe they know before the music does what their hands, their feet are to do, but that illusion is the music's secret drive: the control it tricks them in to believing is theirs; the anticipation it anticipates. In between record changes, while the girls fan blouse necks to air damp collarbones or pat with anxious hand the damage moisture has done to their hair, the boys press folded handkerchiefs to their foreheads. Laughter covers indiscreet glances of welcome and promise, and takes the edge off gestures of betrayal and abandon.[84]

Jazz musicians often indulged in a practice called "Walking the Bar": the entire band would stand on a bar, or on a bandstand behind a bar, with their instruments in hand, and begin to jam. As a group, they would walk back and forth, swaying in step and in rhythm, blowing their horns out of sync, acting like clowns, goons, mimes—like a circus show. Audiences seemed to like "stuff like that."[85]

Ultimately, despite jazz's worldwide appeal, views toward jazz remained remarkably complex both at home and abroad. As jazz music permeated the world against the backdrop of McCarthyism and the Cold War, jazz increasingly represented a paradoxical trope about race and American democracy: interracial harmony and racial equality rhetorically resulted from the workings of American democracy—but these ideals had not yet been achieved in modern American life. Amid widespread Cold War conflicts, black cultural ambassadors had to emphasize their "Americanness," not simply their identity as African Americans, to represent America abroad. The tours of black artists in this context also reflected DuBois's prophetic words from 1925, that

> in the world at large, it is only the accident, the remnant that gets the chance to make the most of itself; but if this is true of the white world it is infinitely more true of the colored world. It is not simply the great clear tenor of Roland Hayes that opened the ears of America. . . . [A] foreign land heard Hays and put its imprint on him and immediately America with all its imi-

tative snobbery woke up. We approved Hayes because London, Paris, and Berlin approved him and not simply because he was a great singer.[86]

Moreover, jazz had became associated with the lower stratum of American society because it had thrived among African Americans and Creoles between 1910 and 1930 in the midst of brothels and the crass nightclub life of the red light district in Storyville, New Orleans. Amid segregation resulting from the decision in *Plessy v. Ferguson* in 1896, as jazz expanded into similar venues in succeeding years, it frequently met with disdain. Americans, both black and white, associated jazz with banality, chaos, disorder, and people of ill-repute. Furthermore, because the creators and innovators of jazz were people of color—these included Jelly Roll Morton, Bunk Johnson, and Louis Armstrong—jazz became a stigmatized art form.[87]

In addition, many jazz innovators did not read notated music in the European tradition. Rather, they learned to play and create music through listening, imitating sounds, and pure ingenuity. Consequently, in the United States, in the Soviet Union, and throughout the world, some musical aficionados who represented "high" culture—theater, ballet, opera, and the symphony—regarded jazz as a "low" art form with low cultural origins. Some people questioned its value as art. During World War I and World War II, jazz became more commercial as white musicians began to record and sell jazz and "sanitized" the music to appeal to more conservative white musical tastes. Each new form of jazz thereafter was similarly politicized.[88]

Yet jazz has embodied other ideals as well. To many, jazz also reflected a trope about the culture and values that remained "native" to the United States and from which others derived the true meaning of the country.[89] Precisely because jazz represented a form of African American artistic expression arising out of the experience of racism and segregation, it symbolized a cultural ideal: that even in the most adverse social conditions, an oppressed people could achieve cultural integrity and expressive freedom. Many regarded jazz, a form of the black aesthetic, as an analog of colonial America's struggle for independence, thereby illuminating in part why jazz aficionados have extolled the music as a unique form of American cultural expression.[90] Jazz symbolized the country's expansion from colony to nationhood, reflecting the paradigm of race and culture that shifted during the Cold War: blacks once regarded as "separate but equal" came to signify the ideal of American nationhood. Such paradoxical tropes reflected the tensions that emanated from modernism, racial dualism, and the re-definition of black cultural politics during the Cold War.

Echoing Monson, noted African American scholar Cornel West suggests in *The Future of the Race* that in the struggle for freedom, black artists remained aware that they had a responsibility to represent black achievement to the world in order to sustain and promote democracy and to confront oppression. In West's view, black jazz performers remained quintessential representatives of American culture; he writes that they were "immerse[d] . . . fully in the cultural depths of black everyday life" and, moreover, that they embraced "democratic concepts of knowledge and leadership which highlight human fallibility and mutual accountability," as well as "self-realization within participatory communities."[91] As they contributed to the terrain of cultural and political ferment, the progressive intellectuals of black jazz, including John Coltrane, Louis Armstrong, Duke Ellington, and Charles Mingus, arose as "towering examples of soul-making and spiritual wrestling which crystallize the most powerful interpretations of the human condition in black life."[92] Not surprisingly, those who celebrated jazz at home and abroad honored its racial heritage while admiring it as an ingenious American cultural achievement, a reflection of America's cultural prosperity.[93] The rise of the United States as a great power during this era thus involved a cultural component that both originated from and reflected the dynamism of jazz.

In this vein, the travels of Dizzy Gillespie, Louis Armstrong, Dave Brubeck, Benny Goodman, Earl Hines, Charles Lloyd, Marian Anderson, and many others revealed an American commitment to the modernist ideals of progress and openness, and these artists themselves became models of the dynamism of a democratic system. As the Cold War intensified, jazz diplomacy aimed to portray several important themes about America's Cold War culture. First, it softened the emerging policy of containment by revealing the softer, more civilized side of American society. Second, it conveyed the idea that in an era rife with racial conflict, culture and race relations, in some venues, could engender peace and interracial harmony. Third, it exemplified the country's concrete attempts to improve the status of African Americans even in the midst of social repression. Equally important, the tours helped enhance American prestige and credibility because they elevated culture above the fray of politics and race. Not surprisingly, however, against the backdrop of ongoing racial conflicts, the message the United States employed in an effort to thwart Communism sometimes appeared as an insincere and deeply flawed artifice. Adding to the fray, American cultural officials often infused jazz discourse with elitist and ethnocentric rhetoric that undermined the efficacy of jazz diplomacy. Thus appreciation of jazz tours did not always indicate or engender support for American policies.

Ultimately, American Cold War policy cautiously sanctioned a message, an aesthetic, and an ethos that helped thwart Communist cultural activities, even in the Soviet sphere. The multifaceted jazz aesthetic increasingly appealed to peoples struggling for freedom worldwide, and to those overwrought by Communism in the Soviet bloc. In a unique way, in the words of Lawrence Levine, jazz often gave peoples abroad "a sense of power of control. . . . It allowed [artists] to assert themselves and their feelings and their values, to communicate continuously with themselves and their peers and their oppressors as well. Here was an area in which they could at least partly drop the masks and the pretense and say what they felt, articulate what was brimming up within them and what they desperately needed to express."[94] As jazz remained a vibrant symbol of art's ability to transcend political and cultural barriers, jazz diplomacy placed superpower relations in a complicated cultural context. Jazz distinctly depicted the realities and possibilities of American democracy. It also signified the emergence of a new American ethos on the world stage that contributed to the toppling of Communist regimes.

Chapter 1
Battling the Reds

This year, for the first time in American history, the world is seeing a bigscale drive by the U.S. to best the Russians—not in guns, science, or sports—but in culture. . . .

It's apparently the first time that the Government has recognized the need for battling the Reds on the highbrow front for what's left of the free world.

    —*Variety,* 1955

Even before American jazz musicians became cultural ambassadors, the United States launched performing arts tours in the Soviet bloc to compete with the "Reds" on the cultural front. After the Soviet Union emerged from the ruins of World War II, and Joseph Stalin embarked upon a policy of political and cultural expansion that challenged America's bid for preeminence in world affairs, American cultural policy makers aimed to destroy what they characterized as "myths" and stereotypes about the country that lingered abroad. The "myths" that frequently emanated from America's racial dilemma significantly shaped the international discourse on discrimination, civil rights, and cultural freedom that became proscribed in the 1950s.[1] As W. E. B. DuBois professed in 1957, "the whole colored world, together with the world of socialism and Communism, stand asking whether the United States is a democracy or the last center of 'white supremacy' and colonial imperialism."[2]

Moreover, many countries stereotypically saw the United States as culturally barren and morally imprudent. The United States was quickly replacing Europe "as the major symbol of colonialism through its excessive wealth, superior technology, and racial arrogance."[3] To side with the United States abroad, additionally, often meant accepting military and economic assistance, not cultural revelry.[4] These stereotypes persisted despite the fact that in the 1950s and 1960s, black cultural products—especially jazz, rock and roll, and rhythm and blues—reshaped the American cultural landscape and permeated the cultures of the world. Thus, as black music made a deep impact on the image of American race relations, American artists undermined

Cold War orthodoxies. Through music, blacks and whites at home and abroad assuaged social tensions by sharing a common social and cultural experience, thereby transcending racial boundaries.[5]

Against this backdrop, American Cold Warriors aimed to redefine American cultural values through the presentation of music, Hollywood movies, operas, sports, and dance. They became increasingly convinced that cultural contacts between nations deeply influenced perceptions of race and culture at home and abroad. Cultural contacts shaped attitudes, broadly influenced belief systems, and helped determine how a nation interpreted the world. Culture itself also influenced and reflected a nation's way of life and thus helped delineate which institutions and practices a nation would endorse in international affairs. Before the onset of the Cold War, the United States, although active in the international arena, espoused a policy of isolationism—the idea of a "city on a hill."[6] Yet in the postwar years, as the country acquired a new racial character and assumed the role of worldwide protector of democracy, American officials reevaluated the American mission; they reinforced the idea that racial equality and the survival of American values were not mutually exclusive and had become critical to the survival of the Western world.[7]

In this context, the United States buttressed efforts to revamp its image by participating in a momentous affair in 1955—the Geneva Summit.[8] This pivotal international event, held from July 18 to 23, became critical in redefining the cultural Cold War in the mid-1950s. Countries that attended included the United States, the Soviet Union, France, and Great Britain. Geneva signified a lessening of Cold War tensions and embodied hopes of "removing barriers to normal intercourse between the" East and the West.[9] The main topic at the summit centered on nuclear strategy and Eisenhower's policy of "Open Skies." Yet the summit also laid the groundwork for person-to-person contact between those in the United States and the Soviet Union by advocating reciprocal visits for political figures, performing artists, civic leaders, and many others. Arthur Bronson, writing for *Variety*, had reported just months earlier that a Soviet cultural invasion of the world was occurring.[10] Thus Geneva helped set the stage for future jazz tours in the Soviet bloc.

In his memoirs, Soviet premier Nikita Khrushchev voiced his ambivalence about the summit. He expressed the view that in this nuclear age, "the Western powers were still reluctant to take even the basic measures necessary for laying the foundations of a secure peace." He further asserted that "the Geneva meeting was probably doomed to failure before it even began." Still, he amusingly recalled Eisenhower's suggestion that, regarding tensions, "we could wash them away with martinis." Ultimately, he believed that the summit was an "important breakthrough . . . on the diplomatic front" and claimed that "we had established ourselves as able to hold our own" in international negotiations.[11]

Equally, Geneva symbolized a Soviet desire to pursue a policy of peaceful coexistence with the West. After the death of Stalin in 1953 and a subsequent power struggle, a cultural thaw occurred in the Soviet Union that give rise to a myriad of dynamic cultural activities. Amid this cultural openness, Westerners were allowed to travel behind the Iron Curtain for the first time in the postwar era.[12] The Soviet Union also embarked upon cultural tours with the West in part to acquire information on American technology, politics, life, and culture. It advocated a bevy of activities such as tourism and musical performances. The United States, contrarily, conducted cultural relations with the Soviet Union in order to expose the Soviet people to Western ideas, nurture their demands for freedom and a more open society, and encourage liberalism in the Soviet Union and the Communist bloc. Likewise, cultural policy aimed to create an atmosphere of friendship, warmth, and generosity with the Soviet Union, with the ultimate hope that the Soviet people would assimilate American values. Both sides emphasized the importance of achieving mutual understanding to improve overall relations.[13]

Walter Stoessel Jr., acting officer in charge of European affairs, further justified cultural exchanges with the Soviet Union by arguing that they offered "Communist-indoctrinated" people realistic "knowledge of" the United States and helped to favorably impress them with the American "way of life." Soviet peoples could thus relay positive stories about America "to their friends and relatives upon returning" home. Stoessel also contended that cultural interactions might disabuse Soviets of the notion that the United States is "responsible for" constructing "the 'iron curtain'" between the East and the West.[14]

Despite this astounding breakthrough in superpower relations, some American goodwill ambassadors touring the Soviet Union expressed dismay about their travels. In a letter to Stoessel, members of the American chess team voiced several complaints about their official visit in 1955. Stoessel suggested that the team "refrain from overly effusive public comments and statements regarding the treatment given to them in the USSR." He reiterated that "it is always well, in this connection, to bear in mind" the Soviet Union's "persistent refusal . . . in the post-war years to cooperate with American proposals for cultural exchange." He pointed out that the Soviet Union had just modified its "line somewhat in this regard" and that "such exchanges as the U.S.-Soviet chess competition are permitted by the Soviet government only because they are considered to be useful in furthering the overall political aims of Soviet Communism."[15] While some American artists feared "cultural contacts" behind the Iron Curtain, many remained avid supporters of cultural initiatives.[16] In this vein, Paul Kapp, manager of the Delta Rhythm Boys, suggested that the African American singing group appear as the "first American jazz artists" in Russia. He characterized the singers as the "finest" in black American achievement.[17]

One of the most significant cultural events to arise from the Geneva Summit was the tour to the Soviet Union of George Gershwin's musical *Porgy and Bess*, a striking showcase of African American culture. *Variety* reporter Irving R. Levine pointed out that in the "Geneva Spirit," the Soviet Ministry of Culture "footed the bill" for the entire *Porgy and Bess* tour, leading some Soviet officials to claim that "there is no 'Iron Curtain' as far as the importation of American culture is concerned." Some American officials, however, worried that the musical depicted negative images of African Americans and surmised that it might reinforce ambivalent Soviet opinions about black life in the United States.[18]

By the end of this historic year, numerous Soviet artists toured worldwide in the name of propagating Communist values and ideas. These activities intensified the American desire to rebut ideas of American materialism and cultural backwardness that lingered in the international arena.[19] Importantly, Geneva also represented a definitive achievement for the Soviet Union because it revealed that on the eve of Khrushchev's denunciation of Stalin at the Twentieth Party Congress in 1956, the Soviet Union did not completely remain "unable to break with the past, unable to muster the courage and the determination to lift the curtain and see what had been hidden about the arrests, the trials, the arbitrary rule, the executions, and everything else that had happened during Stalin's reign."[20] Khruschev's speech caused an uproar in the Eastern bloc, and even incited rioting in Poland.[21]

In July 1956 President Eisenhower expressed his continued support for American cultural initiatives "at this moment, when developments on the other side of the Iron Curtain clearly show[ed] that the yearning for freedom remain[ed] alive and vibrant. . . . For maximum usefulness, wide contributions by American citizens and American enterprise [were] essential in this work."[22] *Variety* and *Time* likewise expounded upon cultural policies when they praised the United States' new Cultural Presentations Program (CPP)—Eisenhower's "President's Program"—which sponsored such groups abroad as the Jubilee Singers and the Philadelphia Orchestra.[23]

As cultural tours ensued, a critical Cold War event significantly overshadowed Geneva's success and drastically altered U.S.-Soviet views toward cultural affairs. Attempting to stifle a nationalist movement in Hungary in October 1956, the Soviet Union occupied the country militarily. Khrushchev characterized the invasion with optimism, extolling the socialist cause. He asserted that "by helping the Hungarian people to crush the counterrevolutionary mutiny we have prevented the enemy from impairing the unity of the entire Socialist camp, rigorsly tested during the Hungarian events." According to the Soviet premier, socialist countries had "approved" the invasion "unanimously."[24]

The Soviet invasion unavoidably met with ardent criticism at home and abroad. Some African Americans equated the invasion with racial oppression in the southern United States.[25] Others suggested that U.S. cultural efforts had helped instigate the rebellion.[26] Similarly, Fred Schang, of Columbia Artists Management, and Robert O. Blake, of the Office of Eastern European Affairs, declared that the United States remained eager to sponsor "first-rate" American performing artists to the Soviet Union, but only after "public reaction against Soviet intervention in Hungary had died down to an extent that such appearances would not redound against the American artists at home."[27] Secretary of State John Foster Dulles believed that it was essential to "impres[s] on . . . Soviet leaders [the United States'] strong disapproval of their intervention."[28] He did not know when cultural relations would resume.

In a letter to Soviet official Nicolai Bulganin, Eisenhower proclaimed that the invasion had a "shocking" impact. Most important, he implored that "in the name of humanity and in the cause of peace that the Soviet Union take action to withdraw Soviet forces from Hungary immediately and to permit the Hungarian people to enjoy and exercise the human rights and fundamental freedoms affirmed for all peoples in the United Nations Charter."[29]

As the invasion exacerbated international tensions, the acting assistant secretary of cultural relations emphasized that the United States would not consider Hungary's request for tours. He recommended that "when . . . circumstances warrant consideration of a program of cultural interchange with Hungary, the [Hungarian] legation should submit new recommendations."[30] In November, Harold C. Vedeler, counselor of embassy, claimed that the act of aggression even caused Czechoslovakia to be "preoccupied with security" and to "mov[e] backward toward police dominance."[31] Even in the months before the intervention, Henry P. Leverich, officer in charge of Balkan affairs, had discouraged travel to Hungary, pointing to "adverse developments in U.S.-Hungarian relations."[32]

In the midst of this international uproar, American officials hotly debated cultural policy with the Communist bloc. John C. Guthrie, first secretary of embassy in Moscow, advocated any type of entertainment for the Soviet Union, yet asserted that some "extreme" jazz could offend Soviets "who have a high degree of musical sensibility."[33] The Prague embassy advocated tours to Czechoslovakia for such groups as Jose Limone's Dance Troupe and the Cleveland Orchestra, yet remained uncertain about whether an American group could perform in Czechoslovakia—Czech policy depended on American policy toward the Soviets. The American embassy reiterated that if the "Czech regime could be convinced that an American group was not going to the Soviet Union because of limited time rather than for policy reasons, it would be permitted to perform."[34] Toward this end, Robert Dowling, chairman of the board of the American National Theater Academy, traveled to the Soviet Union and Czechoslovakia in an effort to negotiate a tour for a musical comedy. Llewellyn E. Thompson, an official in Moscow, reported that when Dowling spoke with Khrushchev, it was clear that despite the Soviet premier's ambivalence, he approved of cultural relations. Momentarily, "the Soviet and American people got on well together."[35]

Frequent negotiations did not dispel American fears of Soviet anti-American propaganda. Some U.S. officials believed that the Soviet Union brainwashed its tourists with anti-American ideas. The Czechs endured charges of constructing an "iron curtain of [their] own."[36] Other American policy makers even suspected that Communist artists and athletes might be carrying suitcases full of "Communist propaganda" during their visits abroad. Consequently, such officials urged exercising tremendous caution when interacting with peoples from the Soviet bloc.[37]

In 1959, as Khrushchev and Eisenhower prepared for another pivotal summit and as tensions over the military occupation of Berlin intensified, Richard H. Davies, minister-counselor in Moscow, reiterated the importance of promoting U.S.-Soviet cultural contacts. He observed that when three American painters and a sculptor visited the Soviet Union, American "cultural accomplishments [were] one of the least well known" in the country, and "of all the aspects of American culture, American art is perhaps the most unknown." This, he claimed, resulted in part from the Soviet press's imprudent desire to protect "the purity of Soviet art."[38]

"The purity of Soviet art" indeed faced significant challenges as American popular culture steadily reached peoples behind the Iron Curtain. Such publications as *Variety*, *Time*, and the *New York Times* reported on the increasing popularity of jazz in the Soviet Union. Jazz thrived in the more open cultural environment. Willis Conover launched his jazz and popular music show, *Music USA*, for the Voice of America in the Soviet Union in 1955, while Radio Moscow began to play jazz tunes and rhythm and blues in its broadcasts.[39] Conover became known all over the Soviet Union for his jazz show. The *New York Times Magazine* reported that because of the Soviets' penchant for the music, jazz records were even sold "surreptitiously . . . outside GUM, Moscow's biggest state-owned department store."[40] Soviet jazz musicians also smuggled jazz records into the country from Western and Eastern Europe and traded jazz records on the black market. They likewise engaged in heated debates about jazz. An article in the Soviet journal *Sovetskaia Muzyka* examined the instrumental and stylistic potential of jazz and "easy" music.[41]

Jazz's popularity grew despite the fact that Soviet officials viewed jazz as "bedlam from the decadent West."[42] Renowned Soviet writer Maxim Gorky had vociferously expressed this opinion toward jazz in his 1928 article "The Music of the Gross," and his viewpoint subsequently became an official tenet of Soviet domestic and foreign policy.[43] Because jazz originated among segregated African Americans, it also symbolized the bedlam of class conflict: the music of the oppressed mass proletariat expressing discontent and unshackling the tyranny of capitalist "oppressors." Jazz's appeal in the Soviet Union became so undeniable that Khrushchev attempted to co-opt the music from 1956 to 1962.[44]

As jazz made significant inroads in Soviet society, the Soviet Union launched a "massive 'cultural offensive'" in Asia.[45] At the same time, the People's Republic of China also entered the foray of cultural competition, placing greater emphasis on cultural affairs in the late 1950s. Chinese initiatives caused American officials to identify Asia as a high priority for cultural campaigns and heightened fears of Chinese cultural expansion into the Western Hemisphere. American officials grew concerned that, like the Soviets, the Chinese might use cultural groups to spread Communist propaganda and ideology. Consequently, the United States sought to prevent the Peking Opera from performing in Santiago, Chile, and in other parts of South America. The State Department urged that Latin America and other regions refuse visas for the group. It also advised U.S. embassies to clarify the official American position about the group to other governments.[46]

In this way, the United States "successfully frustrated Chinese Communist efforts" to expand culturally.[47] One official believed that accepting the "seemingly innocuous group" for a tour might "legitimat[e] Chinese Communists" or undermine the "common front" against a regime that the United Nations "branded . . . as an aggressor." He feared that such a troupe could have a "domino" effect by posing a threat to stability in Korea, Taiwan, and Southeast Asia or by reaching "sympathetic" groups in Africa. He even worried that the group might "break opposition to a seat" for China in the United Nations.[48] Moreover, Joseph S. Evans Jr., counselor of embassy for public affairs in Tokyo in 1958, warned that the United States was "losing [the] cultural Cold War in Japan," and in March 1959 George M. Hellyer, counselor of embassy for public affairs in Tokyo, declared that the United States was not prepared to compete with the Communist cultural offensive in Japan.[49]

As the cultural Cold War in Asia intensified, the world continued to debate the progress of race relations in the United States.[50] Such discussions gained momentum in 1955 when the murder of Emmett Till—a fourteen-year-old boy killed after being accused of flirting with a white woman—resulted in domestic and international calumny. Musicians like trumpeter Miles Davis recalled the horror of the incident when he remarked that it "shocked everyone in New York."[51] At the same time, black activists initiated the Montgomery Bus Boycott in December 1955, an event that represented a shift in blacks' political approach to descrimination.[52]

American cultural policy makers saw another dilemma emerge in their efforts to confront Communism and the color line as black cultural internationalism dynamically resurged. In the wake of civil rights struggles in the United States, securing the allegiance of African peoples become pivotal in the American mission to win over the free world. Yet many American liberals characterized Africa as primitive and in need of civilization.[53] The illusory rhetoric of Cold War liberalism echoed the American political rhetoric of the late nineteenth century that encompassed the ideology of social Darwinism. Thus Africa became a Cold War "focal point," "the center of colonial contention"— yet for the purposes of expanding American Cold War policies, not buttressing Africa's political aims.[54] As American officials made attempts to win the sympathy of African nations, they often equated African nationalism with Communism and thus did not support African freedom struggles. Winning the Cold War remained a priority over supporting independence movements.[55] This policy undermined American attempts at political and cultural cooperation, and, not surprisingly, American cultural relations with Africa remained steeped in a political and racial conundrum.

Black internationalism continued to progress under world scrutiny in 1955, when the Bandung Conference took place in Bandung, Indonesia, and in 1956, when the First International Congress of Colored Writers and Artists met in Paris. Such distinguished black artists as Richard Wright attended Bandung. The Bandung Conference was sponsored by India, Pakistan, Ceylon, Burma, and Indonesia. Delegates from twenty-nine nations attended, including six from Africa—from Egypt, Ethiopia, Liberia, Libya, the Gold Coast, and the Sudan (Anglo-Egyptian)—along with representatives from Asia and Latin America, as well as Marshal Tito, the leader of Yugoslavia. By reaffirming a commitment to international freedom struggles and announcing a policy of nonalignment, Bandung represented the third world's disengagement from the politics of the Cold War.[56]

Though Western officials worried that the nations represented at Bandung would fall under Communist influence, many, including Secretary of State John Foster Dulles, trivialized the event. New York representative Adam Clayton Powell Jr. had traveled to the conference despite State Department efforts to dissuade him. Espousing Cold War liberal views, Powell urged delegates to suppress the race question and to denounce China and Russia. Bandung delegates cautiously espoused support for Afro-Asian cultural contacts with the Communist bloc and beckoned the United States to address its racial problems. Powell believed that by advocating such efforts, he kept the conference from unequivocally supporting Communist political strategies.[57]

Still, black cultural internationalism frustrated American policy makers by giving impetus to worldwide criticism of the American race question. When Eastern and Western Europe, Asia, Africa, Latin America, and most notably the Soviet Union publicly disdained the persistence of racial violence and the denial of civil rights to African Americans, they denounced what they saw as a hypocritical divide between American rhetoric and American realities. Thus the race quandary represented a profound threat to national security. Black internationalism also propelled greater controversy into debates about American efforts to develop image building, especially when the USIA presented such movies abroad as *The Negro in American Life*, which depicted themes of "reconciliation and redemption" with regard to race. These themes conveyed the USIA's official Cold War approach to the race question.[58]

Moreover, Cold War reductionism continued to cast a shadow over cultural affairs. American policy makers who viewed the dilemma of race through the paradigm of the Cold War colored official debates about cultural tours. In 1955 controversy arose when the Berlin Philharmonic visited the United States. Musician Arnold Manoff proclaimed that "our own Negro musicians are barred from most American symphony orchestras while [the] Nazi German Berlin Philharmonic is invited to tour. What shameful hypocrisy."[59] Shortly thereafter, in a letter to Carl Ditton, of the National Association of Negro Musicians, Inc., Richard Straus, of the Office of German Affairs at the Bureau of European Affairs, defended the tour by stating that the "conductor was cleared by de-Nazification tribunals," and under certain American laws such musicians were permitted to enter and perform in the United States. The State Department did not have any connection with the trip. Straus hailed the orchestra as a "cultural symbol of free Berlin" and an "expression of gratitude by Germans in general."[60]

Ultimately, the pivotal Cold War events that redirected the American approach to battling the "Reds" in the mid-1950s—most notably, the Geneva Summit, the Bandung Conference, the Soviet invasion of Hungary, and the Communist cultural offensive in Asia—revealed significant tensions in American policy. U.S. policy makers saw an increasing need to thwart official sympathy toward black internationalism as their fears of Communist cultural expansion intensified. Yet the appropriation of black and white American cultural products to counter the Soviets' worldwide effort to win sympathetic Communist allies sometimes unwittingly gave impetus to cultural internationalism. When African American artists performed abroad in the "Geneva spirit," the views of such officials as Edward A. Symans, attaché in Poland, grew increasingly popular. Symans believed wholeheartedly that official performances of African American artists could help mend or ameliorate political breaches and also engender sympathy for American policy goals.[61] Cultural tours helped improve what the United States saw as the faltering and incongruous image of American life that often existed in the international arena.

Chapter 2
Jazz Diplomacy at Home and Abroad, 1954–1957

Jazz is not in ideological favor in Communist countries. Not so much because it is "decadent" but because it is typically Western! But no matter how much the ideologists frown, youngsters pick it up on their receiving sets and belt it out in their jam sessions so that at almost any hour of day or night, jazz can be heard whistled in the street, played in the homes, or coming through a crack in a basement window.
—Joseph C. Kolarek, 1956

With anti-Communist fervor at its height in the mid-1950s, racial oppression in the United States sometimes mirrored the pervasive tyranny in the Soviet sphere, despite campaigns to buttress the image of American democracy.[1] As W. E. B. DuBois wrote in a letter to the editor of the newspaper *New Times* in 1954, "The present attitude in America is to make it impossible for American Negroes to express themselves concerning their situation unless they confine their remarks or writings to fulsome praise of the United States."[2] In confronting this conundrum, the State Department, wary of jazz's racial and social origins, reluctantly became jazz's ally.

President Dwight D. Eisenhower helped lay the foundations for a global jazz diplomacy in the aftermath of *Brown v. Board of Education*—a decision that provided impetus for a worldwide United States Information Agency (USIA) propaganda campaign. Racial realities at home and abroad led policy makers to recognize the need to forge new tactics to conduct diplomacy. Apparently, "USIA efforts and the exchange of black speakers abroad did not adequately confront the looming dilemma of race in the United States. A new approach was needed, especially because several new nations focused more on dismantling colonialism rather than choosing sides in the Cold War. The cultural exchange program provided the apparent solution."[3] Thus in July 1954 Eisenhower "beseeched Congress to allocate funds for Cold War cultural exchange."[4] It became clear that, for Eisenhower, the Cold War would be won on the level of ideas. Thereafter, in August

1954 the U.S. Congress authorized the President's Emergency Fund for Participation in International Affairs. The International Cultural Exchange and Trade Fair Participation Act of 1956 granted this fund permanent status, after which it was renamed the President's Special International Program for Participation in International Affairs; it also became know as the Cultural Presentations Program (CPP). The act of 1956 additionally called for the creation of an Advisory Committee on the Arts (ACA), imbued with the power to help choose the program's participants and to evaluate its effectiveness. Initially, the American National Theater Academy (ANTA) and the State Department jointly administered the CPP. In 1954 the State Department also approved the creation of several panels to select American performing artists to tour abroad for the United States. These included panels for drama, dance, music, and, later, jazz. When the music panel first met in New York City in October 1954, American officials elucidated the CPP's primary purpose: to "counteract Russian propaganda."[5]

The State Department maintained final authority in approving all musical and dramatic selections and advocated the "utmost discretion in the selection of artists."[6] It instructed the panels to approve only the best performing artists the United States had to offer. Toward this end, it established a rating system in March 1957, which, over the years, helped assess the integrity, personal attributes, musical abilities, and "Americanness" of artists proposed for American tours. The panels likewise evaluated artists' suitability in terms of personal character and the racial makeup of their group.[7] The United States Information Service (USIS)—USIA overseas—in part held the responsibility for coordinating these new global efforts. The USIS promoted cultural contacts through various cultural media—the press, brochures, posters, pamphlets, photos, films, and newsreels.[8] Moreover, it assisted in determining what types of artists would perform and which themes performers would emphasize. It also organized receptions, jam sessions, and other social events. In 1955 the director of the USIA expressed his support for this dynamic new chapter of the cultural Cold War and especially underscored the importance of countering Soviet efforts. He declared that

> the basic objectives . . . are to improve the understanding in foreign countries of United States cultural achievements, thereby to refute *Communist propaganda*, and to demonstrate to the people of the world that the United States is genuinely interested in the cultural achievement of its own and

of other peoples. . . . [We must] strengthen the climate of world opinion, and [the] understanding and appreciation of art and culture in the United States.[9]

Significantly, with the launching of the CPP, the "leader of the free world" found innovative ways to create meaning in its cultural life and to communicate this to other cultures. To counter Soviet propaganda, the United States attempted to substantiate claims that it had a superior Western culture and civilization. Policy makers sought to employ the arts to help transcend a compelling ideological, political, and racial divide—by the mid-1950s the world had divided into several ideological blocs established because of the exigencies of the Cold War.[10] Unavoidably, the U.S. government appropriated American culture in the midst of political upheaval at home and Communist revolutions abroad.

The Back Door

Black jazz musicians in the United States faced the pervasive and unyielding restraints of Jim Crow, as the barrier between black and white had become emblematic of the jazz world. Yet both black and white jazz musicians spoke out loudly against discrimination and segregation and made considerable strides in fighting racism. Interracial collaboration became an important component of the fight for justice. Such musicians as Louis Armstrong, Duke Ellington, Dizzy Gillespie, Benny Goodman, and Dave Brubeck fought to gain access for black jazz musicians through "the front door." Numerous musicians participated in marches, in fund-raising events for civil rights organizations, and in a variety of other activities.[11]

Armstrong led his world-famous band the All Stars in the 1950s and 1960s, touring throughout Japan, Europe, Africa, and Latin America. He also traveled to Ghana under private sponsorship in 1956, where he performed for Kwame Nkrumah, who became prime minister upon Ghana's independence in 1957. Yet when he played for a segregated audience in Knoxville, Tennessee, a group of hooligans threw dynamite at the theater where his band performed. Armstrong continued the concert, nevertheless, and the *New York Post* asserted that it "Takes More'n Tenn. Bomb to Stop Satchmo." After an official investigation, it was reported that the White Citizens Council had organized the dissentious act.[12] Armstrong also traveled to Ghana under private spon-sorship in 1956, where he performed for Kwame Nkrumah.

Armstrong expressed a perceptive view of American culture and race relations in a letter to his manager, Joe Glaser. He underscored the important role that a white manager played in forging the finan-cial success of black jazz musicians. He recalled one of his mentors who once stated, "*Dipper*, As long as you live, no matter where you may be—always have a *White Man* (who like you) and can + will put his Hand on your shoulder and say—"*This is My*" N . . . " and, Can't Nobody's Harm' Ya."[13] Armstrong collaborated with such noted white jazz managers and producers as Joe Glaser of Associated Booking Corporation, George Wein of Festival Productions, and George Ava-kian of Columbia Records. All helped organize several tours for the State Department.

Similarly, Duke Ellington noted the pivotal significance of white managers in jazz. In his memoirs, he pointed to a racial paradox that often arose from such relationships. He wrote that

> Louis Armstrong was the epitome of jazz and always will be. He was also a living monument to the magnificent career of Joe Glaser. . . . Don't put the cart before the horse, they say, and at first glance you might think Louis was the horse doing all the pulling while Glaser was in the driver's seat of the cart. Obviously, a cart is a most convenient place to stash the gold. . . . Louis still ended up a very rich man, maybe the richest of all the "trumpet Gabriels." . . . Joe Glaser watched over Louis like the treasure he was, and saw to it that his partner was well fixed for the rest of his life.[14]

Ellington likewise expressed profound dismay at America's racial par-adoxes. In what musicologist Mark Tucker heralds as Ellington's most ardent expression against racism anywhere in his writings, Ellington commented on the U.S.-Soviet space race. He declared that the Unit-ed States had not achieved the scientific success of the Soviet Union because racial prejudice had prevented the nation from attaining the "harmony of thought" that had to "prevail in order for" scientific prog-ress to occur. He further claimed that because "so many Americans persist in the notion of the master race, millions of Negroes are de-prived of proper schooling, denied the right to vote on who will spend their tax money, and are the last hired and first fired in those indus-tries necessary for the progress of the country."[15]

In the same vein, Dizzy Gillespie emphasized the flaws in American democracy that emanated from America's racial dilemma. He challenged segregation when he became one of the first bandleaders to integrate his band in the postwar years. As he introduced be-bop to the world and engendered enthusiastic fans among a wide spectrum Americans, Gillespie demanded "'first class' treatment" for jazz practitioners. He heralded jazz as critical to the modernization of American music. As critics increasingly began to recognize the new jazz styles, he sought to eliminate segregation clauses in musicians' contracts. Gillespie also protested the hiring policies of the music union, particularly in New York, where the majority of jobs for jazz musicians—in Broadway musicals, big bands, radio networks, and television studio ensembles—went to white performers.[16]

Another impetus for integration in jazz came from Jazz at the Philharmonic (JATP), an organization dedicated to eliminating discrimination "on the job" that became equally prominent in the fight against segregation during the Cold War. The JATP traveled throughout North America, Europe, and Asia. Begun by white manager Norman Granz in the 1940s, the JATP sought to give jazz musicians "'first class' treatment" by ensuring that musicians "traveled 'first class'" and "stayed in" the best hotels.[17] Most important, Granz objected to segregated audiences. The organization, which also included recording and distribution companies, produced a considerable number of jazz records on the market. Many musicians who played with Granz became some of the highest paid in the business. Ellington expressed admiration for Granz in his memoirs when he asserted that "Norman Granz is one of those guys I have spoken of as encountering at the various intersections of my road through life, guys who have been there to point out the way."[18] As he sought to dismantle the barriers of discrimination, Granz became widely respected in the jazz world. He observed that

> it didn't make no kind of sense to treat a musician with any kind of respect and dignity on stage and then make him go around to the back door when he's offstage. I don't understand that treatment. . . . It wasn't only anti-black discrimination, it was discrimination against musicians. . . . I insisted that my musicians were to be treated with the same respect as Leonard Bernstein or Heifitz, because they were just as good both as men and musicians.[19]

On one occasion, when Dizzy Gillespie performed with the JATP at a main concert hall in Houston, Granz "removed the signs that said 'white toilets and negro toilets.'" Gillespie remembered a rueful event on that trip, recalling that "between sets, we'd be in the back, shooting dice, playing cards, and this time in Texas, all this money was on the floor. . . . We were shooting dice in the dressing room; the dressing room door burst open. The police came in and took us all to jail, including Ella Fitzgerald. Norman put up a bond and got us out. They asked everybody their name, and I told them my name was 'Louis Armstrong.'" Gillespie's band also encountered similar difficulties in Charleston, South Carolina, where Granz had demanded that concert tickets "be sold without regard to race—first come, first served." In Kansas City, where the group stayed at the Hotel Continental, the management refused to allow Gillespie to swim in the hotel pool. Only after a dispute did Gillespie obtain permits to swim. The management nonetheless forced the band to enter the hotel through the back door.[20]

Other white managers who became remarkable pioneers during these Cold War years included George Wein of Festival Productions and George Avakian of Columbia Records. Both brilliantly balanced the needs of the musicians with the demands of the volatile and fluctuating jazz market, domestically and internationally, and they traversed the terrain of race relations with exceeding agility. Avakian recalls his ardent belief in his musicians' and his own ability to maintain musical integrity, even when the personal idiosyncrasies of such jazz greats as Benny Goodman colored their experiences at home and abroad. Likewise, Wein exhibited keen respect for the artistry and abilities of the musicians. Yet at the same time, he had an astute awareness of the needs of the State Department in this explosive Cold War political climate. His tact, knowledge, and prudence made him integral to the success of jazz diplomacy.[21]

White jazz musicians like pianist Dave Brubeck also opposed segregationist practices. Brubeck, for example, expressed anger at racial restrictions: they prevented him from hiring some of the best musicians in the business who were black. Like Gillespie and Armstrong, he also canceled performances in cities that forbade performances of integrated bands. Brubeck penned a Broadway musical, *The Real Ambassador*, in 1961, which mocked government-sponsored cultural tours. Though the show never made it to Broadway, some of the songs were performed in a poignant birthday tribute to Armstrong at the Newport Jazz Festival. Armstrong himself performed a selection of the show tunes at a jazz festival and also recorded several songs from the show. The musical illuminated the ironies that emerged when black and white jazz artists represented the United States as Cold War cultural ambassadors.[22]

Benny Goodman, one of the most successful swing-band leaders of the era, likewise recognized the ironies of segregation, a practice in the business that he disdained. His immigrant parents were born in the Russian Empire, and Goodman himself was born and raised in a Chicago slum. Although he had a notoriously difficult personality, he, like countless others, encountered enormous obstacles as he attempted to create a fully integrated band and to bring "colored musicians . . . in the front door."[23]

With such controversies emanating from the jazz world, the State Department's Bureau of Educational and Cultural Affairs (CU) did not initially sponsor jazz in cultural tours—jazz's ambiguous, paradoxical reputation evoked ardent controversy. Despite the globalization of jazz, one of the music panel members lamented that a "snobiness . . . toward jazz" existed in the United States and that many Americans were ashamed of the music. At home and abroad, many associated it with the margins of American society—lower-class African Americans.[24] Moreover, American jazz also represented black cultural nationalism and posed a revolutionary challenge to the status quo.

In this vein, American officials and jazz aficionados debated the efficacy of appropriating jazz and cautiously came to embrace "America's classical music" in cultural efforts. Jazz's rise as an instrument in the U.S.-Soviet Cold War rivalry intensified late in 1955 and early in 1956, as the CU learned that American jazz and dance music had a significant, dedicated, and avid following in the Eastern bloc. In the wake of the Geneva Summit, Vice Consul Ernest A. Nagy praised a performance by the Czech Karel Vlach Dance Band in Budapest, Hungary.[25] He avowed that the American cultural influence remained striking and clear and that the United States could capitalize on its widespread appeal.

The Karel Vlach Dance Band performed at Margaret Island Tennis Stadium in Hungary in July 1955. Nagy reported how the "Czech orchestra play[ed] American jazz in Hungary" to women in "low cut evening gowns," and proclaimed that both the instrumentation and the orchestra's "dress" reflected "unmistakable . . . American influence."[26] Twelve thousand people heard the band in Magyar Memzet, where it rendered interpretations of several popular American jazz tunes. Nagy amusingly claimed that the "degree of reception was in direct proportion to the 'haziness', for want of a better term, of the number. The louder, faster, more intricate, more improvised, more daring the number, the better was the reception." The group performed such tunes as Irving Berlin's "Blue Skies" and George Gershwin's "Rhapsody in Blue," as well as songs modeled after Les Brown's "cool styling."[27]

Nagy enthusiastically characterized the Czech reaction to the band as "memorable" and exhilarating. This reflected jazz's extensive appeal among young people worldwide, he claimed. Consequently, he urged that the State Department employ jazz to buttress American cultural initiatives. He asserted that

> this American product, one of America's outstanding contributions to the art forms of the world and perhaps our most popular export, remains singularly unexploited. I fear that most of our leading people do not like or understand jazz for various reasons and are, in fact, ashamed of jazz music. I am sure that a performance in Budapest by Norman Granz's Jazz at the Philharmonic troupe or by either Les Brown, Woody Herman, or especially the Stan Kenton orchestra would be worth more from a propaganda and public relations standpoint than six weeks of VOA [Voice of America] broadcasting or high level conferences.[28]

For Nagy, Hungarians' and Czechs' hunger for American jazz also reflected the increasing cultural openness of the Hungarian regime. He proclaimed that "this orchestra could only have survived the past ten years, let alone prospered and grown in stature, as the result of an overwhelming demand from the people which had to be fulfilled no matter how basically 'reactionary', 'decadent', or 'cosmopolitan' its music might be to Communist ideolots."[29] Roy Schmidt, president of Hungary's Hot Club for jazz, agreed that a popular American jazz group would have considerable appeal in Hungary.[30]

Another event that "helped catapult jazz into Cold War cultural exchange" occurred on November 6, 1955. In a front-page article, the *New York Times* announced that the "United States Has Secret Sonic Weapon, Jazz." It then questioned why the government did not employ jazz in its cultural programs "to promote democracy" and urged wholeheartedly that American officials use jazz to nurture yearnings for freedom abroad, especially among the youth.[31] To add to the fervor, magazines including *Time* and *Down Beat* keenly highlighted jazz's propaganda value. *Time* commented that the propaganda value of jazz had grown immeasurably around the world because of Willis Conover's jazz program, *Music USA*. It asserted that the radio show epito-mized the spirit of the United States.[32] Similarly, critic Barry Ulanov acknowledged that jazz appealed to people of all ages, worldwide. Yet he cautioned that American jazz tours would not be effective if presented as nothing more than "carbon copies" of the real thing. He recommended that officials handle jazz as "delicately as literature or abstract art" when attempting to communicate to cultures in the West and the East. More important, he urged that the United States show greater respect for its own music before sending it abroad, declaring that, perhaps, "we shouldn't rush so eagerly into this propaganda pro-gram. . . . [I]f we fight well enough, intelligently enough, and success-fully enough for jazz at home, then we can take up the task of letting everybody around the world know just how brilliant the accomplish-ment of American jazz men is."[33] New York Congressman Adam Clay-ton Powell Jr. had also become a vocal advocate for including jazz in cultural tours.

Unavoidably, when the CU chose the Dizzy Gillespie orchestra, an integrated group, as the first American jazz band to represent the United States abroad on a tour to the Middle East, the announcement evoked ardent, heated protests from both the public and members of Congress.[34] The decision came about in the midst of mounting Cold War tensions in the Middle East that eventually led to the contentious Suez crises and after which the world censured the Western alliance.

As debates about the tour ensued, some Americans vehemently disapproved of the musicians' salaries. The CU reported that the gov-ernment had approved a sum of $92,000 dollars for a ten-week tour.[35] One individual implored the State Department to "justify . . . wasting" money on Dizzy Gillespie, whom he called a "colored 'hoat' trumpet-er."[36] Another observer disliked the fact that Gillespie's band received $2,150 per week for his tour—more than the president's salary. Still, another citizen adamantly demanded "to know the name of the weak-minded individual or individuals responsible for this criminal waste of the taxpayer money. For years I have heard that the State Department was the hideaway of more nuts than any other Department in Wash-ington and that's going some." He further expressed his desire to "see that the idiot responsible for this waste be discharged. . . . I can furnish you hundreds of horn tooters of both races just as good as the one mentioned in this article for about $25.00 per week and expenses."[37]

However, when Adam Clayton Powell informed Gillespie that Eisenhower approved a tour to the Middle East, Gillespie, aware of the international situation, expressed both delight and surprise, the tour spiritedly engendering pride in him. In his memoirs, he recalled how he "took it as an honor, really, because they had many people they could've chosen as the first one to represent the State Department on that tour. I felt highly honored, and I like the idea of a big band that wouldn't cost me any money ... and I sort've like the idea of representing America, but I wasn't going over there to apologize for the racist policies of America." Thus in part his sense of duty as a black artist and intellectual in the public eye led him to represent the U.S. government abroad.[38] He stated to a reporter for the *Philadelphia News*, "I want to show Easterners that Negroes do all right over here."[39]

As such controversies ensued, Gillespie's band helped propel jazz and cultural containment into new and restless Cold War arenas. His band came to symbolize the fruits of American democracy and the vitality of "America's classical music," traveling to Latin America, the Middle East, and Southeast Asia.[40]

The *New York Times* reported that Gillespie's "Rover Bop Boys" began their tour of these Cold War–torn regions in mid-1956.[41] Jazz scholar Marshall Stearns accompanied Gillespie on the tour to give lectures on the history of jazz. Audiences responded enthusiastically to Gillespie's music because he imparted a spirit of democracy and engendered a positive image of race in American life. The embassy in Dacca, East Pakistan, for example, declared that the Pakistani people saw jazz as a "radical innovation" and quickly grew accustomed to it. Although Gillespie's tour did not achieve commercial success because of competing events, it proved "successful in its basic aims," according to William L. S. Williams, the American consul general.[42] Young people embraced Gillespie's jazz with zeal. In his incomparable report, Williams emphasized jazz's aesthetic appeal. He asserted that while performing on his last night in Dacca, Gillespie and his singer played extended encores as listeners cherished his powerful and expressive musical interpretations. They infinitely enjoyed how the "blare of his trumpet section" could "reach right into the very back row of the theater and shake a customer by the scruff of the neck." Gillespie played anthems "with verve, style, and flourish," candidly and mundane.[43]

Williams also heard a youngster play on a "homemade one-string violin." The boy seemed rather frightened when Gillespie extended a kind gesture and allowed him to accompany him to his hotel for an informal jam session. Thereafter, the boy became particularly enthusiastic when Gillespie invited him to perform in a rickshaw; it was an impromptu show that astounded and impressed local fans. Williams recalled that another meaningful event took place when Gillespie played a spontaneous jam with a local flutist.[44]

Importantly, Williams also reported that throughout their stay, the entire band remained "well mannered and cooperative" and were keenly aware of the State Department's objectives. Williams did not have any "doubt that Dacca acquired an ear and a taste for American jazz" and that Gillespie "pioneered promising new territory."[45] Likewise, Marshall Stearns, in a report for *Down Beat*, noted that initially in Dacca, jazz was an unknown product, but by the last night a concert hall was "jumping with new" jazz fans. On a more personal level, Stearns recalled how Quincy Jones, who played piano for Gillespie on the tour, extended a kind gesture when he "bought a complete outfit for a sailor" in Dacca.[46] Overall, both Stearns and Williams characterized Gillespie as vital to the new cultural program. Not only did he achieve goodwill and appeal to diverse audiences, but he also inspired new appreciation of the jazz art form.[47]

Most important, when fans and admirers asked Gillespie about racism in the United States, Gillespie advocated America's Cold War views toward the American dilemma. He stated that "they could see it [racism] wasn't as intense because we had white boys and I was the leader of the band. That was strange to them because they heard about blacks being lynched and burned, and here I come with half whites and blacks and a girl playin' in the band. And everybody seemed to be getting along fine. . . . [T]hose white guys were working for me. We have our problems but we're still workin' on it." Gillespie thus characterized the race question cautiously, yet optimistically, by professing that although "a hundred years ago, our ancestors were slaves, I'm sure its gonna be straightened out some day. I probably won't see it, completely, the eradication of racial prejudice in the United States, but it will be eliminated."[48]

As the tour gained "momentum," the band continued to buttress the American image when it performed in Turkey. Many events illuminated the band's broad aesthetic appeal. "Audiences normally not easily" moved in Ankara "went wild, shouting, whistling, and demonstrating that Turkey's reputation as a 'square' country was undeserved."[49] Gillespie often ended his performances with an indigenous anthem and "The Star Spangled Banner." Stearns characterized the band's "fire, cohesion, and impact" as "unbelievable." The press commented that

Gillespie's visit had become "a sweet dream for many Turks to have a chance to listen to a real jazz orchestra."[50]

On another occasion, when a dispute about the race of audience members arose, Gillespie proclaimed to the Associated Press, "I won't have any segregation here. I won't play until the people outside the fence are let in."[51] Thereafter, at the Turkish-American Association, some casually dressed laborers "happily entered the Association compound and joined the crowd." Additionally, Gillespie met with a Turkish trumpeter who, according to the Public Affairs Officer (PAO), played just as well as top American jazz men like Roy Eldridge or Miles Davis.[52] To show his appreciation, the musician gave Gillespie "a pair of Turkish slippers."[53]

Many other incidents similarly revealed audiences' overwhelming fascination with the group. When the musicians encountered a "pretty girl" who had become a fan, they learned that she was a renowned ballerina who had "sold her shoes" for a ticket to Gillespie's concert. In Karachi, Lorranie Gillespie, Dizzy's wife, who also accompanied the band on the tour, met a chambermaid who delighted in Gillespie's music and mused that the band might be "a gang of wealthy and eccentric capitalists." Furthermore, in Istanbul, Stearns and Gillespie attended a United Nations' party for entertainer Danny Kaye, where the "two celebrities gently clashed."[54]

The band continued to engender enthusiasm when, as the *New York Times* observed, American "Culture Roll[ed] On" in Syria. There, some of the "would-be hipsters . . . yelled 'Rock it and roll it!'" during performances, while others amusingly "clapped on the wrong beat." The newspaper also observed the band's fascination with the "fabulous wealth of some of the guests." Upon meeting one guest, Gillespie asserted that "this cat's got enough money to burn a wet mule."[55] On a different note, the *New York Post* shrewdly indicated that in Damascus, Gillespie's "lady trombonist" was "booed" by a male audience and then "fled in panic" because she became startled by the striking cultural differences among Middle Eastern women.[56]

The band also toured Greece, where their success seemed surprising in light of provocative and contentious cultural events that had recently taken place. A group of young people had conducted anti-American demonstrations and attacked the American Library in Athens. Gillespie also encountered substantial competition from Russian cultural groups. Stearns commented to the *Saturday Review* that Gillespie, who was keenly aware of the cultural tensions, became concerned that Athenians would not welcome the band.[57] Yet when he performed, youngsters expressed their ardent zeal and appreciation for his music. Some even "scared" Gillespie when, in admiration, they mobbed him and hauled him "over their heads." They simultaneously greeted him with "cheers of Bravo Dizzy." *Variety* characterized Gillespie's achievement in Greece as "glorious." Gillespie asserted that "I made it safe out of South Carolina and now I'm going to get it in Greece."[58]

Gillespie also received unfavorable reviews from a reporting officer who believed that the artists were not briefed properly about American objectives. To him, they appeared "arrogant" and "insulting." Most important, Soviet competition appeared ominous. The Russian Folk Ballet performed at the same time and drew large audiences. The USIS did not want to cave in to Soviet pressure by canceling Gillespie's performance—the Soviets might construe such a gesture as "a sign of weakness" and exploit it in propaganda. Consequently, Gillespie sometimes "played to half empty houses."[59]

In commenting on what he saw as Gillespie's waning appeal, the PAO claimed that his "dizzy" behavior did not amuse Athenians—the musicians once arrived over an hour late to a buffet dinner, he remarked.[60] Moreover, expressing an elitist view, he believed that the more "conservative" and "snobbish Athenians" favored the "high arts" like opera and the symphony, not jazz. The elite, he proclaimed, even "disparage[d]" jazz's African American origins. Thus Gillespie did not help dispel the notion among more "sophisticated opinion-leaders that the United States has no cultural arts which they can appreciate." Accordingly, the reporting officer discouraged jazz for future presentations in Athens and indicated his preference for such presentations as *Porgy and Bess*, a production that had triumphed in Greece despite the tense political atmosphere during its 1955 tour. Overall, he expressed the view that Gillespie did not help improve the image of American culture and life.[61]

Stearns viewed the band's visit to Greece in a different light. He recalled that even members of the Russian Folk Ballet had a chance to hear a Gillespie concert, despite the disapproval of Soviet officials. Stearns asserted that the ballet's spokesperson, who "looked just like a movie version of a commissar, chunky, determined and grumpy," wanted to hear more "sentimentality" in Gillespie's music and eventually grew enamored of the group. This, he believed, significantly decreased cultural tensions.[62] Gillespie also achieved this goal when he performed in Cairo and Beirut, according to Stearns.

U.S.-Soviet cultural relations became further tested, however, when Gillespie helped the United States launch cultural containment into Eastern Europe, a region that continually struggled to define its own independent culture while under the control of Moscow's ubiquitous authority. Gillespie's band found an enthusiastic reception in Yugoslavia. Yugoslavia's leader, Marshall Tito, had successfully challenged Moscow's central authority by establishing less oppressive Communist rule in the country, and Yugoslavia's reception of Gillespie reflected its increasing cultural autonomy. The Yugoslav jazz federation served as the local sponsor for the group.[63] Joseph C. Kolarek, PAO to Belgrade, described what he saw as Gillespie's incomparable appeal during his performance: "Jazz lovers, diplomats, and gentle white-haired ladies alike jostled elbows and squeezed sardine-like into Belgrade's Kolarac Hall on May 9 for the only first-hand contact the Yugoslavia public had to date with American jazz . . . the longest musical ear-beating in history."[64] Afterward, jazz aficionados felt deeply inspired by the concert. Kolarek concluded that Gillespie's performance had become a "triumph for the West"—it extolled "self-expression" as a defining facet of American culture. Young and old alike "bounced, clapped, whistled, and indulged" as Gillespie "belted . . . a lighter note into the drab, serious tone of Communist life."[65]

Kolarek also believed that Yugoslav officials had become more tolerant of American artists because they increasingly exhibited European musical influences. Though some Yugoslav audiences and critics disliked Gillespie's music, others, including a reporter for *Republica*, praised the "democratic . . . organization of the orchestra" and hailed the image of blacks and whites playing together harmoniously. Gillespie's black female trombonist especially impressed fans, many of whom grew "wild" about her playing. Kolarek, who wanted the band to tour again in 1957, believed that Gillespie could help establish a strong foothold for American jazz in the country. Thus he avidly praised Gillespie's role in promoting cultural containment in Yugoslavia and, simultaneously, all of Eastern Europe.[66]

Stearns expressed similar views when he recalled that on one occasion, fans stormed the stage and "serenaded" the musicians. Even a local Yugoslav reporter became a new jazz fan, despite official pressure. Likewise, during a discussion following one of Stearns's lectures at the Zagreb Music Conservatory, Yugoslav jazz fans professed that they revered the spirit of protest that American jazz artists embraced. Moreover, pianist Quincy Jones made many friends and inspired local musicians. While in Abada, Jimmy Powell, Gillespie's clarinetist, extended a gracious goodwill gesture when he gave a reed to a clarinet player who "almost cried" after receiving the gift.[67]

Overall, Gillespie's tour ended with a grand forte, according to Stearns.[68] Gillespie's evocative music significantly helped reshape the American image and make new friends in the face of ardent Soviet competition. Later that year, in the midst of the Soviet invasion of Hungary, President Eisenhower expressed appreciation for the United States' more open cultural relationship with Yugoslavia. In a letter to Tito, he declared that "our two countries have . . . supported international cooperation in an increasingly interdependent world"; moreover, he proclaimed that although the Soviet Union had denied the people's wishes for greater freedom, "your efforts have consistently been in the direction of greater independence for the country."[69]

Evidently, escalating tensions in Cold War politics had not diminished the effectiveness of jazz diplomacy. In promoting cultural containment, Gillespie effectively revealed the softer, more civilized side of American life and often buttressed the image of American race relations. Accordingly, the State Department sent the band on a subsequent tour to Latin America in the same year, where he jammed with musicians in such places as Quito, Ecuador; signed autographs; and delighted audiences in such cities as Quayaquil, Ecuador, and Montevideo, Uruguay.[70] Gillespie again helped bring American jazz into new international venues. To introduce audiences to his music, the USIS even prepared a detailed pamphlet on the band entitled *What You Should Know About Jazz and Dizzy Gillespie*.[71]

After Gillespie's momentous cultural tours, American officials increasingly sanctioned jazz as an effective weapon in the cultural Cold War. One even advocated sending modern bands because the "name" guys had already gained popularity, just like the "'old timers' of Hollywood" like Clark Gable and Joan Crawford.[72] Yet jazz policy continued to undergo considerable criticism. Many Americans sought "an explanation of [the] 'jazz band' incident."[73] One businessman claimed, "I am one of those who are now becoming definitely alarmed over the amount of government spending and the apparent inability of our officials to control this spending to any degree whatsoever. . . . I refer to the article accounted for in the *New York Times* . . . detailing the cost of sending Dizzy Gillespie into Pakistan at the cost of $141,000. . . . I cannot help but feel that someone is slipping up on a very important job."[74]

Another member of the business community characterized the program as "preposterous." He believed that it remained "a well known fact that the people in foreign countries care nothing for Dizzy Gillespie's band. All they want is American-Dollars. . . . The whole program is a deplorable farce." Disenchanted with the Republicans, he retorted that the "last thing South America needs is a Negro jazz band," and "why send one to Africa where they all came from anyway?"[75]

The uproar continued when, in a letter to a member of the CU, a woman stated, "I myself became too angered to express myself rationally and logically, despite a try at a cooling-off period. . . . I sincerely hope that if the State Department has . . . again planned on sending jazz groups abroad, it will soon reverse its decision."[76]

In their replies to such inquiries, such cultural officials as Maurice S. Rice, deputy chief of the Public Services Division, ardently justified jazz tours, pointing to the "positive response of the public abroad to this aspect of American culture." He believed that jazz "contributed effectively to the development of cultural exchange with other peoples."[77] John P. Meagher, chief of the Public Services Division, similarly argued that jazz music had resulted in "large dividends . . . in the form of new understanding of the variety and quality of" cultural life in the United States.[78] American officials further justified jazz diplomacy by declaring that the State Department regarded Gillespie as an "effective demonstration of the creativity and vitality of" American life.[79] Likewise, Marshall Stearns, also instrumental in institutionalizing jazz diplomacy, underscored the tour's significant impact by characterizing it as a "sparkling new idea in the jazz world which worked out famously."[80] On another occasion he observed that jazz represented the fun, spontaneous, "generous side of American life."[81] Upon returning to the United States, Gillespie's band played at the White House, where President Eisenhower bestowed honorary plaques on all of the musicians. During the ceremony, Gillespie was immersed in a conversation with Senator Hubert Humphrey when the president called him to the stage to accept his award. Eisenhower shouted "Dizzy . . . Gillespie. Dizzy, Dizzy." Gillespie turned to the stage and said casually, "Right over here, Pops."[82]

Not surprisingly, as the race question persisted, the tours heightened Gillespie's desire to end segregation. Having just returned from an official mission to "offset reports of racial prejudice in the United States," Gillespie became determined to "fight against racial prejudice and end all those reports" circulating around the world.[83]

Amid this controversy, the State Department had reportedly approved Armstrong for a tour to Latin America in mid-1956, which it eventually canceled because the CU could not agree on a fee for the band.[84] Armstrong traveled privately to Latin America and Ghana before it had gained its independence. *Variety* praised Armstrong when it reported: "our loudest B sharp to you, Ambassador Armstrong"; and it enthusiastically characterized him as an appealing alternative to the "commie squares."[85] The Columbia Broadcasting Company (CBS) spent $25,000 to sponsor Armstrong in Accra, where, "from the moment he walked on down the plane steps, the Gold Coast gleamed with 22-carat jive." Though some fans had "roughed him up" out of excitement, Armstrong kept his composure. He even inspired an elderly woman at Achimota College to dance to such tunes as "Royal Garden Blues."[86] Moreover, while Ghanaian high-life bands celebrated his visit, he also met with Kwame Nkrumah, whom he "promised . . . so faithfully that [he'd] return there for the big moments [independence] which lasts for about a week."[87] The *New York Times* characterized Armstrong as "a cool, sweet note in the diplomatic hot war." Armstrong, who was interviewed by Edward R. Murrow while in Africa, had returned to the land "where the blues and the colored people had their first awakening."[88]

Despite Ghana's ardent expressions of African nationalism, Wilson C. Flake, ambassador to Ghana, downplayed the factor of race during Armstrong's visit. He later argued that Armstrong's group made a smashing impact because the group represented exemplary "Americans in their particular field," not because the musicians were black or had African origins. He argued that Ghanaians appreciated Armstrong in the same way that they admired the Westminster Singers— "a white group"—because they exhibited "outstanding" artistic talent. He summed up by remarking, "Let's forget color and let the chips fall where they may."[89] Such keen disagreements regarding race and the American image echoed the growing ideological tensions between blacks and whites in American society, among CU officials, and in the jazz world.[90]

Bandleader Benny Goodman also toured for the United States in the late 1950s. He helped bolster the American image in Asia, where the United States waged the cultural Cold War before its far-reaching military involvement in Vietnam in the 1960s. A region dominated by French influence and wrought with political turmoil, Southeast Asia most notably remained a hotbed of the Cold War as Communists attempted to come to power in the region. Some officials contended that Goodman's indispensable tour advanced cultural containment because it helped impart American cultural values to Asian peoples. Similarly, audiences learned that the United States was a nation with more than just "fancy cars."[91] Like Gillespie, the fact that Goodman played with an integrated band increased the band's symbolic appeal. Goodman recalled that observers and the press often asked him about the progress of civil rights and America's racial dilemma.[92]

Goodman's 1930s style swing orchestra toured Southeast Asia just as the offshore island crisis in Quemoy and Matsuo strained relations between the United States and the People's Republic of China—Eisenhower considered using nuclear weapons to eliminate the Communist threat in the region. During Goodman's six-week tour, which began late in 1956, the band performed in such places as Bangkok, Indonesia, Malaya, the Philippines, Japan, South Korea, Taiwan, Hong Kong, South Vietnam, Burma, and Cambodia.[93] In Phnom Penh, Cambodia, the PAO recommended that the United States participate in an American cultural festival and urged contact with those Cambodians who sympathized with American cultural objectives. He recalled that Goodman

> was staged in front of the Royal Palace before a seated audience of about 1,500 invited and uninvited Cambodian guests plus what should have been a howling mob of 25,000 jazz-mad Kmers. Again, the music was complicated, but the melody lingered on, and it is safe to assume that the King of Swing . . . reached the hearts, if not the vocal chords, of his audience. A private party immediately following the public concert was also well-attended by some 200 high-ranking Cambodians, including the King and Queen, who appeared to enjoy Mr. Goodman's music immensely.[94]

The PAO coolly lamented the fact that the prince of Cambodia "preferred to sulk in his tent" rather than attend a jam session with the band. Eventually, however, Goodman played a concert for the prince, and overall, Goodman demonstrated his immense personal and musical appeal.[95] The reporting officer hoped that the Cambodian elite would continue to endorse American cultural objectives.

Because of logistical problems, Goodman's band did not achieve as

much success in South Korea, according to the PAO. Likewise, in Tokyo, an official called Goodman's scheduled appearance a "fiasco" that
"still rankles"—the embassy had to cancel Goodman's performance
due to the band's unscheduled stop in Taipei.[96]

Nonetheless, the *New York Times* ardently praised Goodman's tour
overall, asserting that in Thailand, where Goodman performed at the
International Trade Fair, the band bolstered U.S.-Thai relations more
than any other cultural exchange previously had. Goodman decidedly
broke down cultural barriers, especially when the band performed in
the palace of King Phumphol Adulet, who loved the music so much
that he asked the musicians to play four jam sessions. The band also
performed in the homes of Thai musicians and fans and displayed an
"uninhibited and unaffected appreciation of every kindness shown
them." Simultaneously, the group revealed a love for Thailand's "gaudy
wonders." Their performance of Thai songs elated audiences. As they
visited clubs and dance halls, "bonds of sympathy and understanding"
emerged. Some band members enthusiastically learned to write their
names in Thai.[97] Likewise, *Variety* reported that during Goodman's
"Swing-Ding" in Singapore, though he played during a Singapore holiday, audiences deeply appreciated his music. Thirty-five hundred fans
shouted for Goodman's jazz during his concerts, and his music captivated local musicians. Even clubs in Singapore hosted jam sessions for
the group.[98]

Goodman's tour helped cement his status as a Cold War cultural
ambassador and a symbol of American exuberance. Like Gillespie, his
band created new audiences for jazz and established important cultural contacts in volatile Cold War regions. Goodman often softened
the image of American culture among Southeast Asian peoples. After
returning to the United States, Goodman attempted to secure an official invitation to tour the Soviet Union. Toward this end, he invited
Soviet composer Dimitry Shostakovich and Soviet official Tikhon
Khrennikov to a concert at Basin Street East in New York City. He also
met Utrech Utysov, a noted Soviet advocate of jazz.[99] It was not until
the early 1960s, however, that Goodman successfully brought his celebrated style of jazz to the Slavic land where his parents were born.

In 1957, as Cold War crises enveloped the world, U.S.-Soviet Cold
War competition in Africa significantly intensified, and the context of
the Cold War in Africa dramatically shifted. West Africa in particular
became a focal point when it experienced rapid political, social, economic, and cultural changes.[100] After a series of political maneuvers,

the British accepted Ghana's motion for independence, and Ghana gained its long-awaited independence in March 1957. Kwame Nkrumah was inaugurated as the prime minister of Ghana and became the first African leader to bring his country to independence in the postwar era.[101] In the wake of this movement, the State Department increasingly recognized Nkrumah's enigmatic appeal. He declared a policy of neutrality in the Cold War and became the most powerful leader on the African continent.[102]

In an effort to secure the allegiance of Ghana and other African nations, the United States sponsored Wilbur De Paris's New Orleans Jazz Band, an all-black group, for an African tour. Many African American jazz musicians proclaimed cultural affinity with Africa and fervently expressed this sentiment in their music.[103] Yet cultural tensions escalated when, in Algeria, political and domestic turmoil arising because of the Algerian civil war forced De Paris to cancel his appearance.[104] Regarding the crisis, Eisenhower wrote in his diary that "he . . . hope[d] that the United States could find some way to mediate in that useless struggle."[105] Moreover, in Southern Rhodesia, the American consul, who focused on attempts to improve multiracial cooperation, preferred an "occasional Negro artist of the virtuosity and personality of" William Warfield to help dispel prevalent cultural and social prejudices.[106]

De Paris also visited the French and Belgian regions of the Congo— Brazzaville and Léopoldville (Kinshasa), respectively; he likewise performed in Elisabethville (Lubumbashi).[107] When the band traveled to Dar es Salaam, Tanzania, John Anderson Naunda, a member of the city's Jazz Club Federation, underscored that jazz deeply influenced images of race and democracy, maintaining that African jazz musicians sought to emulate American jazz performers. In an adulatory letter to the American consul, he extolled the links between jazz and liberty, and between black culture and black nationalism. He stated that "Africans felt it a unique opportunity of being honored by the visit of such a band, and that our faith and trust in the U.S.A. Government is [sic] very great. . . . We also believe that in spite of the present state of world affairs, the United States Government will always display to all other nations that she is the true Champion of Liberty and the greatest Benefactor to all underdeveloped peoples all over the world."[108]

Overall, American officials praised De Paris and extolled the efficacy of jazz as an instrument of global containment. Reflecting upon the enthusiasm De Paris engendered, Cushman C. Reynolds, the PAO, asserted that for "Americans, at least, it was a little unreal—however delightful—to sit out of doors in the starlit African night and hear a high-caliber live orchestra play the *Saint Louis Blues*. And it was heartwarming to see a man of Mr. De Paris' personal caliber in action. He had the crowd with him even when he refused a request to play 'rock n' roll' ('Bobby sox stuff,' he said) . . . fast."[109] When De Paris visited the Sudan and Tunis, the ambassador remarked that his band became one of the top American performers to appear—De Paris became a hit with Sudanese jazz fans, especially the students. This occurred not only because of the musicians' "splendid" performances but also because of their personal appeal—they candidly discussed American racial problems. From beginning to end, the audiences "got with it" until they heard "the final growl of Mr. De Paris' trombone."[110] Such leaders as the minister of agriculture attended the concert, along with members of the business community. Additionally, De Paris gave an interview with the USIS for Tunis radio and socialized with French and Tunisian cultural groups. The Tunisian press and the PAO all embraced De Paris's music.

An official in Addis Ababa, Ethiopia, similarly believed that De Paris helped improve the American image in that country. De Paris's performances at the Haile Selassie Theater, his charity jam session, and the benefit for an Ethiopian children's center appeared "highly" effective. This resulted in part from jazz's popularity in Ethiopia, as well as from favorable publicity and "the close cooperation given the Embassy by private, municipal, and military musical groups."[111] Curiosity about the race question also sparked interesting conversations. The group reportedly impressed an Ethiopian body guard who amusingly expressed profound surprise when he learned that blacks in the United States could buy "material possessions"—they bought their own houses and cars, he mused.[112]

As De Paris continued his tour through Casablanca and East Africa, according to a reporting officer, he continually attempted to reinvent his music in an effort to echo modern times while staying true to the traditions of New Orleans jazz. De Paris believed that musical "interpretation must come from the heart."[113] Significantly, however, the American consul in Nairobi believed that the race question sometimes undermined the effectiveness of cultural containment and led to embarrassing incidents. First, De Paris had to turn down performing in a local segregated nightclub "because of the implied support of segregation that would have been involved."[114] He also refused an appearance for the European Hospital Fund. The band not only had a previous engagement but also would have performed and helped "raise money for a building to which they would not be admitted." Ultimately, De Paris's tour became a powerful portrait of black American cultural achievement that momentarily obscured racial conflicts.[115] The tour also reflected U.S. efforts to foster cultural contacts with the British in Africa by emphasizing "multi-racialism."[116] In Nigeria, still under British rule, an official had urged working toward common goals, ultimately hoping to promote the "assimilation of Americana."[117]

On the home front, the tours of Gillespie, Goodman, and De Paris ignited passions in some musicians that reflected their aversion to the American mainstream and provoked yet one more "battle" about the place of jazz in the Cold War world.[118] Such battles gave rise to disputes that complicated American efforts to use jazz as an instrument of global containment. The CU regarded many of the new musical styles in the 1950s and 1960s as turbulent and subversive and did not include them in cultural tours. Reflecting the tensions between culture and ideology that persisted at the height of the Cold War, for the CU, it had become too perilous for the United States to endorse subversive or radical art forms in an era in which subversive and radical activities were characterized as un-American.

Additionally, the United States strove to endorse the status quo; as it sought to promote the message of integration, it did not seek to encourage radicalism through its cultural programs, especially when sponsoring activities in tumultuous Cold War arenas. Mainstream styles of jazz, not the jazz avant-garde, safely represented democratic ideals and the dynamism of American cultural traditions and, most important, the move toward integration and racial harmony in American society that was mocked in Soviet propaganda. Thus jazz diplomacy challenged jazz musicians to accept the responsibility to be exemplars of their art and simultaneously embrace America's Cold War aims through their music. Such dynamics sometimes became a source of contention for American policy makers, who shaped the political statement jazz artists sought to make when confronting the American image abroad. The musicians took part in cultural tours because they had confidence in jazz's ability to cultivate feelings of solidarity with peoples outside of Europe while presenting a more democratic view of American life. They did not endorse the idea that their activities as cultural ambassadors had simply become one more facet of Western imperial domination. Instead, they believed that by becoming involved in exchanges, they provided an "alternative to it."[119] In subsequent years, Glenn G. Wolfe, director of the CPP staff, proclaimed that jazz was "certainly no substitute for the great symphonies, and . . . must be kept in its own context."[120]

Aware of such controversies, Robert G. Hill, assistant secretary for cultural relations, defended jazz as the country's unique contribution to world culture and declared that it helped create a "truly representative" panorama of American music while illuminating the country's "exuberant, pioneering spirit."[121] The appropriation of jazz in the late 1950s buttressed the policy of cultural containment by capitalizing on jazz's worldwide appeal, by responding to the international demand for black cultural products, and by encouraging racially integrated cultural contacts in Communist regions.

Jazz diplomacy thereafter heightened an appreciation of the multilayered cultural nuances of American life. In this new era of the Cold War, many embraced jazz for its aesthetic appeal as it helped improve the image of America's racial dilemma in new global arenas. It simultaneously reinforced the notion of American exceptionalism as the Soviets intensified their global cultural offensive. Amid Cold War disputes, African American musicians struggled for cultural autonomy, and jazz music at home and abroad became saturated with the ethos of the times. Jazz musicians challenged America to embrace the ideal of black equality as jazz emerged as a uniquely American expression of the vitality and contradictions of American democracy. The music waxed powerful and provocative and was also recognized for its energy and vitality among youth worldwide—especially in the Soviet Union, where the youth were hungry to share in the cultural idealism of the jazz musicians from the Western world. Jazz helped impel the ideological disunity that increasingly came to characterize Cold War cultures worldwide. It crossed over color lines, class lines, and lines of taste and morality. It tested the limits of American freedom and challenged whites' tolerance for African American musical ideals.

As they traveled abroad, jazz ambassadors represented the frayed soul of a divided people—and a divided nation—in a rapidly changing Cold War world. They provided spiritual inspiration to peoples and nations that sought to affirm their identities as citizens of the world and embrace political causes through their music. The musicians' achievement echoed the sentiments of such musicians as Miles Davis, who declared that "if you put a musician in a place where he has to do something different from what he does all the time, then he can do that. . . . I've always told the musicians in my band to play what they *know* and then play *above that*. . . . [T]hat's where great art and music happens."[122]

Chapter 3
Jazz Means Freedom, 1957–1960

> To play such music, to make so many people happy for so many years, is [a]
> far, far better thing than . . . to command armies, [or] lead nations.
> —Ralph Gleason, 1958

Just months after Wilbur De Paris's historic tour to Africa, the school
desegregation crisis in Little Rock, Arkansas, set off a chain of events
at home and abroad that dramatically altered the course of jazz diplomacy: from 1957 to 1960 jazz policy makers became reluctant to
sponsor black jazz musicians in cultural tours and questioned the efficacy of using black jazz in cultural policy. In the view of the Bureau of
Educational and Cultural Affairs (CU), the use of black jazz musicians
might heighten attention on America's racial problems. Contrarily,
conservative, mainstream white jazz bands would offset controversies
about race and help avoid a common exposé associated with jazz and
Little Rock—"regime propaganda linking jazz to" the subjugation of
blacks in the United States.[1] The activities of expatriates and free jazz
performers added to the perceived chaos the United States sought
to quell. In this vein, Little Rock signified a critical turning point in
America's rhetorical approach to Cold War cultural relations. It was
not until the independence of French West Africa in 1960 that the CU
again began to sponsor a majority of all-black and racially integrated
groups in its jazz tours.

The Little Rock crisis played out when Arkansas governor Orval
Faubus defied a federal court order and refused to integrate Central
High School. President Dwight D. Eisenhower sent federal troops, as
well as the National Guard, to the town to try to protect the black
students who were integrating the school. Violence and rioting ensued
as the federal troops escorted a group of nine black children into the
school. The Little Rock Nine came to symbolize America's paradoxical racial image in the Cold War era: they underscored that the leader
of the free world was committed to democracy only in theory, rather
than in actual practices.[2] In the words of Thomas C. Holt, Little Rock
exemplified how blacks worldwide remained "anchored in a past time,
but always looking to a future time."[3] To add to the fervor, in Octo-

ber 1957 the Soviet Union launched *Sputnik*, the world's first satellite. Symbolically, this represented a Russian triumph and an American defeat in the race for space.[4]

As Little Rock and *Sputnik* reshaped the global context of cultural containment, the Soviets intensified anti-American propaganda campaigns and emerged as the most vocal critic of the incident in Arkansas. Eisenhower became deeply concerned that Little Rock imperiled "national security" especially because America's adversaries worldwide celebrated the country's embarrassment.[5] Historian Cary Fraser argues that Little Rock caused the United States to shift its policies and practices with "colored nations." As the United States sought to counter its image as a "bastion of white supremacy," it saturated the world with black cultural products, launching a steadfast effort to contain the international censure arising from the event.[6]

In the fallout after Little Rock, debates about race, culture, and the ethos of jazz inescapably proceeded unabated in America. As this critical link between ideology and culture emerged in the CU's jazz policy, Ellington remembered that

> when you think of the lost time and effort President Eisenhower spent trying to settle the Little Rock situation, in fact the time being lost all over the South as well as places in the North over the school desegregation ordered by the Supreme Court in 1954, you'll get the idea of how and why the Russians may be having breakfast on the moon by the time you read this. It seems to me that the problem of America's inability so far to go ahead of or at least keep abreast of Russia in the race for space can be traced directly to this racial problem.[7]

Similarly, such musicians as Charles Mingus ridiculed Faubus in a recording "Foibles of Faubus," his music becoming an overt "satiric" "parody" that embraced an expression of defiance and self-assertion against southern racism.[8]

The most explosive controversy surrounding Little Rock arose when Louis Armstrong decisively canceled an official State Department tour to the Soviet Union. In a provocative article, a reporter declared that the lessening of international tensions boded well for an Armstrong tour to the Soviet Union—but the Little Rock crisis changed that.[9] Little Rock impelled Armstrong to divulge one of the most fervent expressions of America's racial paradox during the Cold War. On September 19 the *New York Times* reported that in Grand Forks, North

Dakota, "Louis Armstrong, Barring Soviet Tour, Denounces Eisenhower and Gov. Faubus." Armstrong asserted that "the way they treat my people in the South, the government can go to hell." Moreover, he reportedly remarked that "it's getting so bad a colored man hasn't got any country." Armstrong, "a voice long quiet in world affairs," had "unloaded a verbal blast echoed virtually around the world." He even called President Eisenhower "two-faced" and claimed that Eisenhower was an "uneducated plow boy" who "let Faubus 'run the country.'"[10]

Armstrong subsequently remarked to the *Pittsburgh Courier* that

> I wouldn't take back a thing I've said. I've had a beautiful life over 40 years in music, but I feel the downtrodden situation the same as any other Negro. My parents and family suffered through all of that old South. . . . My people . . . are not looking for anything . . . we just want a square shake. But when I see on television and read about a crowd spitting on and cursing at a little colored girl . . . I think I have a right to get sore and say something about it.[11]

American officials inordinately worried about the propaganda value that the "Reds" might derive from Armstrong's "verbal blast."[12] One reporter commented that "Satchmo's Words Rocked [the] State Dept." and caused a "political earthquake."[13] Similarly, an official denounced Armstrong's "insult to beloved President Eisenhower" and adamantly discouraged State Department funding. Another professed that "as an American," he protested "most vigorously anyone who has made such a statement as 'the government can go to hell' being sponsored by any branch of our government."[14]

The public reaction to Armstrong's "blast" grew equally controversial. The *Gazette and Daily* pointed out that "Negro Entertainers Back Up Armstrong's Action in Cancelling Trip."[15] Yet while some of Armstrong's friends supported him, others, including the popular entertainer Sammy Davis Jr., vehemently criticized his provocative candor.[16] In a letter to the State Department, an individual called Armstrong a "sacred cow" and declared that he objected to his tour, "not because I think his music is drivel, which it is, but I certainly can't see how" a musician who makes such a remark about the government "can be any sort of an effective salesman for it."[17] Others expressed the opinion that Armstrong's comments "disqualified" him as a goodwill ambassador.[18] The *Miami Herald* likewise reported that Armstrong's remarks "destroyed his 'good will' usefulness behind the Iron Curtain."[19]

The controversy arising from Armstrong's "blast" simultaneously revealed that profoundly entrenched nineteenth-century ideas of white racial superiority remained deeply ingrained in the American cultural landscape. In a trenchant letter to the State Department, a woman proclaimed that Armstrong should be thankful "every day" that "he isn't still in slavery. I believe in equal but *separate* rights." The taxpayers, she professed, did not "give a hoot what any country thinks of our way of life." She did not believe that race and integration remained significant amid the "facts of international life." In her ardent protests, she also exclaimed that

> the very idea of the heads of this government being so very stupid . . . surely there must be something wrong.
>
> Aren't they aware this country was given to Christian people, the Anglo-Saxon race, not the negro race, even tho you politicians have about sold it out for the Negro vote.
>
> The very idea of the tax payer money being given to a negro, one of a heathen race of people, to represent our nation to a Communist Country which has only one aim, that is to destroy this race, Anglo-Saxon. A prophetess has spoken. . . . The saddest story ever told.[20]

Notably, those who defended Armstrong included American jazz critic Ralph Gleason. Gleason firmly denounced Armstrong's critics and praised his ability to stand up and talk back to the president. He simultaneously expressed the opinion that the verbal dispute reflected the resilience of American democracy: he believed that Armstrong experienced no significant reprisals after making his cacophonous comments. In Gleason's view, Armstrong had taken jazz, the "legacy of the Negro race, and had given it to the world."[21]

Significantly, after Eisenhower sent federal troops to Little Rock to resolve the crisis, Armstrong had a change of heart. The *New York Times* reported that "Eisenhower's Action [Is] Lauded by Satchmo."[22] In a telegram to President Eisenhower, Armstrong exposed his politically savvy approach to race and culture and revealed that he remained an astute observer of social affairs. He proclaimed: "Dady if and when you decide to take those little Negro children personally into Central High School along with your marvelous troops please take me along. O God it would be such a great pleasure I assure you. My regard to brother [Attorney General Herb] Brownell and may God bless you President. You have a good heart."[23]

Armstrong later told *Variety* that he extolled jazz's international appeal and its potential to "lessen world tensions," especially in the context of U.S.-Soviet relations. He professed that "everywhere I have gone in the world, I have been well received and understood." He even recognized that Russian musicians had a love for jazz—for while performing in West Germany, Armstrong had met Russian musicians who had "slipped over the iron curtain." Armstrong then insisted that he supported the idea of touring the Soviet Union, proclaiming that when "you sit down to play jazz, to blow with Satchmo, there is no enmity. One man rule has no influence in such a background."[24]

Amid the fervor, an American businessman voiced his surprise at how Armstrong "changed his tune" after Eisenhower sent troops to Little Rock. He asserted, "I can visualize the contempt which even colored races must feel for a Government which would send such a man out as a representative of the American people. It would smack of boot-lickin', and meet with a well deserved sneer." He avidly professed that Armstrong was "no longer the disciple abroad of unity and the opportunities for advancement, whatever the color of a man's skin"; he then sharply derided Armstrong as an "instrument for those who would destroy" the United States.[25]

As controversies ensued, U.S. officials sought to effectively implement cultural containment without relinquishing broader Cold War interests. They deeply feared potential alliances of powerful African and Asian states with the Soviet Union. Seeking to reach prominent sectors of these societies, especially in such politically important countries as Ghana and Vietnam, officials debated the propaganda value of sponsoring black cultural figures.[26] An American official in Turkey requested such artists as William Warfield, who was "good for propaganda purposes" because he was an accomplished African American performer.[27] The secretary of state received a pressing request from an official in the Middle East in September 1957. It suggested that in such regions as India and Africa, the United States immediately should counter the effects of Little Rock by printing an Associated Press wirephoto in newspapers that depicted "Vice President Nixon presenting the winner's trophy to Miss Althea Gibson, the first Negress ever to win the National Women's Tennis Championship."[28] Most notably, the CU sponsored world-renowned opera singer Marian Anderson on a tour to Asia in 1957. Because she performed an art form derived from Europe, she presented African Americans as a vibrant component of American and international life, showcased the exuberance of American culture, and helped redress the American dilemma without the racial stigmas and implications of jazz.

Anderson became a highly appealing U.S. cultural ambassador despite expressing initial reluctance to the tour because of the race problem. When she performed in Seoul, Korea, the reporting officer characterized her visit as "the most important cultural exchange event of the year." During a dinner, she talked with many prominent Korean musicians, and young Korean women looked up to her as a "respected leader." The official also believed that she had acquired "a reputation and social standing which very few people could emulate." When she responded to questions about American race relations, according to an official report, the "colored lady who sang a song at the inauguration of the President of the United States" expressed her deep hope that the U.S. race problem would be "cured."[29]

Anderson also impressed the king of Bangkok as she launched "the most memorable cultural event in Thailand since the war." Mesmerized by her great "artistic and dramatic abilities," the king allowed her to shake his hand in public, a gesture that was contrary to Thai custom. Additionally, when a young Thai girl wrote an essay that appeared in Thailand's Young Women's Christian Association (YWCA) bulletin, she praised Anderson effusively. The youngster especially expressed her appreciation for black American spirituals that, to her, keenly elucidated the idea of black oppression. Such songs "made her heart which was sad for her people to feel better." The young girl also commended Abraham Lincoln.[30]

Anderson's visit likewise symbolized the unshackling of racial barriers in Rangoon, where the embassy indicated that her performance "afforded a number of Burmese leaders (many perhaps for the first time) an opportunity to meet a truly outstanding American Negro. Her simplicity, sincerity and spirituality, traits of character highly esteemed among the Burmese, won an immediate and appreciative response. . . . [She represented] opportunities afforded by a democratic society."[31]

The singer met with continued success in Saigon, according to Thomas D. Bowie, counselor of embassy for political affairs, as Cold War tensions escalated further.[32] In North Vietnam, under the leadership of Ho Chi Minh, Communist nationalists had begun their quest for control of the North and the South. After the North Vietnamese Communists defeated the French at Dienbienphu in 1954, the Eisenhower administration increasingly sent military advisers and economic aid to South Vietnam. With U.S. support, Ngo Dinh Diem became the leader of the South and ruled until he was assassinated in 1963.[33] These events foreshadowed the political and social conflicts in Vietnam that perilously eclipsed other Cold War rivalries in the 1960s.

Anderson's broadcast on Radio Saigon's Voice of Vietnam became the "first exception to the rule that no American singer of any sort should be heard on that channel."[34] She also visited a refugee camp and gave a concert at a motion picture house—Majestic Theatre—where audiences were mostly European and American. Equally important, Anderson met with President Ngo Dinh Diem. Afterward, Bowie claimed that the "benefits from Miss Anderson's tour . . . went far beyond merely the cultural performances in the theatre; the Anderson personality and the charm of the entire party were felt wherever they appeared, whether it was at a diplomatic reception or at a refugee camp, and they presented their side of America in the best imaginable way."[35]

In Madras, Anderson's performance equally improved the American image, according to the American consul. Again, her personal impact proved indispensable. She became more honored than any American artist that year, he professed.[36] One of the most effusive reviews of her visit appeared in the *Hindu* in November 1957. Describing her in glowing terms, the newspaper extolled her middle-class upbringing in Philadelphia as well as her great achievements overcoming racial obstacles. It declared that she "has had to beat down prejudices arising out of colour, class and sex." The article also highlighted her courage in dealing with the incident in 1939 at Constitution Hall—the Daughters of the American Revolution, a conservative women's group, had prevented her from performing because she was black.[37]

In Manila, an official professed that "she loom[ed] much larger than the ordeal of Little Rock, which after all, will pass, whereas Marian Anderson is of all time."[38] The *Philippines Herald* likewise praised her for her "personal merit and character," which prevailed over "all barriers, even those of racial prejudice."[39] Similarly, the *Manila Chronicle* observed that the United States "is not all jukebox" and that presenting "Miss Anderson and her voice to our part of the world is making up for Orval Faubus. He is barbarian and . . . a rustic disgrace, because the real America, as well as the rest of the good world, hails Marian Anderson."[40] Likewise, Manilans exalted Anderson when presenting a bust to her at the All Nations Women's Group Tea. She received praise for showing American "good-will and the spirit of brother-hood," something to which Manilans declared they also aspired.[41]

After Anderson's tour, a movie about her travels, *The Lady from Philadelphia*, was made for Edward R. Murrow's *See It Now* program, which appeared on CBS television. Many applauded the film, lauding Anderson for building "bonds of fraternity" and "binding peoples of the world regardless of color and customs." Her popularity soared.[42] The *Saturday Review* described her tour in glowing terms. It emphatically proclaimed that Anderson, as depicted in *The Lady from Philadelphia*, vividly epitomized American ideals in the context of anti-Communism: she conveyed the idea that "formerly slaves to white masters from the West" were now their "own masters free to choose between the Communists and us." The movie professed that slavery and a "poverty of spiritual values" would result if newly independent countries chose Communism over American industry and culture. Anderson epitomized the promise of the nation through her stunning "sense of song" and her impassioned artistry. She symbolized the potential of Western civilization to triumph over Soviet foes—her tour was a "propaganda triumph."[43]

Another propaganda triumph that helped generate praise for black artists was the tour of the Florida A&M University Players to Africa in 1958. As the African continent moved toward independence, the group played in Addis Ababa, Ethiopia, where, according to Stephen W. Baldanza, Public Affairs Officer (PAO), Haile Selassie, the leader of Ethiopia, "expressed his pleasure at seeing 'Afro-Americans' in such a large number at one time." He observed that Selassie generally exhibited a feeling of "affinity" toward African Americans who visited the continent.[44]

Burt F. McKee Jr., PAO to Cairo, likewise commended the group when he boldly asserted that "the greatest impact made by the group was on a person-to-person basis rather than on a cultural one. Wherever they went, they were recognized as American Negroes and were greeted with cries of 'welcome.' This was not only true of the 'Musky' (market place) . . . but also when the group walked through the streets of Cairo."[45]

McKee also declared that a young black man working on the Afro-Asian youth conference remained eager to converse with the group and to learn more about American life.[46] Likewise, the Florida A&M University Players were "mobbed" at Cairo University; and in Ghana,

Henry A. Dunlap, PAO, asserted that "there can be no question but that the appearance of the Players in Ghana had a net effect favorable to the United States," not only culturally but also socially.[47]

These historic tours, however, did not help dispel the paradox of race, which resonated loudly on the world stage. Wilson C. Flake, ambassador to Ghana, put forth the view that the American policy of sending blacks to perform in cultural presentations might have backfired. He discouraged sending black artists to the region, arguing that "mediocre" black performers could do a disservice to the program. He contended that

> Ghanaians . . . like to see Americans who really have something to offer, regardless of ethnic origin. In fact, there is an ever-present danger that the Ghanaians may think that we tend to discriminate against them in a sense by sending a number of persons from one ethnic group out of all proportion to the population ratio in the United States. Even some thoughtful American Negroes who have visited here have expressed to me some concern about the emphasis on racial factors when we are choosing Americans to come here for cultural presentations. Some of them have felt, and I most certainly agree, that we are doing the American Negro himself a disservice when we send mediocre Negroes here for cultural presentations.[48]

Likewise, in April 1958 Cushman C. Reynolds, PAO to Khartoum, declared that

> it is a well known fact here that the United States has a racial problem as does the Sudan. The lamentable incidents at Little Rock certainly did much to focus world attention on this problem and resurrect widespread condemnation of the treatment of the Negro in the United States. It is well to show other people in every way possible that we are at least trying by legislation, if not by other means, to remedy the evils of racial discrimination. But it would seem that by over stressing our earnest endeavors to proclaim that we have goodwill to all men, we may be drawing too much attention to the fact and thus defeating our purpose. . . . We are not fooling anyone here in Khartoum by so far selecting only Negro artists to come to the Sudan.[49]

Thus Reynolds, like Flake, claimed that overemphasizing the factor of race could undermine the goals of cultural containment. He further asserted that "in fact, it would seem to stress to the people here that they are of a different color, and will undoubtedly bring forth some rather caustic remarks from Sudanese friends." Reynolds urged that the United States send white performers to Africa in order to present "balance" in the cultural program and to represent the United States more "correctly."[50]

The shift in emphasis on black musicians who performed art forms other than jazz also resulted in part from the need to offset the impact of black expatriates abroad. The CU recognized that expatriates significantly contributed to the country's waning international image and thereby attempted to restrict their international activities. The paradoxical complexity of the cultural forces shaping the policy of cultural containment expanded in many venues. In Latin America, Josephine Baker, who had become a citizen of France, openly criticized the race problem, and in the early 1950s the State Department convinced governments in the region to ban her performances.[51] Additionally, the American embassy in Paris emphatically denied her request for a conference with President Eisenhower, predicting that such a meeting could only have a detrimental effect. When the embassy informed her of its decision, it reiterated that "her past record of abusive statements toward the United States would seem to more than outweigh any possible statement she might make."[52]

At home, expatriates like W. E. B. DuBois and Paul Robeson had their passports revoked in the early 1950s. Robeson had criticized American involvement in the Korean War because black troops who fought in Korea did not receive official recognition for their valor. Many in the press discredited his opinion.[53] DuBois was indicted and fined when he refused to sign a State Department document denying that he was a Communist.[54] When the State Department revoked his passport, he professed that "it [was] curious to see America, the United States looking on herself, first, as a sort of natural peacemaker, then as a moral protagonist in this terrible time. No nation is less fitted for this role. . . . Instead of standing as a great example of the success of democracy and the possibility of human brotherhood America has taken her place as an awful example of its pitfalls and failures."[55] Such incidents further ignited DuBois's belief in the virtues of Soviet socialism. After his passport was reinstated in 1958, he visited the Soviet Union, and in a letter to the foreign editor of the *Literary Gazette*, he wrote:

> For this experience, I stand with bared head before the miracle of the Union of the Soviet Socialist Republics, before a great nation. . . . I know that this

miracle has been accomplished in the face of the armed attack from nearly every civilized nation in the world including my own; that it has been carried on doggedly in the midst of economic boycott and a vicious slander and barrage of lies which reached a depth of infamy which this world has seldom if ever seen before. . . . I am astonished at the wealth of ability and strength and moral courage which the Soviet Union has given the world in the Twentieth Century.[56]

As DuBois's political philosophy evolved, he espoused the belief that black Americans should create their own nation within a nation. Segregation could be "positive," he asserted; integration, however, remained a "distant ideal," under the "veil" in a nation of white supremacy.[57] John G. Day, second secretary of embassy at the Hague, regarded DuBois as a perilous voice in international affairs. When he heard DuBois speak for the Council of the Arts in September 1958, he characterized his speech as "brief, rapidly delivered, and full of hate for" the United States. Reportedly, DuBois voiced fierce "anti-Americanism," reflected in his declaration that the U.S. government strove for war in order to save capitalism.[58]

Shortly thereafter, in October 1958 DuBois attended the International Congress of African and Asian Writers in Tashkent, Uzbekistan.[59] And in Prague, the embassy observed that he had avid supporters in the Soviet Union, many of whom claimed that "the brave fighter of the coloured people in the United States not only publicly declared that the socialist countries are the hope of the peace and mainstay of the colonial nations and oppressed minorities, but also fought for years against defeatism and the spirit of Munich among his own people."[60]

In the same vein, singer Ruth Reese represented a contentious voice in Europe, according to John W. Piercey, labor attaché in Oslo. He grew concerned because she emphasized the negative aspects of American race relations in a speech at the University of Oslo during a private tour, criticizing southern governments and white supremacist groups—the Ku Klux Klan and White Citizens Council. She asserted that "530 atrocities against Negroes in the South . . . had gone unpunished." These included bombings of schools, churches, homes, and synagogues. Significantly, according to Piercey, Reese did not balance such criticism with "an account of the gains made in some relations," such as school integration. He proclaimed that she "left the general impression of unrelieved terror and oppression of the Negro race in the United States." She "excoriated" Eisenhower's handling of the Little Rock crisis, professing that the United States should "sweep before its own door" before criticizing others.[61]

Policy makers likewise believed that Robeson's impact in Eastern Europe and the Soviet Union appeared ominous, especially after a classic Cold War confrontation had begun: the heated dispute between the United States and the Soviet Union over the political division of Berlin. Robeson became a devout supporter of Communist regimes and traveled to Berlin in 1960.[62] The American embassy in Berlin believed that "Communist fronts or regimes" sponsored some of Robeson's appearances, including one in Berlin. A reporting officer asserted that Robeson had become a member of what he saw as subversive front organizations, such as the Council on African Affairs, the African American Peace Council, and the Civil Rights Congress.[63] Robeson also expressed support for the Soviet zone in Berlin at the Third Annual Press Festival of Art, where he sang "Fatherland No Enemy Shall Threaten You." To add to the fervor, he had allegedly claimed that black Americans would not take up arms against the Soviet Union. He decried democracies as "pro-fascist" and when commenting on Little Rock stated that "he would have asked 'thousands of Negroes from all over the U.S. to go there armed' and he was sure nothing would have happened."[64] Though the American embassy in Berlin advocated boycotting Robeson's performances, it surmised that "disavowing his political intent could prove counterproductive."[65] Howard Trivers, chief of the Eastern European Affairs Division, sought to diffuse Robeson's impact by declaring that he was not representative of most black Americans. He argued that Robeson might have greater appeal in Asia and Africa.[66]

Robeson also traveled to Moscow in 1960, where he engaged in numerous artistic and intellectual activities: he appeared on Soviet television, attended a mass meeting at an industrial plant, and listened to a reading of works by Anton Chekov. Additionally, he made a presentation to Soviet artists at the World Peace Council.[67] Llewellyn E. Thompson, U.S. ambassador to Moscow, reported on Robeson's efforts to promote Soviet-black cooperation through spirituals and jazz. Such Soviet newspapers as the *Literary Gazette* and *Trud*, he noted, praised Robeson's artistic and political endeavors, as Robeson also expressed keen admiration for Khrushchev. *Trud* thus declared that Robeson represented a "bright searchlight [that] . . . illuminated the path to a new world, to a world without wars and human suffering."[68]

In a statement about American race relations, Robeson reportedly had claimed that

> a few days ago a jury in the state of Mississippi acquitted nine white racists who in April of last year lynched Negroe Chauffeur Mack Parker. The American people should understand that one cannot continue to talk about basic democracy when in our country such things happen. . . . Naturally, in the Soviet Union racial discrimination is an unthinkable thing. Your country does everything possible to aid the countries of Asia and Africa. . . . [In the end] peace will conquer war.[69]

Not surprisingly, American racial attitudes and the activities of black expatriates reinforced perceptions abroad of America's cultural paradoxes. Officials from Malaysia and Singapore who visited the United States expressed their belief in the "stereotype of the average American as an ignoramus." Apparently, an American official concluded, Malaysians assumed that they knew "more about the Americans than they kn[e]w about themselves."[70]

These factors shaped the context that led policy makers to continually emphasize the need to present white groups for jazz tours. W. K. Bunce, counselor for public affairs in New Delhi, recommended a white performer—Gerry Mulligan—for a tour.[71] An official in Rio requested such jazz groups as Woody Herman's band, while the embassy in Czechoslovakia pointed to the popularity of Dave Brubeck.[72] In Poland, Edward A. Symans, attaché in Warsaw, believed that for propaganda and cultural purposes, a white jazz group "would rekindle waning sentiments and strongly reinforce relationships still alive."[73] Ultimately, even after American embassies throughout Africa—from Senegal to the Congo—made numerous requests for jazz, especially for Louis Armstrong, the CU chose Dave Brubeck to represent the country on the next jazz tour.[74] Brubeck's group was all-white, except for the African American bass player, Eugene Wright. Not surprisingly, some black jazz musicians sharply opposed the CU's choice.[75] A deep rift in jazz policy had clearly emerged.

Brubeck traveled abroad for the CU in 1958 against the backdrop of contentious Cold War disputes, his music embodying the white mainstream values of Cold War America that had come to define the parameters of commercial jazz in the 1950s. Significantly, his group traveled to Poland, South Asia, and the Middle East, but did not tour Africa. This policy came about in part because the Eisenhower administration continued to identify relations with Europe as a priority over those with Africa and sought to buttress cultural containment in the Soviet sphere. Like Gillespie's, his music engendered passion in this region and helped break down Cold War cultural barriers in neutral nations.[76] The USIS presented Brubeck's jazz as the artistry of the "elite" high culture—the "finest modern music" in the United States.[77] Amid the fervor of Little Rock, jazz policy keenly reflected DuBois's proposition that "all art is propaganda and ever must be, despite the wailing of the purists."[78]

In March 1958, when Brubeck's "'Cool' or 'horn-rimmed' jazz came" to Poland, official reports often pointed to the aesthetically noteworthy aspects of the grueling tour.[79] Brubeck apparently appeared as a novelty to those used to New Orleans—style jazz. Roman Waschko, the impresario for Poland who introduced many of the onstage performances, conveyed the distinctive American character of jazz to enthusiastic audiences. Jazz aficionados especially enjoyed Brubeck's more modern selections, and as young people flocked to his concerts, some older listeners, although "puzzled" at the sound of jazz, expressed deep affinity for his music. After meeting with noted Polish musicians, according to the cultural attaché, Brubeck performed for students and youth in Krakow, who filled the "Rotunda Auditorium" to see him.[80]

Additionally, at the Literary Club, "the 'cats' gathered to hear and be heard." The atmosphere became "charged with youthful and uninterrupted enthusiasm." Audiences less familiar with jazz markedly grew to like the improvised arrangements of such celebrated melodies as "St. Louis Blues" and "Some Day My Prince Will Come." Jazz again engendered new fans and proved its appeal as a "modern international language."[81]

Importantly, the American cultural attaché emphasized that jazz's popularity among Polish youth made jazz a vital cultural product: jazz remained a unique symbol of the dynamism of America's Cold War ethos. Brubeck's jazz gained respectability and revealed that many Poles did not consider it "undesirable" or "linked with hooliganism." Thus Brubeck helped to "update" jazz in Poland, a critical goal of cultural containment.[82]

Brubeck also buttressed American interests in Ankara, Istanbul, and Izmar, Turkey, where, according to the PAO, he received rave reviews both personally and musically. As the band departed, "two boys who had gone to the airport stood shaking their fists at the plane, and [a] young French horn player, with tears running down his cheeks cried, 'It's terrible, terrible! We are like children without a father now that he . . . is gone!'"[83] Though not all of the fans' reactions "matched the emotion of this little scene," many revealed that audiences avidly relished the music. The band attended receptions and informal talks, and mingled with Turkish musicians and composers. Brubeck also met jazz enthusiasts in Turkey's "largest urban centers."[84]

In India, contrarily, Brubeck sometimes encountered friction because of ardent denunciations of American race relations that had arisen in the wake of Little Rock. This especially concerned American officials. India remained the world's largest democracy and declared a policy of nonalignment in the Cold War, making its allegiance critical in the Cold War rivalry. Moreover, many listeners were not very familiar with jazz, and even W. K. Bunce, counselor for public affairs, declared, "I am a little afraid of it myself."[85]

Nevertheless, Brubeck reportedly helped transcend cultural and political barriers in the country and played a pivotal role in shaping the American image. When he performed in Madras, many people yearned for jazz in an atmosphere of "cultural conservatism" and delighted in the spontaneous joy of "creating lacy and Gothic sounds." The band also held a jam session with important musical figures. Likewise, Bunce maintained that in Calcutta, although "both the ignorance and aversion to jazz had to be handled," Brubeck generated considerable interest in jazz, thereby helping to achieve pivotal cultural objectives. Bunce characterized Brubeck as the perfect person to bring American jazz to India for the first time. His sophistication, his virtuosity, and his "improvis[ed] . . . melod[ies] and rhythm[s]" heightened his eminent appeal.[86]

Similarly, in June 1958 his group became "a 'smash' hit in Bombay." During his concerts, he appealed to a wide spectrum of Indians, which included "hard core jazz lovers," and he even managed to charm fans of classical music, who increasingly saw a link between modern jazz and classical Indian music. The embassy staged concerts at a major stadium, and the band even played in Rajkot on an old piano not touched by "a musician for thirteen years." Significantly, many youngsters attended his concerts, some of whom wanted to travel with the band. The solos by Brubeck's drummer, Joe Morello, Bunce recalled, became a "rhythm that every person in the audience understood without explanation or instruction." The drummer's "wizardry . . . proved to be a talk[ing] point for days afterward." Jazz had become "an entirely new experience in Rajkot."[87]

The band members engaged in offstage activities as well. They held meetings and demonstrations with classical musicians, during which the musicians spontaneously improvised on Indian instruments like the sitar and the "baya."[88] Throughout the tour, the band received press comments extolling their great artistry and what John T. Reid called "sax appeal."[89] Brubeck likewise performed in East Germany and Afghanistan, both critical arenas of Soviet cultural competition. Overall, Bunce characterized Brubeck's band as the "most congenial" group he had encountered and referred to Brubeck as the "best in progressive jazz."[90] Brubeck portrayed the exuberance of American culture while revealing an openness to the ideals of internationalism.

Although Brubeck helped advance the policy of cultural containment in turbulent Cold War regions, he endured tremendous hardship upon returning home. A volatile dispute arose that caused a furor in the jazz world. Brubeck scheduled a series of performances at a group of southern universities, but they canceled his concert dates because Brubeck's bass player, Eugene Wright, was black. The colleges had devised rules that stipulated that interracial bands could not perform on their campuses. Brubeck repudiated the "lily white" clause in his contract by refusing to replace Wright with a white musician.[91] He lost a reported $40,000 dollars as a result of the cancellation. Brubeck himself expressed his dismay at the incident, calling it "unconstitutional" and "ridiculous"; he stated that "all we want is that authorities accept us as we are, and allow us—and other integrated groups—to play our music without intimidation or pressure."[92]

Jazz critic Ralph Gleason recalled that both the *New York Times* and *Variety* reported the story incorrectly by claiming that Brubeck had agreed to the "'all-white' clause." Gleason himself praised Brubeck's action, just as he had praised Armstrong's denunciation of Little Rock months earlier.[93] Brubeck believed wholeheartedly in jazz as a symbol of democracy and would not give in to racial prejudice in the South.[94] His alto saxophone player, Paul Desmond, agreed, and Wright lamented that "it's a shame we can go travel all over the world and not have problems and come home and have such a 'silly problem.'"[95] Such paradoxical incidents reflected the racial and cultural contradictions that were inherent aspects of jazz diplomacy and the American ethos in these trying times.

Not long after, jazz trombonist Jack Teagardan toured for the United States in 1959 and created a "splash" abroad. His band helped the United States implement cultural containment in former British possessions as well as in other volatile parts of Asia.[96] The world had seen the increasing division of Asia into Communist and non-Communist blocs in the 1950s, most notably in Korea, Taiwan, and Vietnam. Moreover, the offshore island crisis and Chinese nationalist leader Chiang Kai Shek's continued demands for control of China exacerbated U.S.-Asian relations. Fearing cultural dominoes in Asia, many cultural policy makers sought to reach a wide spectrum of communities, from indigenous and folk groups to the Vietnamese elite.[97] From Hue to Saigon, American officials assessed how the Vietnamese might respond to American cultural products. An American official believed that while Burl Ives and Harry Belafonte might achieve astounding success, an artist like Elvis Presley, because of his excessive effervescence, might "spell the end of the post's cultural effort."[98] In Hue, an official asserted that "since the end of the Communist strife," the culture remained conservative and isolated but "receptive to Western music." Though the Golden Gate Quartet, a black singing group, had been a "great hit," he did not believe that the more unfamiliar 1920s style jazz would become "completely acceptable . . . for another two or three years." He also remarked that it would "be a long time before the music of the Brubeck style could be successfully presented here."[99]

Nonetheless, Robert C. Schnitzer, the general manager of the American National Theater Academy (ANTA), pointed to Teagardan's astounding success. Schnitzer noted that in such places as Karachi, Ceylon, Bombay, the Philippines, Malaya, Hong Kong, South Korea, and Okinawa, Teagardan charmed and delighted audiences. Like Brubeck, he performed with unabated exuberance, and even though he suffered a serious illness while abroad, he refused to quit the tour.[100] Many winsome events took place. In Kabul, a "cape-covered woman" who was not allowed into the main performance area listened to Teagardan's music outside of the performance space as camels sauntered by. In Bombay, young girls cheerfully adorned each of the band members with garlands. Additionally, Teagardan, like Goodman, played for the king and queen of Thailand. He performed jam sessions with the king, who even played a tune on the clarinet. In Cambodia, he met the "piano-playing king and the saxophonist prince," and the king bestowed on him a "medal for meritorious service to the arts."[101]

Teagardan received equally rave reviews in Saigon as Cold War tensions escalated further. Howard Elting Jr., counselor of embassy in Saigon, believed that jazz would widely appeal to educated Vietnamese. Although he acknowledged that the older generation exhibited a "condescending tolerance of jazz," he extolled Teagardan's music by avowing that his band might be "well on the way towards universalizing jazz in Asia." He highlighted jazz's overall popularity in the region when he declared that if jazz "spreads more widely [to] the lands of the Indochina Peninsula, nobody over there will believe that jazz [came] up the Mississippi from New Orleans. They will think it came up the Mekong."[102]

Herbie Nichols's band, a white group, also performed abroad on an official tour in Asia and the Middle East. In such cities as Cairo and Athens, he exhibited great artistic appeal among audiences. American officials praised Nichols's personal contacts and referred to the musicians as exceptional cultural diplomats. When Nichols arrived in Calcutta and Bombay, his performances sold out.[103] At the Regal Theater, the band fraternized with the governor of Bombay. The musicians also gave concerts at Xavier College, the Bombay American Women's Club, the American Businessmen's Club lunch, and the Bombay Jazz Club. At the Rhythm House Music Store, "[c]rowds thronged" to hear Nichols. His appearances thereby advanced American objectives by showcasing America's unique musical tradition and promoting "the best" artists the country had to offer. Throughout the tour, "a steady stream of callers day and night . . . wished to see and speak to Mr. Nichols." Nichols played before over 8,000 fans, becoming "one of the most effective ANTA shows . . . held in Bombay," according to Daniel P. Oleksiew, the PAO.[104] Nichols's potent cultural appeal also became clear in New Delhi, where "classic American jazz in a theater environment . . . allow[ed] the true genius of the music to cross the footlights."[105] In contrast, in Colombo the reporting officer maintained that Nichols did not effectively represent American musical life. He asserted that even professional people familiar with "the popular musical field had to be lectured on Nichols' place in the development of jazz." Jazz artists existed "in a different category," he averred.[106] While Nichols's jazz "rang familiar to the ears of many Ceylonese," others had little knowledge of 1920s- and 1930s-era jazz. Additionally, the embassy sponsored too many performances in Colombo, according to an official, and the group sometimes had to play in uninviting venues— once they performed in an "old barn." Moreover, the official surmised that the performers' attitudes had changed by their last stop because "thirteen weeks of close living and constant traveling had created internal dissension." Equally important, the group did not participate in many offstage activities.[107]

Jazz diplomacy became tested again during Herbie Mann's tour to Africa in 1960. Some American officials undermined policy goals by displaying blatant ethnocentrism. The PAO in Sudan disliked what he called Herbie Mann's "cavalier, condescending attitude" off-stage—to him, Mann seemed arrogant and self-absorbed. In addition, he believed that the Sudanese disdained modern jazz and preferred Dixieland—"melodic, danceable jazz with enough 'gut bucket' beats and rhythms to make feet tap and hands clap." He also expressed the elitist view that the Sudanese were "uncultured" and preferred "action . . . of a virile nature involving physical skill and requiring no need for explanation." Overall, he concluded that a rodeo would have proved much more appealing, because, like jazz, a rodeo was about as typically American as a hot dog.[108]

The extensive press coverage throughout Mann's tour portrayed Mann's jazz more favorably than did official reports. The *Bantu Mirror*, for example, professed that "people of all races [were treated] to a wholesome dose of jazz." The *Tangier Gazette* enthusiastically asserted that Mann "helped brin[g] jazz back to Africa."[109] Evidently, jazz diplomacy in the wake of Little Rock harbored an era of increasing paradoxes.

Not surprisingly, musicians continually bolstered the emerging links between jazz and the cause for social justice.[110] Such efforts took a noted turn in 1959 when the National Association for the Advancement of Colored People (NAACP) sponsored a benefit concert entitled "Jazz for Civil Rights" in the name of the "Fight for Freedom." Such jazz greats as Miles Davis, Art Blakey, Randy Weston, Billy Taylor, and Horace Silver performed. The NAACP hailed the concert, declaring that the musicians exhibited "the solid merit which built their reputations" and had "a core of idealism" that signified their "devotion to a great cause."[111]

Also in 1959 Duke Ellington became the first jazz musician to be awarded the Spingarn Award by the NAACP.[112] Bandleader Benny Goodman presented Ellington with the medal on the SS *United States*. Goodman proclaimed that he was "honored" to award the medal to an American citizen "who achieved fame, distinction, and honor in the field of popular music" and who could "enrich our culture and enhance our national prestige." For Goodman, Ellington remained one of the country's "popular heroes"—a man who could "capture the imagination, inspire the youth and bring joy to the hearts of millions."[113] In his acceptance speech, Ellington eloquently remarked that he had become encouraged by the fact that Soviet premier Nikita Khrushchev would soon visit the United States to observe the workings of "democracy." More important, when asked "why" he "thought American jazz was so much in vogue in other countries," he stated, "I thought the reason was that jazz means freedom and that today, freedom is the big word around the world." He professed that "if jazz means freedom, then jazz means peace because peace can come to mankind only when man is free."[114]

Such sentiments rang true in mid-1960, another decisive turning point for jazz diplomacy during this phase of the Cold War. Several factors contributed to this shift: the emergence of free jazz, the burgeoning of social protest, and the intensification of the Cold War rivalry in Europe. The social and political revolutions at home and abroad that gave rise to the counterculture of the 1960s also inspired the modernization of jazz. As the repressive era of the 1950s gave way to an age of cultural ferment, jazz musicians faced a critical aesthetic dilemma: they increasingly embarked upon a search for "heroes, symbols, [and] myths." An aesthetic rebellion took place, and free jazz—a new, radical form of jazz—rose on the American cultural scene.[115] Jazz simultaneously lost its American and international audiences to rock and roll, and the music became more eclectic. In attempting to find their niche in this new Cold War culture, many young jazz musicians faced profound racism and encountered even greater hardships than their more experienced predecessors.[116]

It was Ornette Coleman's album *Free Jazz* that emerged as the most revolutionary music of the decade. Coleman became the innovator by adopting the theory of harmolodics, emancipating himself from established chord progressions and pitches, and creating ingenious tempos with dynamic rhythmic twists. Jazz scholar Gary Giddins has called *Free Jazz* "an illuminating fantasia that inspired the new music movement and has yet to be equaled."[117] Instead of using chords to accompany melodies, a free jazz musician might use his or her instrument to "paint colors," just as an avant-garde painter would use brush strokes on a canvas. The free jazz artist also manipulated pitches in remarkable ways, mimicking the sounds of animals, cars, trucks, screams, cries, and other manifestations of life.[118]

As free jazz developed, and as postmodernist trends began to stir in the jazz world, jazz artists further deconstructed the traditional elements of their music, and free jazz burgeoned into a widespread movement at home and abroad. African American innovator John Coltrane, a paragon of free jazz and a redoubtable figure in twentieth-century American music, also wrestled with conformity and rebellion as he embarked upon an aesthetic exploration of new sounds and rhythms. In an article published in 1960, "Coltrane on Coltrane," he commented that at "[a]bout this time, I was trying for a sweeping sound. I started experimenting because I was striving for more individual development."[119] He composed such classic jazz tunes as "Giant Steps," "My Favorite Things," and "A Love Supreme." Some called Coltrane a passionate mystic, always thriving and searching for new forms of musical expression. In 1963 Coltrane composed "Alabama," a piece dedicated to those killed during the tragic bombing of a black church in Birmingham, Alabama.[120] He became a radical innovator who challenged the traditions of the cultural status quo.[121]

Other trailblazers, like Cecil Taylor, helped spearhead the free jazz avant-garde and dismantled the artistic confines wrought by Cold War culture. For Taylor, who felt the tension of being a black musician in middle-class white America, music became a "way of holding on to Negro culture, because there wasn't very much of it around." Albert Ayler, who experimented with free jazz, emerged as a "master of the 'dirty tone,' that calling card of the African-American musical tradition with a lineage predating King Oliver and Robert Johnson."[122]

Equally provocative, free jazz innovator Archie Schepp became one of the most outspoken jazz artists of his day. Schepp played what he called race music—music that was profoundly connected to the struggle of African Americans for social equality. As a pivotal voice in the Black Arts Movement, Schepp sought to use his music as a "political and social force" that symbolized "the pressures of the time, just as the field hollers of farm workers reflected the pressures of the time."[123] Schepp embraced the Marxist notion of the artist's function in society. Music historian James Bakst characterizes this function as a

> political and economic force implied in Lenin's "Theory of Reflection." . . . Reflections of contradictions in the external world intensify the content of art worlds, give representations of life to the people of mass movements, protest, [and] revolts, and show the people as the fighting and impelling force in history.
>
> A composer becomes a progressive innovator and creator of advanced

contemporary music when he joins popular liberation movements, defends the interest of the masses, accepts the ideas of socialism, and spurns indifference to politics.[124]

Not all jazz musicians, however, welcomed this formidable music. Miles Davis professed that when Coleman appeared in New York, he "turn[ed] the jazz world all the way around."[125] Outsiders at home and abroad often disdained the emergence of free jazz—it dismantled established notions of art and order at a time when many looked for a way to sustain order in the wake of increasing upheavals against the "establishment."[126]

Another development that set the stage for jazz diplomacy in mid-1960 was the burgeoning of civil rights and social protest. African American artists continued to express an affinity for the international black cause as blacks at home and abroad fought what George Fredrickson has called "an analogous form of racial oppression."[127] Eventually, in the words of Elliott Skinner, these struggles resulted in "political emancipation . . . from European racial hegemony."[128]

In the 1960s social protest became a more prevalent component of the American struggle for racial equality. The sit-in protest movement had started in February 1960 in Greensboro, North Carolina. At the same time, the activities of Martin Luther King Jr. and his Southern Christian Leadership Conference (SCLC) received worldwide attention. When the Student Nonviolent Coordinating Committee (SNCC) was founded in April 1960, vociferous student demonstrations increasingly occurred nationwide. In May 1961 Freedom Riders, who became emblems of nonviolent protest, intensified the movement to bring fairer treatment to blacks in bus terminals and train stations in the South.[129] Further, when some activists were beaten by whites in Birmingham, Alabama, the incident provoked fervent international calumny, and people of color throughout the world looked upon the event with marked disdain.[130] This racial conundrum deepened when King was jailed in Birmingham. Senator John F. Kennedy called King's wife, Coretta Scott King, to express his dismay at the incident and to help free King from jail. The United States Information Agency (USIA) surmised that such developments keenly influenced international reactions to cultural overtures from the West;[131] they sparked ardent skepticism toward cultural policy and the American race question that found expression in the works of such celebrated African American artists as poet Langston Hughes.[132] In jazz diplomacy, American policy makers responded by increasingly endorsing the notion of "jazzocracy"—a democratic country unified racially and politically through the arts and jazz—to implement the policy of cultural containment.[133]

In Europe, the dispute over the military occupation of Berlin and the U-2 incident again caused Africa's problems to become dwarfed in the eyes of "Europe-first" Cold Warriors. The U-2 crisis arose in May 1960 when the Soviet Union shot down an American spy plane that had flown over Soviet air space. Afterward, Eisenhower, fully aware of American espionage flights over the Soviet Union, attempted to save face—he publicly declared that it was a civilian plane that had flown off course, a statement causing embarrassment for the United States.[134] Eisenhower did not know that the pilot had survived and was being detained by the Soviets. Khrushchev made this known just before he and Eisenhower were scheduled to meet for a summit in Geneva. In the aftermath of the U-2 incident, these talks did not take place.

These developments, along with the independence of French West Africa in June 1960, led the CU to reclaim black jazz in cultural programs. The CU appropriated black jazz not only in an effort to convey the core liberal values of social justice, egalitarianism, and democracy but also to create sympathy for the U.S. position in the world.[135] Simultaneously, it worked to assist newly independent nations in their evolution toward a multiracial democracy and "groped" for a way to "enhance multi-racial cooperation."[136] Not surprisingly, the CU rebuffed the music that arose out the free jazz movement, fearing it because it advocated protest and rebellion against existing social and political structures. As in the 1950s with the rise of black nationalism, President Eisenhower did not seek to further "stir up unrest" in Africa or other regions of the world.[137] Revolutionary forms of jazz music might inspire rather than quell the drive for rebellion against the West already brewing on the international stage.

The CU's choice of mainstream jazz in this new context also reflected its belief that mainstream musicians embraced a different notion of freedom than the jazz rebels. In order to appeal to a broad spectrum of people across racial and political boundaries, mainstream artists "wanted to claim the banner of freedom, but they also wanted to distance themselves from the term's association with individual license and whimsical choice." The idea of freedom came to mean not simply the idea of free enterprise, and ultimately "private choice," but also the freedom to move the music into a larger "social setting" in an attempt to correspond to the country's larger "needs" and broader goals. Freedom meant seeking collaboration and social participation while receiving affirmation as individual participants in the political and social structures of the day. Ultimately, freedom came to mean participation in a republican democracy.[138]

The ideas of simultaneous improvisation and collaboration, of "self-expression and solidarity," became equally appealing to audiences in the Soviet sphere, as Soviet musicians also aspired to embrace new trends in aesthetic and political agitation.[139] Like many American musicians, Soviet musicians grappled with how to "align" their music with a "deeper political purpose."[140] While American jazz musicians who traveled on cultural tours sought to dismantle the structures of American racism, Russian youth, jazz lovers, and fans sought to surmount the political structures of Soviet Communism.

Echoing the 1950s, the policy to globalize the jazz mainstream often met with brusque criticism and caused restlessness in the jazz establishment. When discussing a possible tour for his group, jazz clarinetist Tony Scott commented to *Down Beat* that the State Department requested that his group remain all-white. The State Department, he asserted, preferred "watered down" versions of jazz played by white musicians.[141] Critic George Hoefer, writing for *Down Beat*, similarly expressed a significant caveat regarding jazz diplomacy. In an editorial, he argued that the United States employed jazz bands abroad simply to entertain other nations and not to create mutual understanding or bridge Cold War cultural differences. He urged that the United States and its embassies rethink their approach to jazz tours if this were true. He claimed that the State Department only reevaluated its policy toward black jazz musicians when Marshall Stearns suggested including more black jazz groups in the program.[142]

As the United States recognized the need to expand cultural containment after Little Rock and capitalize on the cultural and political fervor brewing abroad, the CU chose Louis Armstrong for the next jazz tour to Africa.[143] It was as much this changing Cold War atmosphere as Armstrong's tremendous appeal that led to his unparalleled and exuberant welcome by African peoples. By the end of 1960 Armstrong, who disdained Communism, had become the most controversial jazz artist to tour abroad for the United States. His tour took place in the wake of the Sharpeville massacre in South Africa, which had banned his group and his music.[144]

Armstrong's band, the All Stars, brought the spirit of "jazzocracy" to Africa in a new and volatile Cold War context. The CU initiated the tour with "a massive promotional campaign" for Pepsi Cola, showcasing Armstrong on exciting posters: "in Armstrong's hand, instead of the familiar horn, was a glistening bottle of Pepsi Cola." Pepsi also printed "five special Pepsi-Cola bottle caps on which Armstrong's likeness was printed under the cork."[145] *Variety* reported that in Accra, "Satchmo to Hit Spots in Africa for Pepsi-Cola."[146] Richard Berstein, the PAO to Accra, hailed Armstrong with the "slogan," "Pepsi Cola Brings Out Louis Armstrong."[147]

As the tour ensued, enthusiasm for "Ambassador Satch" reverberated throughout the continent. *Down Beat* remarked that when he arrived in Ghana, Armstrong, "dressed in his native robes[,] poured a pint of Scotch on the ground as a libation to the gods and chanted 'Akwaba,' the Ghanaian word for welcome."[148] When Armstrong discussed his powerful appeal as a cultural ambassador, he did not reflect on the political climate, remarking to a reporter that "the reason I don't bother with politics is the words is so big that by the time they break them down to my size the joke is over. . . . I'm just a trumpet player."[149] Armstrong expressed his deep affinity for Africa when he asserted, "I feel at home in Africa—more so now since I've been all through the place."[150]

After Armstrong's pivotal tour, the *Journal American* referred to "Ambassador Satch" as a "Good-Will Asset" who "captivated" Africans "[a]t a time when Kremlin agents were whipping up African feelings against" America.[151] The tour revealed that it remained paramount for the CU to convey not only American material and technological prowess to new nations but also America's cultural vigor, especially in light of the fact that many "new nations imported their concepts of American culture from Europe." An American official reiterated that jazz diplomacy established a strong American cultural presence in new nations as well as a "shared devotion to cultural values that transcend[ed] political differences."[152]

The jazz tours of these years nonetheless underscored the fact that the paradox of race, global diplomacy, and American anti-Communism increasingly imperiled the American image. After Little Rock, American policy makers continued to express ethnocentric views toward jazz and new nations. Although a proponent of jazz, Lawrence J. Hall, PAO, for example, observed that such artists as Herbie Mann had made jazz popular for "its rhythmic qualities rather than . . . its melodic or harmonic qualities." Hall believed that Moroccans did not understand jazz because it diverged from Middle Eastern music. Yet he claimed that the 1930s style swing bands remained popular because "melody is paramount" in their music. Additionally, Hall remarked that "progressive jazz" with its "complex harmonics" might not have much appeal. He even considered Moroccans "much more at ease when shouting and clapping hands to the beat of a jazz drummer."[153] Likewise, several American officials perceived people in some African nations as backward or as "outsiders" and feared their fervent nationalism in the same way that they feared the activities of African American expatriates. The racial paradox that consequently emerged in jazz diplomacy loomed large as the United States employed African Americans to improve its image and to counter widespread Soviet influence abroad.

The changing dynamics of the Cold War, race, cultural affairs, and jazz helped illuminate the volatile role that jazz diplomacy played in cultural policy. In the wake of Little Rock, jazz diplomacy increasingly engendered both pride and pessimism in audiences at home and abroad as conservative ideas of jazz reached new parts of the globe. Jazz diplomacy also grew increasingly complex because it helped augment American influence in arenas where none might otherwise exist. In these venues, American officials continually emphasized jazz's transcendent aesthetic and cultural appeal. Such officials as Robert C. Schnitzer of ANTA commended the musicians' personal and musical aplomb abroad and called jazz "one of the most useful weapons we have in our arsenal."[154]

By the end of the year, John F. Kennedy had been elected president in a close race and turned his attention to Cold War exigencies in Europe and Asia. The world recognized that Eisenhower's policies toward race and integration had not significantly improved the status of blacks at home or abroad. Kennedy, however, expressed greater support than Eisenhower for the cause of black justice and gained black advocacy in the United States by championing the African cause. Thus jazz paradoxically came to represent the vitality of American culture and society at a compelling turning point in the cultural Cold War. Unavoidably, in efforts to revitalize the image of the country, jazz diplomacy significantly highlighted American weaknesses.

Still, jazz's profound global influence among the youth became abundantly clear to American officials, especially in the Eastern bloc, where the Soviet Union had suppressed rebellions and installed Communist leaders. Similarly, in such cities as Seoul, Beirut, Cebu, and

Addis Ababa, American jazz inspired young new fans and fostered an appreciation of African American culture. Even in Reykjavík, policy makers acknowledged that "interest in modern jazz [was] very wide."[155] Jazz tours especially did "wonders combating the [Soviet] idea that jazz is a degenerate art form."[156] Thus jazz became an instrument for expanding Western power—and black culture became a paradoxical symbol of that power, especially in the aftermath of Little Rock. Decidedly, in the *Saturday Review*, Stearns declared that jazz in foreign lands, more than American art forms derived from Europe, revealed the "sincerity, joy, and vigor of the American way of life"—a phenomenon that knew no political boundaries. Discovering the vitality of "America's classical music" was like the "old story of finding the blue bird in your own garden."[157]

Chapter 4
The Paradox of Jazz Diplomacy, 1961–1966

But our culture and art do not speak to America alone. To the extent that artists struggle to express beauty in form and color and sound, to the extent that they write about man's struggle with nature or society or himself, to the extent they strike a responsive chord in all humanity, art and the encouragement of art are political in the most profound sense, not as a weapon in the struggle, but as an instrument of understanding of the futility of struggle between those who share men's faith[;] art is the great democrat, calling forth creative genius from every sector of society, disregarding race or religion or wealth or color.
—John F. Kennedy, 1962

The inability of the Bureau of Educational and Cultural Affairs (CU) to contain international criticism of cultural affairs became even more acute in the 1960s against the backdrop of domestic racial conflicts and the Vietnam War. These dual injustices amplified the paradox of jazz diplomacy on the world stage to such an extent that they compelled a profound reassessment of jazz policies: under the scrutiny of the informationalists, jazz diplomacy no longer seemed viable, and the CU consequently suspended jazz tours. It did not reinstate them until the mid-1960s, when the resurgence of internationalism in the CU and the expansion of black cultural production led the CU to reevaluate jazz diplomacy in a transnational context. Even as jazz, an analog of American freedom and racial equality, spoke to America's cultural modernity, the American image grew increasingly enigmatic amid the Cold War confrontations between Communism and democracy that engulfed the world.[1]

As in the late 1950s, in the 1960s civil rights struggles most clearly reflected America's changing national ethos. Black activist Clayborne Carson profoundly impelled the "black awakening" when he helped form the Student Nonviolent Coordinating Committee (SNCC) as the Left attacked the evolving liberal consensus. The decade became characterized by constant and compelling cultural, social, and political "redefinition."[2] Yet as the world of ideas acquired new meaning in foreign affairs, American policy makers still viewed jazz through the prism of containment and the Cold War—as a trope that reflected the cultural "affluence" of American society and the uniqueness of American democracy. Jazz tours paradoxically aimed to depict racial equality, integration, American exceptionalism, and even the idea of republicanism, both as cultural aspirations and realities on the world stage.

Jazz musicians like Louis Armstrong embodied the spirit of republicanism the United States sought to propel abroad, conveying an image of America in which blacks and whites "contribute to and enjoy the fruits of democracy."[3] In 1961, in a sentimental and perceptive letter to jazz scholar Leonard Feather, Armstrong expressed this view of the jazz ethos:

> I'd like to recall one of my most inspiring moments. It was in 1948. I was playing a concert date in a Miami auditorium. I walked on stage and there I saw something I thought I'd never see. I saw thousands of people, colored and white on the main floor. Not segregated in one row of whites and another row of Negroes. Just all together—naturally. . . . I thought I was in the wrong state. When you see things like that you know you're going forward.[4]

Likewise, he affirmed his belief that black music could play a role in the fight against racism by dismantling cultural and racial boundaries. He asserted that "these same society people may go around the corner and 'lunch' a Negro. But while they're listening to our music, they don't think about trouble. What's more they're watching Negro and white musicians play side by side. And we bring contentment and pleasure. I always say, 'Look at the nice taste we leave. It's bound to mean something. That's what music is for."[5] Armstrong's beliefs and his music signified jazz's ability to transform cultural identities and ideologies among jazz practitioners, aficionados, and fans.[6]

Despite Armstrong's inimitable impact on cultural affairs, by 1960 elitism and ethnocentrism remained common among American Cold Warriors in the CU and abroad and continually undermined the efficacy of jazz policy. Two kinds of elitism emerged. First, some officials put forth the view that American culture had grown more sophisticated than the cultures of Europe and expressed beliefs in cultural hierarchies—high and low culture.[7] Only mainstream jazz, not avant-garde or free jazz, represented American high culture. Other forms of jazz reflected low- or "middle-brow music of Broadway tunes and blues-based improvisations."[8] In international circles, however, many regarded free jazz as a component of high culture and believed that it represented a unique Western art form. For them, it was not just a type of entertainment of which the "sole purpose" was to elicit an "intrinsic perceptual interest" or have a "fleeting" influence on "aesthetic sensibilities." Free jazz as art "require[d] . . . active involvement," was "highly charged with content, and profoundly influence[d]" one's sense of self "and the world for years to come."[9] American cultural officials, especially informationalists, often downplayed the significance of these cultural nuances. Second, officials frequently expressed elitist attitudes toward race. Although the CU characterized jazz as a component of America's superior cultural heritage, it did not embrace the black freedom struggles at home or abroad that helped shape that heritage. Consequently, it also shunned free jazz because such music embodied the ideologies of revolutionary and black cultural nationalism. Third, as European empires crumbled, cultural tours that increased U.S. contacts with people of color often reinforced policy makers' paternalistic notions of black peoples as primitive and backward.[10]

Such elitism became apparent when officials like Gordon Arneson, director of the Office of Cultural Exchange, delivered a keynote address to the CU in January 1961. Although he praised many aspects of cultural relations, he also claimed that in attempting to appeal to "new cultures avid for things" from the United States, the United States would "have to lead them [to] American culture using simpler forms." "These nations did not understand" the United States "too well," he maintained. "Simpler" art forms included cowboy shows, ice shows, athletic groups, and choruses, not the more "sophisticated" art forms like the ballet, opera, symphony, or dramatic theater. Accordingly, Arneson urged that the United States send cultural attractions to Africa that included variety and novelty shows because they contained "color, fast pace, music and spectacle." He sought to cater to what he called "less sophisticated audiences," particularly in "new" countries that were "not so familiar with . . . Western culture." Further, Arneson believed that Armstrong had made a favorable impression throughout Africa and "created the best possible kind of good will" for the United States, despite the cultural "primitiveness" of the continent.[11]

Also exposing the paradoxical aspects of cultural relations, Robert Beninder, an observer of cultural affairs, characterized American global diplomacy as "one more front in the Cold War." Although he pointed out that it sometimes softened people's sentiments toward the country and could change the hard realities of diplomacy by assuaging the "cultivation of hate" toward America, he also asserted that global diplomacy dangerously surpassed its original intentions. He declared of foreign peoples that "you may hate the rich uncle who sends you cash but not the singer" who sings you the blues: the Russian women cried for Van Cliburn; the students who attacked Vice President Richard Nixon in Venezuela in 1958 threw parties for the Howard University choir; and folk artist Charlie Byrd, who performed in Chile, received a standing ovation on the night of the Cuban missile crisis. Thus cultural policy often created greater cynicism about the American ethos.[12]

The deepening paradox of cultural affairs also became clear when African leaders and scholars who frequently visited the United States on official tours experienced racial antagonism firsthand.[13] Discrimination "against non-white visitors" in the United States, which began in the nineteenth century, frequently took place, especially in the South. Notably, in a letter to President Kennedy, James Dennis Akumu, an African scholar who visited the United States under the American Leaders Program, expressed his sincere hope that the United States would help African Americans out of despair. He recalled that he had traveled

> around the country alone and even in the deep South where at times . . . I was a bit depressed by the position of the Negro. I, however, saw changes taking place, both by legislation and some by force, organized [by] groups like [the] NAACP, [the] Urban League, CORE and the Southern Regional Council, [the] Christian Leadership Council, and [the] students non-violent movement. I am convinced the present Administration will do more for the Negroes. . . . I would have liked [to visit] the Electrical Union which has achieved much, but I was told it does not as yet accept the Negroes.[14]

The transnational awareness of the confounding and paradoxical nature of the American race question became more problematic for the CU as the complexity of cultural containment grew.[15] The African American athlete Wilma Rudolph triumphed at the Berlin Olympics in 1960, and Soviet premiere Nikita Khrushchev ordered the construction of the Berlin Wall in 1961.[16] Additionally, mounting tensions in Cuba and the Congo caused rifts between the superpowers that resonated for years thereafter. During the Bay of Pigs calamity in 1961,

America's failed attempt to overthrow the Cuban leader Fidel Castro became an international embarrassment.[17] In the wake of the Congo crisis early in 1961, Moscow had grown angry at the downfall of social-ist leader Patrice Lumumba, especially after the United States helped install a nonaligned government under a moderate prime minister re-ceptive to the West. The United States also supported the conservative leader Josef Mobutu in the civil war.

In order to confront the changing dynamics of Communism and the color line, President Kennedy acknowledged the need to reinforce the efficacy of culture in the Cold War rivalry.[18] Under Kennedy, USIA activities expanded. He also created the position of assistant secretary for educational and cultural affairs in February 1961 and appointed Philip H. Combs to this new post.[19] In 1963 Carl T. Rowan became the first African American to be appointed the director of USIA. In addition, Kennedy initiated a new policy in Africa by wooing neutral nations.[20] This new approach became clear in American relations with Guinea, which had achieved independence in 1958 and had begun to seek monetary assistance from the United States. Although President Sekou Toure had become a radical socialist, he suspected the Soviet Union of a "teacher's plot in 1961" and cut off relations with the coun-try. Guinean officials also accused the Soviet ambassador of "flooding the country with propaganda and cultivating close contacts with" the youth. Consequently, they expelled the Soviet ambassador—a drastic action in the cultural Cold War. Moreover, Guinea banned "all cultural centers operated by foreign missions," including the United States. It also accused the United States of sponsoring a "counter-revolutionary plot" and banned American films, the United States Information Ser-vice (USIS) library, and English lessons.[21] While Toure remained "cour-teous but cool" diplomatically, the United States sought to increase its "credibility and good-will" by appearing "friendly and sympathetic" to Guinean interests. U.S. policy makers remained concerned that Guin-ea would "ente[r] the red wedge," despite its policy of nonalignment.[22]

The United States feared this in part because the Communist cul-tural offensive had grown formidable in several African countries. In Morocco in 1962, for example, M. R. Yves Mas, editor of the newspa-per *Petite Moraccaine*, revealed that in just a few months the Soviets had exported several provocative cultural products to Morocco: the Moscow Circus, the Bolshoi Ballet, and Russian phonograph records. The Soviet Union spared no money or effort to "squeeze the last bit of propaganda from [its] presentations," he claimed. They also requested that Mas's newspaper publicize the sale of Russian records and run full-page ads for the circus.[23]

In the face of the Soviet onslaught, the paradox of race profoundly undermined U.S. interests after an African American, James Meredith, registered at the University of Mississippi in Oxford in September 1962. White mob violence ensued, and President Kennedy sent federal marshals to the school to suppress the disorder. As in Little Rock, American policy makers argued that federal intervention reflected the government's sincere interest in promoting integration and racial equality.[24] The USIA portrayed the government as the "hero" of civil rights that had helped to rescue its ill-fated black citizens from misfortune.[25] Yet the Soviets capitalized on this incident, and their umbrage seemed unwavering in the eyes of the world.

Not surprisingly, showcasing jazz and black performing artists to highlight blacks' improving status in American life and to rectify perceptions of American race relations appeared illusory to many peoples and nations.[26] In 1961 esteemed African American writer James Baldwin offered an eloquent expression of such a paradox in *Nobody Knows My Name.* He stated that "the American Negro can no longer, nor will he ever again, be controlled by white Americans' image of him. This fact has everything to do with the rise of Africa in world affairs. . . . Any effort, from here on out, to keep the Negro in his 'place' can only have the most extreme and unlucky repercussions."[27]

The United States nonetheless attempted to employ jazz in emerging African states to display the resilience of American culture and promote the idea of "jazzocracy." Late in 1962 a black 1920s style New Orleans jazz band—Cozy Cole's jazz review—traveled throughout Africa on an official tour.[28] Cole toured from October 1962 until early 1963, in the wake of the Cuban missile crisis. He promoted an image of American prosperity and cultural abundance as he brought jazz to new parts of the globe. During his concerts, the immense appeal of jazz among African youth became clear. Even French youth in Marrakech, "quite out of character for the French," were "screaming like demented banshees" when he performed. They "tried to hoist a battered Cozy Cole to their shoulders and parade him around the stage."[29] *Variety* portrayed Cole's tour as an impressive feat—"top cultural diplomacy."[30] Cole's astounding tour became one of the most successful U.S. cultural presentations in Africa in the 1960s.[31]

As Cole triumphed abroad, however, tensions between containment and the color line continued to undercut the viability of jazz diplomacy. Early in 1963 Kennedy delivered his evocative "Special Message to the Congress on Civil Rights." In it, he declared, "Let it be clear, in our own hearts and minds, that it is not merely because of the Cold War, and not merely because of the economic waste of discrimination, that we are committed to achieving true equality of opportunity. The basic reason is because it is right."[32]

Martin Luther King Jr. expressed similar sentiments when he led the historic March on Washington and gave his momentous "I have a dream" speech. King enunciated his "dream" for "an oasis of freedom" in southern states and for a nation of equality among people. Historian David J. Garrow characterized the speech as the "rhetorical achievement of a lifetime."[33] As USIA covered these events in radio broadcasts and other media, honorary marches took place worldwide, and many notable black artists living abroad expressed reverence for King's pronouncements. They included James Baldwin, who admired King's march from a nightclub in Paris. Numerous American jazz musicians had attended a meeting that Baldwin organized to show support for King's march and to fervently embrace the African American cause. Even actor Anthony Quinn became involved in the meeting.[34] Poet Maya Angelou and other cultural figures showed their support from Accra, Ghana.[35]

Kennedy's and King's civil rights initiatives met with praise in such countries as Chad, where the American mission showed *Press Conference USA*, a film about race relations. African officials, students, and friends heartily commended Kennedy's civil rights efforts. The mission also displayed an exhibit of King on a main street in front of the mission.[36] The reporting officer, however, expressed an elitist attitude toward Chadian people when describing the film's impact. He claimed that "so few Chadians have any background at all to understand the detailed ramifications and nuances of U.S. race relations that the high principles and humanistic philosophy of a Dr. King would surely—and so easily—drop out of sight in the well of Chadian ignorance on the subject."[37]

Thus, although many new nations seemed impressed by how the U.S. government had "gone to bat for the Negro," they recognized that a crisis of American mores endured.[38] How could black art embody the soul of American culture and the essence of American civilization when black Americans were an ill-treated people? As an "intellectual heavyweight" in "the purist sense of the word," W. E. B. DuBois, who became a Ghanaian citizen in 1963, had foreshadowed the cultural contradictions that emerged in the Cold War arena.[39] In 1923 he declared that

> art is not simply a work of art, it is the spirit that knows Beauty, that has music in its soul and the color of sunsets in its handkerchiefs; that can dance on a flaming world and make the world dance, too. Such is the soul of the Negro. . . .
> This is the best expression of the civilization in which the white race finds itself today. This is what the white world means by culture.[40]

This paradox became even more glaring after a civil rights march in Birmingham, Alabama, in 1963, where police used water guns, police dogs, and fire hoses to disperse peaceful protesters. Kennedy ordered federal marshals to the city to quell the violence, and the Soviet Union capitalized on this incident with sweltering anti-American propaganda. Moreover, on May 21 the governor of Alabama, George Wallace, attempted to prevent the integration of the summer session of the University of Alabama. Such incidents starkly undercut the message of racial progress that the United States Information Agency (USIA) attempted to portray in propaganda campaigns and led many world leaders to reassess their support for American policies.[41] In the wake of racial unrest, freedom rides, student protests, marches, church bombings, and the missile crisis, such officials as Mark B. Lewis, Public Affairs Officer (PAO) to Ghana, pointed out that, overall, Birmingham had significantly harmed the American image and resulted in "lost ground." He called the consequences of the episode "serious"; in Lewis's view, although cultural presentations often "enhance[d]" the American image and such incidents as Oxford resulted in an exalted view of President Kennedy "even in the leftist press," the paradox of race in America had manifested itself on the world stage too frequently.[42]

On June 11, 1963, shortly after Birmingham, President Kennedy spoke to such issues in his "landmark" civil rights address. In a televised speech, he declared, "We preach freedom around the world, and we mean it, and we cherish our freedom here at home, but are we to say to the world, and much more importantly, to each other that this is a land of the free except for the Negroes; that we have no second-class citizens except Negroes; that we have no class or caste system, no ghettos, no master race, except with respect to Negroes?"[43]

Kennedy likewise addressed the public about the horrors of nuclear war and the importance of arms control with the Soviet Union. His speech met with international praise. He expressed the view that both harmonious race relations and arms control, if achieved, could help sustain more prosperous relations with the Soviet Union.[44] In a circular to all diplomatic posts, Secretary of State Dean Rusk revealed that he shared these views. He asserted that in order to counter negative reactions to American racism, the United States had to take "decisive action."[45] Further, in an address to the Senate Commerce Committee in June, Rusk professed that "discrimination because of race, religion, and national origin was simply incompatible with American democracy. But I also argued that how we handled civil rights in the United States strongly influenced our relations with the rest of the world."[46]

When Senator Strom Thurmond of South Carolina "asked" Rusk if he "favored recent civil rights demonstrations and marches," Rusk remarked, "Well, Senator, . . . I would not wish to make a blanket statement, but if I were denied what our Negro citizens are denied, I would demonstrate." Rusk recalled that "Thurmond was horrified."[47]

Amid these passionate declarations by America's stanch Cold Warriors, the paradox of race again deepened when, on September 15, 1963, four young black girls were killed after white supremacists bombed the Sixteenth Street Baptist Church in Birmingham. This brutal event profoundly reinforced the image of the United States as a cultural wasteland. As President Kennedy expressed his "outrage," the Soviet Union energetically lambasted the incident.[48] In the jazz world, the paradox of race most poignantly reverberated on the world stage when Duke Ellington brought the message of "jazzocracy" to the Middle East on an official tour. Ellington met with resounding praise worldwide. A remarkable feat in a fretful Cold War world, Ellington convincingly portrayed the idea of American cultural exceptionalism to foreign peoples.[49] He reflected on his travels in his memoirs. In his "Notes on the State Department Tour"—an "eloquent, descriptive, vivid, portrait" of his trip—he described how he admired the "riches" and "splendor" of the region in which he performed. He further proclaimed that "we [were] not required to restrain ourselves in the expression of our personal, political, social, or religious views. As citizens of a great country, there [were] no restrictions on our tongues. We [were] to speak as we think in or out of favor of the U.S." He also characterized his performances as "haunting, formidable, beautiful, and compelling."[50] The *Foreign Service Journal* declared many years later that Ellington had triumphed during a pivotal moment in the Cold War.[51] However, 1963 ultimately became a turbulent year for jazz diplomacy. During Ellington's travels, on November 22, President Kennedy was assassinated, and the remainder of the tour had to be canceled.

Against the backdrop of unyielding domestic unrest, the American image waned to such an extent that cultural policy makers saw the need to drastically redirect cultural containment policies. As early as January 1963 *Variety* had claimed that the State Department had ordered a moratorium on all cultural tours, while in February *Down Beat* reported that the government planned to dismantle the cultural program.[52] By the middle of the year, the CU underwent vast changes, and the cultural Cold War nearly come to a halt. This occurred for several reasons. First, the CU had sent surveys to embassies around the world to reexamine cultural affairs, and numerous embassies generated critical accounts of cultural efforts. Second, the CU fired ANTA, which had administered the program since its inception, and reactivated the Advisory Committee on the Arts (ACA).[53] Though established in 1954, the ACA had remained inert until 1963.[54] Equally important, some members of the music panel, which had become increasingly divided between "kulturalists" and informationalists, attacked the competence of PAOs in Africa, contending that they did not understand the role of jazz or black artists in cultural affairs and that their elitism undermined cultural efforts.[55] In March 1963 even the director of the Cultural Presentations Program (CPP) exclaimed that "Africa is Africa, whether it is North, Central, or South."[56] On another occasion, he retorted that Africans knew only "the beat, rhythm, and missionary hymns" and called Armstrong's jazz meaningless to Africans. A member of the musical panel criticized what he saw as the panel's blatant ethnocentrism, declaring that it approached Africa "as if it were some dark continent."[57] Fourth, officials believed that U.S.-Soviet competition for the allegiance of African leaders called for a shift in jazz diplomacy—by the end of 1963 over thirty African countries had become independent.[58] American officials surmised that jazz diplomacy could no longer engender the support of educated leaders and intellectuals. Not only had the Communists—the Soviet Union and China—immersed Africa with stupendous cultural products, but Europe also often sent various "sophisticated" performing arts troupes to the continent: Germany sponsored a chamber music group, while England sent a Shakespearean company. It seemed that much of Africa remained steeped in the more "sophisticated" cultures of France, Belgium, Spain, and the Netherlands. Thus, to successfully achieve American aims, the CU advocated sending "sophisticated" examples of American "high culture" to Africa, including an orchestra or a chamber group.[59] Lastly, the paradox of jazz diplomacy had become so deleterious to the American image that the CU deemed it had "saturated" Africa with jazz—it did not want to further reinforce this paradox by endorsing the notion that jazz was all the United States had to offer.[60] These developments consequently led the CU to suspend all jazz tours.

This decision precipitated the most explosive controversy the American cultural bureaucracy had seen since the inception of Eisenhower's CPP. The State Department acquired complete responsibility for administering the CPP. Thereafter, it appointed Roy E. Larsen, chair of the executive committee of Time Inc., as the new ACA chair, and Glenn G. Wolfe, a foreign service officer, as the new director of the Office of Cultural Presentations.[61] Additionally, Lucius D. Battle, who later served as an ambassador to Egypt, had taken the helm as assistant secretary of state for educational and cultural affairs in June 1962. The CU requested that Larsen and Wolfe thoroughly reexamine American policies toward the appropriation of the performing arts.[62]

Larsen and Wolfe prepared an extensive report in which they censured the informationalist view of diplomacy and called for an internatonalist approach to cultural affairs. They succinctly distinguished between the artistic and political purposes of cultural policy. They urged that the use of art remain "apolitical" despite the CPP'S "broad political purposes." They also discouraged cultural affairs from becoming an instrument of anti-Soviet political propaganda, advocating instead that artists appeal directly to a nation's people—"in the capitals, cities, and . . . villages"—with cultural, not political, aims in mind. Such contacts would enable American artists to grow "closer" to citizens of other countries. Additionally, they discouraged "competitive displays of cultural accomplishment," calling them "wasteful." Newly independent nations, they claimed, remained eager for contact with American culture. Therefore the United States could focus on showcasing its unique character, vitality, and exuberance by illustrating the ability of a democracy, "a free people," to nurture a "flourishing national culture." The "highest peaceful arts" could help instill a vision of a common future with new governments and inspire them to embrace the American cultural ethos. They contended that the universal language of the arts, by "breaking down social and political barriers," would gradually lead others to accept American "ideals and objectives." Moreover, by appealing to intellectuals, according to Larsen and Wolfe, American ideas would gradually filter down to the masses and eventually "become generally accepted." Finally, they encouraged American officials to make constant attempts to "convey and reconvey . . . the reality of American cultural conditions until it finally replaces legend," for "[o]ld myths, fictions, and stereotypes die very hard."[63]

As the CPP underwent rigorous scrutiny and fell prey to debates between Cold War "kulturalists" and informationalists, Kennedy espoused an internationalist view toward the arts. In an eloquent statement at Amherst College in October 1963, he expressed the opinion that the arts should help build bridges of understanding rather than serve as a political tool. Kennedy declared that the arts were the "fiber of our national life" and asserted, "I see little of more importance to the future of our country and our civilization than full recognition of the place of the artist." He urged American citizens to "never forget that art is not a form of propaganda; it is a form of truth," and "[i]n serving his vision of the truth, the artist best serves his nation." He further proclaimed that "in a free society, art is not a weapon and it does not belong to the sphere of polemics and ideology." He hoped for "an America which commands respect throughout the world not only for its strength but for its civilization as well." He looked "forward to a world which [would] be safe not only for democracy and diversity but also for personal distinction."[64]

By the end of 1963 cultural internationalists had expressed a clear voice in American policy and challenged Cold War cultural ideologues to reframe cultural containment policy. James Baldwin alluded to the impact of such a paradox on the country when he proclaimed:

> the nation has spent a large part of its time and energy looking away from one of the principal facts of life. This failure to look reality in the face diminishes a nation as it diminishes a person, and it can only be described as unmanly. And in exactly the same way that the South imagines that it "knows" the Negro, the North imagines that it has set him free. Both camps are deluded. Human freedom is a complex, difficult—and private—thing. If we can liken life, for a moment to a furnace, then freedom is the fire which burns away illusion.[65]

In succeeding years, policy makers reassessed jazz diplomacy as

U.S. involvement in Vietnam escalated. By 1964, with jazz on hold, President Lyndon B. Johnson pledged to continue Kennedy's legacy and vowed to defeat Communism in Asia.[66] At the same time, the world witnessed Johnson's keen efforts to pass Kennedy's civil rights bill as his commitment to ensuring equality and a better life for African Americans deepened.[67] Blacks fought for and exercised their right to vote, employing a variety of tactics to secure their civil liberties, from nonviolent protests to the rallies of Stokely Carmichael and SNCC. The rise of Malcolm X, Black Power, and the Black Panther Party added to the social and political fray.[68]

As racial violence permeated the American social landscape, Secretary of State Rusk extolled Kennedy and Johnson because they both "encouraged us to do what we could in our personal and official lives to promote social justice." Rusk expressed the view that "we live under the . . . light of world publicity, partly because of our power and position but also because we have committed ourselves historically to these simple notions of freedom, still the most explosive political ideas in the world."[69] Likewise, jazz musicians—from avant-garde to the traditional devotees—grappled to redefine their niche in America's new and volatile social order. While the passage of the Civil Rights Act of 1964 and the Voting Rights Act of 1965 markedly enhanced the declining image of the United States and boldly symbolized the American commitment to racial equality, in the words of George Fredrickson, they ultimately "failed" to redress black Americans' problems. The consequent "aftermath" of the "ghetto insurrections of 1965—1968" "encouraged a bitter and rebellious mood in the black urban communities of the North and West."[70] Thus the Soviet Union continued its "digs" at American democracy and further exploited renowned civil rights events in extensive propaganda campaigns. Despite USIA efforts, many Soviet people still believed that Americans treated African American citizens "no better than . . . caged animal[s]."[71]

Johnson felt a formidable tension: he believed that "as President and as a man, I would use every ounce of strength I possessed to gain justice for the black American." And he observed that although "the barriers of freedom began tumbling down," "[t]he long history of Negro-white relations had entered a new and more bewildering stage."[72] Exemplifying this dynamic, in February 1964 Martin Luther King Jr. was jailed in Selma, Alabama, and later that year he received the Nobel Peace Prize in Norway.[73]

Westerners like the French also expressed increased "sensitivity and resentment" toward U.S. initiatives, especially in Africa.[74] This rift in Franco-American relations arose in Conakry, for example, as American visitors felt tensions "in the boat club and the tennis club and in all their contacts with the French."[75] Moreover, although U.S. cultural containment policy continued to foster Africa's "reliance on the West" and encouraged social progress along nonracial lines, such events as the murder of civil rights activist Medgar Evars generated an "emotional content of criticism" not before seen.[76] Newspapers like the *Ghanaian Times* "flay[ed] the U.S., American capitalism, American civilization, and U.S. society generally." *Time* and *Newsweek* commented that the dilemma of race demanded elimination, not "crocodile tears."[77]

Malcolm X's travels to Africa and Europe in 1964 caused further concern among American officials who believed that his activities undermined Cold War policies—he reportedly reiterated the "evils" of "Americanism" and underscored the harsh realities of black life in the United States. In 1965 the State Department sent James Farmer, president of the Congress of Racial Equality (CORE), to Africa to counter Malcolm X's provocative statements; he and many American speakers attempted to redefine the American ethos on the continent.[78] While speaking in Chad in 1964, for example, an American specialist lecturer, Raleigh Morgan, a language professor at Howard University, asserted that American courts did as much as possible to improve racial problems in the United States.[79]

Such speakers became important in shaping cultural containment in part because African students abroad often fervently denounced discrimination in the United States. Some ardently defended Soviet socialism. These vocal declarations significantly influenced the cultural dynamics between the United States and its North Atlantic Treaty Organization (NATO) allies. In 1964 African students in France—from Algeria, Morocco, and Tunisia—who denounced American race relations, according to Carl T. Rowan, held the United States "last in general esteem" with regard to racial progress in Western countries. The students ranked France and the Soviet Union higher than the United States in the area of cultural achievement.[80]

Likewise, an African student in the Soviet Union criticized U.S. race relations and defended the Soviet Union when commenting on an article entitled "The African Revolt." Published in an African newspaper, the article sharply denounced the Soviet's treatment of blacks.[81] The Soviets feared the article might exert influence in parts of Africa and

Asia because of its graphic depictions of racial conflicts. In response, the student published an article in *Izvestia* claiming that discrimination did not exist in the Soviet Union; he simultaneously took "the expected swipe at racial discrimination" in the United States. He declared that in his opinion, the United States "would do better [to] try first to do anything to help your courageous countrymen, American Negroes, and then examine the imaginary discrimination in the Soviet Union." He also pointed out how Africans in the United States were "forced out of restaurants and hotels and beaten up." Even in Europe, he claimed, blacks suffered injustices perpetuated by American soldiers. The Soviet Union, he argued, contributed to the struggle against colonialism and racism.[82] Many African students abroad shared these critical views.[83]

To counter the impact of such views, American officials often sponsored informal discussions among youth in Africa and Europe. The American ambassador in Paris attended the premiere of *In White America*, a documentary recital of the history of African Americans produced by the Paris Theater Workshop. Blacks and whites in Paris also formed an informal group called Paris Supports American Racial Integration, or P.S. The group declared that it would raise money to help those who fought for racial justice in the United States. It praised such events as the March on Washington.[84]

Yet U.S. support for such initiatives seemed less tenable after another compelling racial incident severely damaged American prestige: Bloody Sunday. In March 1965, during a protest march in Selma, Alabama, whites physically assaulted scores of black and white protestors, and policemen even killed a black man who demonstrated for civil rights. State troopers simultaneously blocked the marchers, beating them with nightsticks and diffusing them with tear gas when they refused to disperse.[85]

The rueful events in Selma led President Johnson to make noble attempts to counter worldwide criticism of the country. He addressed the U.S. Congress in a provocative speech, "The American Promise," recalling in his memoirs that he "wanted to talk from [his] own heart, from [his] own experience."[86] In his address, he invoked the legacy of Abraham Lincoln and proclaimed that the United States had an obligation to fulfill the promise of Lincoln's Emancipation Proclamation. He asserted that "the time of justice has now come. I tell you I believe sincerely that no force can hold it back. . . . Equality depends not on force of arms or tear gas but upon the force of moral[ity]; not on recourse to violence but on respect for law and order. . . . All of America must have the privileges of citizenship regardless of race." He further insisted that "rarely are we met with a challenge, not to our growth or abundance, our welfare or our security, but rather to the values and the purposes and the meaning of our beloved nation. The issue of equal rights for American Negroes is such an issue. [If] the U.S. does not attend to this . . . [w]e will have failed as a people and as a nation."[87] Johnson sent this speech to all African leaders, and it became a hallmark of his symbolic diplomacy, thereby revealing the extent to which the race crisis in the United States had become an acute crisis of American values.[88] In a similar vein, Louis Armstrong denounced the racial injustice in Selma when visiting Copenhagen and Prague. In Copenhagen, he told a reporter that he "became physically ill after watching a television news program showing Selma Police action against civil rights marchers in the Alabama city." He also proclaimed that "they would beat me . . . if I marched."[89]

Another jazz pioneer, Archie Schepp, saw a disturbing link between violence toward blacks in the United States and the bombing of the North Vietnamese. He noted that in both instances, violence emerged against peoples of color engaged in ardent freedom struggles. He stated:

> I am for the moment a helpless witness to the bloody massacres of my people on streets that run from Hayneville through Harlem. . . . But I am more than the images you superimpose on me, the despair that you inflict. I am the persistent insistence of the human heart to be free. I wish to regain that cherished dignity that was always mine. My esthetic answer to your lies about me is a simple one: you can no longer defer my dream. I'm gonna sing it. Dance it. Scream it. And if need be, I'll steal it from this very earth. . . . Our vindication will be black, as Fidel is black, as Ho Chi Minh is black.[90]

"The racial dimension of the Vietnam war" thus caused grave concern among black artists, some of whom embraced Marxist principles to ease the political and intellectual burden of democracy.[91]

Racial incidents simultaneously highlighted what Walter LaFeber calls "a glaring, embarrassing contradiction at the center of U.S. policy in Africa"—American support for the apartheid government in South Africa.[92] South Africa condemned international efforts to end apartheid and reaffirmed its commitment to white rule. A resolution issued by the Organization of African Unity, which was established in May 1963, equated the United States morally with South Africa. In South Africa, civil rights were equated with rebellion, and with the widespread suppression of civil rights in the United States, racial "repression" in South Africa buttressed relations between the two countries. In this respect, the two countries resembled one another more than any other two countries in the postwar era.[93] The United States sought to preserve strategic and economic interests in South Africa as it attempted to define a "middle road" with regard to South African apartheid. In later decades, as George Frederickson has illuminated, the Black Power and civil rights movements in the United States gave impetus to the movement for black freedom in South Africa.[94]

South Africa made a deep impression on such African American artists as Canada Lee and Sidney Poitier; both traveled to the country to film *Cry the Beloved Country*. During their travels, they witnessed the barbaric treatment of South Africa's black population.[95] Even such jazz musicians as Miles Davis deemed that American racism and South African racism were "the same."[96] In this context, policy makers saw great value in "working with non-white artists" in the country, such as those at the Union Artist Organization. They sought to foster their goodwill, trust, and respect.[97]

The racial conundrum in southern Africa caused cultural tensions to escalate further in 1964 and 1965. In January 1964 American officials became aware of a letter protesting the scheduled appearance of the popular singers Chubby Checker and Nat "King" Cole in southern Africa. Ironically, jazz had already gained tremendous popularity in some of southern Africa's cultural centers, including Johannesburg. When the American consul general in Salisbury became aware of the "Warning Letter Addressed to Nat 'King' Cole and Chubby Checker," he requested police protection for the singers.[98] The protesters criticized the fact that black Americans could accept an invitation to perform in Portuguese-controlled Mozambique and Angola. They abhorred the idea that during such a controversial era, blacks would play for whites "just for the sake of a dollar or a pat on the shoulder." They believed that the "Portuguese regard[ed] the black people as beasts" and that it was "as certain as the sun rises that [they were] going to entertain Portuguese soldiers who spend the whole day shooting black people." To the letter writers, blacks seemed "not unlike slaves."[99]

In light of such disputes, many performers refused to perform in southern Africa. The white British singers Dusty Springfield and

Adam Faith declined a tour to South Africa because of stipulations that they had to play before segregated audiences. The prime minister of South Africa refused to allow the performers to insist on integrated audiences and thus "dictate" his international stance on the issue.[100]

American efforts to redress these paradoxes grew more complex as Communist initiatives remained unyielding—cultural groups, including Soviet dancers and acrobats, as well as the Chinese acrobatic troupe, performed throughout the world.[101] Furthermore, cultural containment had not decreased Europe's "cultural monopoly" in Asia, Africa, and Latin America.[102] The CU made attempts to reinvigorate cultural efforts in such places as Cotonou, Dahomey, where the mission opened two USIS clubs, the John F. Kennedy Club and the Cotonou Music Club. It sponsored numerous events frequently attended by keen jazz fans. Some members even lectured on jazz, while others received jazz recordings and instruments.[103]

American officials urged that the United States redefine cultural containment policy just as an urban uprising in Watts, California, shocked the world—thousands of blacks looted the city, and the National Guard was summoned to quell the violence. In addition, cultural and racial borders boorishly surfaced in the American jazz world when the Pulitzer Prize Committee at Columbia University denied Duke Ellington a Pulitzer Prize. Nat Hentoff, a prominent jazz critic, averred in the *New York Times Magazine* that the decision represented a grave injustice, for Ellington and his music keenly spoke to what it meant to be both American and African American.[104] In *Cats of Any Color*, jazz scholar Gene Lees illuminates that the paradigm of black invisibility frequently guided the decisions of the jazz establishment.[105] Ralph Ellison, author of the American classic *The Invisible Man*, also saw a clear bias against Ellington in the committee's decision and indicted the American musical establishment. He declared that "it would seem that Ellington's greatness has been recognized by everyone except those charged with recognizing musical excellence at the highest levels."[106] Composer Aaron Copeland expressed similar regrets. Showing his characteristic aplomb, however, Ellington told *Newsweek*, "I've absolutely no disappointment. . . . Fate's trying to keep me from becoming too famous, too young."[107]

The racial divide in the jazz world became accentuated by criticism of U.S. involvement in Vietnam, which especially surfaced at home and abroad in August 1964 after the Gulf of Tonkin incident. After alleging that the North Vietnamese attacked U.S. ships in the gulf, Johnson enunciated—and the U.S. Congress passed—the Gulf of Tonkin Resolution, which approved of U.S. military action in the absence of a declaration of war. While praised at home, it met with worldwide calumny.[108] President Johnson asserted that as domestic and international incidents developed, "it was clear from the viewpoint of the Presidency at least, that both events foreshadowed dark days of trial ahead. I believed that the nation could successfully weather the ordeals it faced only if the people were united."[109] The Gulf of Tonkin Resolution underscored the image of American aggression and militaristic anti-Communism.[110] Johnson became especially divided after he ordered that troops be deployed in Vietnam in mid-1965 and initiated an extensive bombing campaign, "Operation Rolling Thunder," in the North.[111] U.S. military escalation in Vietnam changed world opinion of the United States to such an extent that American involvement in the war eventually dwarfed the impact of racial events on the American image. In the mid-1960s, the paradox of Vietnam replaced the paradox of race on the world stage, and Vietnam became the linchpin by which the world measured American credibility as a democracy.[112]

The dual injustices of racism at home and the Vietnam War abroad gave rise to a new era of cultural expression. Jazz musicians, artists, and cultural pacifists used their music and art to challenge the status quo.[113] Musicians like Archie Schepp, Duke Ellington, and Cecil Taylor wrestled to embrace their responsibility to promote social activism while helping to reshape society and achieve greater order and stability in public life.[114] Sonny Greer observed that through the years, "Duke has been deeply concerned about his race and its problems." Ellington asserted in the mid-1960s that "you're supposed to command respect for the race, whatever you do."[115] Similarly, such jazz innovators as John Coltrane also hoped that music could help transcend the racial divide. Through his "sonic exploration," he reached new structural and expressive heights with such tunes as "A Love Supreme," and he acquired a plethora of new devotees. Reflecting his spiritual evolution toward utopian idealism, he also professed that "if [someone] loves our music," it "has nothing to do with questions of skin color." It is "an expression of higher ideals, to me. So therefore, brotherhood is there. . . . With brotherhood, there would be no war."[116]

In this new context, while depicting the "brutally honest" facets of American cultural life, cultural policy makers focused more keenly on portraying how the United States attempted to "change things."[117] In Ghana, after Nkrumah's overthrow in 1966, the CU encouraged "meaningful communication" with the youth abroad while exposing them to certain ideas about peace and democracy; it underscored "practical" ideals guided by an open, fair, and just notion of human rights in which race relations appeared to improve day after day more quickly than in the past.[118] Not surprisingly, the topic of the Vietnam War often arose in international discussions abroad. In London, African and European students inquired about "Vietnam, Watts, [and] Kennedy." American visitors, such as Roy Wilkins of the NAACP, lawyer Wiley Branton, sociologist C. Eric Lincoln, and writer Langston Hughes, explored such questions in their conversations with English audiences.[119] Such topics also came to light in November 1966 during an embassy meeting with youth at a counselor officer's residence in Lumbumbashi, Democratic Republic of the Congo.[120]

Amid controversy, black artists continued to transform the global context of cultural affairs, which became increasingly multifaceted with the rise of Little Richard, Elvis, Bob Dylan, the Beatles, Abby Lincoln, and the "Motown Sound" of Stevie Wonder, Smokey Robinson, and the Supremes, among others. American popular music moved into new venues, and new forms of African American culture increasingly grew popular around the world. Significantly, public taste for bebop, hard-bop, and cool jazz declined, and jazz lost its audiences to rock and roll. Many reminisced about Billie Holiday's "Strange Fruit" and the popular Café Society of the 1950s.[121] Still, big bands like Ellington's orchestra toured Europe extensively, and musicians like saxophonist Johnny Hodges, pianist Jimmy Jones, and others felt widely accepted. Jones recalls a lively performance in Italy with Ellington and Ella Fitzgerald. Although not void of bigotry, many European cities offered African Americans a venue for expressive freedom markedly unfettered by the constraints of institutionalized racism.[122]

Paris, however, remained a place where black people from all over the world met to share their artistry and discuss transnational cultural developments.[123] Shortly after President Johnson took office, American expatriate Josephine Baker spoke for the group "Americans Abroad for Johnson" at a rally given at the Eiffel Tower Restaurant in Paris, duly expressing her hopes for racial equality in the United States.[124] Typifying a more open racial atmosphere, according to Tyler Stovall in *Paris Noir*, Paris presented

> an alternate model of black experience, [and] underscores the centrality of race in American history: blacks in the French capital were able to achieve

a level of success usually unavailable to either brothers and sisters in the States. . . . [T]he fact remains that in different ways most African Americans in Paris have not only enjoyed life there, but derived something of value from the experience.

. . . [T]he black American community in Paris has been an exceptionally accomplished one . . . [and] symbolized the potential of African American life in general once it is fully liberated from the shackles of racism.[125]

Aware of the vibrant transnational expansion of black culture, the CU again reevaluated the efficacy of jazz diplomacy. In a policy statement, the CU defended the power of jazz and black cultural products in promoting American Cold War aims; it declared that "in Sub-Saharan Africa, the performing arts are in a very early stage of development. A new culture is emerging, blending the old African culture with modern influences. American performers, particularly Negroes and American films, have been an important element in this modern influence."[126] The CU pointed to the power of jazz diplomacy in another pivotal policy statement when it noted that "American jazz is a unique contribution of this country to the world's cultural scene. It is a form of art universally known and appreciated. It is eminently designed to meet the human urge for and love of rhythm. It is in a sense the truest form of individually improvised music that merges into a joint presentation of artists that have the gifts of skill, musical talent, rhythm and the feeling for team work."[127] Moreover, the CU acknowledged that the globalization of jazz and black culture amid the international turmoil of the mid-1960s signified an important link between race, jazz, and cultural containment. It claimed that

we were aware of the fact that an integrated group of performers could go a long way to put the race question in the United States into proper perspective. Two entertainment acts, the Shirleys and the Riches, were selected not only because of their artistic standing, but also because they projected the image of the out-going friendly Americans and of a fine American family. . . . The Vice President of the Republic of Niger told our Ambassador that the Cozy Cole group was the most effective weapon against the di-tribes [sic] of radio Moscow with obvious reference to the race problem.[128]

This surge in internationalism, which had gained momentum in 1963, impelled the CU to reintroduce jazz in cultural policy. It attempted to reestablish jazz as a symbol of American prosperity, surmising that "jazzocracy" might serve as the best way to bolster the American image in the new context of race and the Vietnam War. An official in Adana reported on the "new youth cultural center" and noted that when the USIS launched the Adana Jazz Club, fifty-five "young people" attended the opening. The USIS also sponsored monthly meetings in the American Library, where local jazz enthusiasts could listen to American music and foster camaraderie.[129]

Nonetheless, the CU's choice of bands for the next jazz tours reinforced the notion that, despite its awareness of the importance of black cultural production in the mid-1960s, the CU was still playing it safe: it chose Woody Herman, a white leader of a New Orleans-style jazz orchestra, for the next jazz tour to Africa, and a black group, led by Earl Hines, to travel to the Soviet Union.

In the wake of these tours, the themes of jazz and internationalism continued to permeate cultural policy debates, and President Johnson keenly recognized the critical role culture played in "thawing the cold war." He avidly declared that

> groups like the Philadelphia Orchestra played for Soviet audiences[;] while the Bolshoi Ballet danced for Americans, Van Cliburn played the piano in Moscow; David Oistrakh played the violin in New York. Each country sent the other exhibits of its goods and its best technology. A relatively small but significant number of Americans and Russians got to know each other and came to realize that men and women on the other side of the Iron Curtain were much like themselves.[130]

Johnson shared the convictions of ardent internationalists in the cultural establishment: Charles Ellison, the director of the Office of Cultural Presentations in 1965, and Charles Frankel, the assistant secretary of educational and cultural affairs in 1966. Void of elitism, like Larsen and Wolfe, they expounded upon cultural affairs by extolling how the appropriation of the performing arts helped bolster the American ethos abroad. Ellison called attention to the "power of music and the arts" to influence foreign affairs. Such cultural products as the symphony, music festivals, Broadway theater, ballet and modern dance, and jazz and folk artists typified the cultural forces of the Cold War world. Most important, he defined culture as a mode of living to which musical achievement remained integral. He asserted that a nation must "have a way of life that is respected and is capable of meaningful communication with other nations at many levels" if it is to serve as a "leader in world affairs." And "music, which is universal, has an important place in that way of life." Also, he claimed that it was doubtful that a "society of the future can be truly great if its arts are not." In this vein, Ellison exalted the potential of culture to shape world societies in the 1960s, a decade in which he believed the arts had become more important than in the past. Although the arts could not solve all of the difficulties wrought by the Cold War, they could "serve as a solvent—if not a solution—and [could] help to wear away, slowly and over time, the impressions and misunderstandings among men that so often make their problems." With the increased "world-wide interest in the arts," Ellison beckoned American citizens to share the nation's musical ethos with other people and avowed that the performing arts—like no other cultural form—could help the United States fulfill its worldwide cultural "mandate." The arts could transcend all barriers—political, economic, social, and others—and reach people from all strata of society.[131]

In 1966 Charles Frankel echoed such sentiments in a lecture to the Bureau of Educational and Cultural Affairs. Unlike Gordon Arneson in the early 1960s, he propounded an eloquent liberal defense of cultural internationalism. He insisted that music had become a component of American foreign relations not simply because of the changing character of American culture but also because of the changing character of diplomacy in the Cold War era. Frankel referred to this phenomenon as the "rise of citizen diplomacy," which symbolized the transformation of foreign affairs in the twentieth century. He characterized intercultural contact as the most "important single cause—some have even insisted the only cause—of the movement out of social inertia into social change."[132]

Such change did not appear "accidental." Cultures had not "triumphe[ed]" over others because of wars or empires rivaling each other, but because of the new era of "cultural traffic—of people, news, ideas, ideologies, fashions, machines, and passions." These contacts, deeper and more extensive than in the past, resulted in a new international "neighborhood" with "color and dimension." In this new order, "less powerful" nations exerted cultural influence upon those more powerful. Frankel recommended that the United States redefine its national interest in terms of this cultural revolution: the "free exchange of ideas, the free movement of people, and the meeting of individuals as individuals without regard to borders" guided freedom struggles and shaped the movement toward democracy around the world.[133]

As internationalism resurged, the CU recognized that jazz's global appeal could help dissolve international borders in the new context of race and the Vietnam War: both the Soviet Union and the CU sponsored a myriad of artists at the Festival of Negro Arts in Dakar, Senegal, in 1966. In his compelling "Dakar Journal," Ellington extolled the transnational exchange, declaring that "after writing African music for thirty-five years, here I am at last in Africa."[134] Echoing this sentiment, Leopold Senghor, poet and president of Senegal, hailed negritude and Ellington in a homage to his music:

> Oh! the dull beat of the rain on the leaves!
> Just play me your "Solitude," Duke till I cry myself to sleep![135]

The impact of the jazz ethos had became apparent in many regions of the world—from Sweden to Japan, from Moscow to Canada, from Bulgaria to Thailand. In Stockholm, American jazz musician Oscar Brown performed at Stockholm's most popular nightclub.[136] In Japan, Ellington's saxophonist Johnny Hodges became surprised by fervent and enthusiastic fans.[137] The first jazz festival in Japan was produced in 1964 by manager and producer George Wein of Festival Productions.[138] Canadians similarly appreciated jazz, as writer Philip Jack proclaimed in *Coda*, Canada's jazz magazine. Many Americans performed at the Monterrey Jazz Festival in Mexico in 1966.[139] Likewise, jazz and Western cultural influence had inundated Chiengmai, Thailand, where boys and girls who referred to each other as "Chiko Chikkie" had begun "dressing in tight slacks and shirts loitering around together and generally tri[ed] to emulate their conception of beatniks and offbeats."[140] In Poznan, Poland, officials encountered problems with "hooliganism," apparently because of the "riotous" influence of "Western music, films and dances," prevalent in youth clubs.[141]

Such developments pointed to a proverbial intellectual debate in the jazz world that racked the CU internationalists: is jazz the intellectual property of black jazz musicians, or is it the exclusive cultural property of "America," with no racial distinction defined by the color of its practitioners?[142] Even more, had jazz simply become the intellectual property of world cultures?

By 1966 the CU's embrace of the jazz ethos reflected its acknowledgment that to fight the Cold War, the United States had to reclaim jazz as its own intellectual property. The CU recognized jazz as part of a worldwide artistic and intellectual phenomenon that prevailed over language barriers, as American Cold Warriors attempted to demonstrate the intellectual maturity of the United States while conveying respect for new and emerging nations and peoples in the Soviet sphere. By the mid-1960s, unlike the 1950s, the pivotal impact of jazz internationalism had impelled the CU to embark on a new era of Cold War cultural expansion.

Chapter 5
Jazz Behind the Iron Curtain, 1961–1966

Man, if they'd just let me run things my way, this world would be a swingin'
place.
　　　—Louis Armstrong, 1961

Internationalist impulses strikingly intensified in the Soviet bloc as
both modern and traditional jazz gained greater respectability. American and Soviet officials recognized the unyielding appeal of jazz
among Soviet people as audiences markedly grew. Soviet jazz debates
raged and often centered around jazz as Soviet intellectual property. By the mid-1960s official cultural contacts with jazz and African
American performers increased immeasurably amid the turmoil of
the Vietnam War and contributed to a shift in America's cultural priorities—the Bureau of Educational and Cultural Affairs (CU) increasingly approached Soviet jazz in the context of internationalism and
accordingly redefined its approach to cultural diplomacy with Soviet
bloc nations. The United States confronted a Cold War arena with a
complexity and a dimension not seen earlier.

To propel cultural containment into the Soviet sphere, American
cultural activities often targeted those countries that had grown increasingly independent from Moscow by espousing national Communism in the 1950s and 1960s. Policy makers encouraged Eastern
European countries to follow Yugoslavia's example by claiming their
political "freedom from Moscow" and by maintaining close cultural
ties with the West.[1] The Soviet Union's pursuit of world Communism
had created an ideological divide that inordinately heightened the uncertainty of cultural affairs.[2]

Several African American performers embraced this uncertainty
and traveled to the Soviet bloc countries, helping to buttress interest in black cultural products. Francis W. Bakonyi, an African American singer, toured the Soviet bloc with a Bulgarian opera troupe late
in 1961. Bakonyi was married to a Hungarian refugee.[3] Likewise, the
African American singer Margaret Tynes performed in Budapest in

January 1962 and, according to the U.S. mission, was met with warm praise. An official attributed her dramatic appeal not only to her artistic talent but also to Budapest's "attempt to promote favor with" both African Americans and Africans. Her "hearty, rather than subtle" performances, her "unrestrained, sensuous" dancing, and "her acting a trifle 'hammy'" while giving it her all engendered "popular enthusiasm."[4] Similarly, when opera singer Martina Arroyo toured Poland, she received an enthusiastic welcome in Szczezecin, Poznan, Koszalin, Olsztyn, Bydgoszca, Wroclow, and Rzeszow.[5] When the African American quintet the Platters toured Poland, Poles celebrated their performances in such cities as Gdansk, Krakow, and Lodz.[6]

Ironically, in December 1962 an American businessman recommended that black businessmen travel to the Soviet Union to help counter what he saw as the negative stereotypes abroad of African Americans as merely "entertainers and athletes."[7] The assistant secretary of cultural affairs agreed that black businessmen in the Soviet Union "might well be given greater authenticity" and dispel stereotypical images of African Americans.[8]

More poignant criticism of cultural and race relations stemmed from Eastern bloc visitors like Emil Herbst, who received a grant from the American Leader's Program and who was in the United States during the Cuban missile crisis. He met with African Americans at Atlanta University and described the state attorney general as "a very intelligent man, a segregationist who defends with his heart what he knows in his mind to be wrong and doomed." Herbst, according to a report, clearly came away from Atlanta with a measure of sympathetic understanding of the racial problem.[9]

Another visitor, M. Gornicki from Poland, also illuminated controversial views of race, according to the *Wall Street Journal*. In an article, "Big Business Is Not against Integration," the *Journal* declared that "Wall Street [Is] Cleared of Bias by a Pole." It claimed that Gornicki, who spent most of a four-month trip to the United States in the South, found it "a bit too much to see postage stamps of the Statue of Liberty and a liberty motto issued by a nation in which 20,000,000 Negroes have a position of second class citizens." Gornicki's "scathing comment[s] about discrimination" suggested that Wall Street could help redress discrimination if it supported integration. This, he believed, could help boost markets. Overall, however, he proclaimed that he saw "no sign of [a] sunny dawn" in American race relations.[10]

Such views reflected the many ways in which cultural relations with the Soviet bloc had become rife with paradoxes as American culture continued to thrive—especially after Khrushchev's co-optation of jazz from 1956 to 1962.[11] Edward L. Freers, chargé d'affaires ad interim in Moscow, pointed to the significance of such diplomatic developments as early as 1960 when the American musical *My Fair Lady* toured Russia. He asserted that Soviet people relished performances and that American culture had clearly triumphed in the country. Moreover, he argued that Cold War events inspired rather than detracted from warm personal relations among artists—many artists urged that "in spite of everything, let us continue to be friends and let us show you that we mean it." The Soviet people, Freers avowed, regarded American culture as a "vital, many-sided, free, expressive, and multi talented force which is part of [the Soviet] way of life."[12]

This dynamic became clear in 1964 after another African American opera singer, Betty Allen, also played to enthusiastic audiences in Bulgaria. The reporting officer appreciated her exceeding aplomb and her "warmth and [her] willingness to chat," qualities that added to the goodwill of her visit. Richard E. Johnson, chargé d'affaires, asserted that "if the regime feared that her appearance might clash with the propaganda image of the American Negro, it seems strange that it would elect to fill the seats with its primary indoctrination target— Bulgarian youth." Allen sang classical music and African American spirituals.[13] In the same year, however, official uproar arose in Bulgaria when an African American cabaret artist performed the "Twist." Before rendering a "Saturday night show in a Varna nightclub," Bulgarian officials ordered the performer to "stop doing the Twist routine" at the end of his act because the party secretary of the Restaurant Division of the State Concert Bureau disapproved of the dance. Controversy further ensued after the musician pointed out that he had signed a contract with the Bulgarian circus that acknowledged that he could include the "Twist" in his show. Bulgarian officials, nevertheless, refused.[14]

In this vein, the United States and Soviet bloc officials heatedly debated the place of jazz in public affairs. Notably, Poland's Cultural Committee had rejected Louis Armstrong, Martha Graham, and Robert Shaw for tours and expressed a preference for Benny Goodman. Goodman, however, turned down an offer to perform in Poland.[15] An event that symbolically prevailed over this Cold War cultural divide was the visit of the Polish jazz group the Wreckers to the United States in July and August 1962. The band performed at the International Jazz

Festival in Washington, D.C. The first jazz festival of its kind in the city, it reflected a new, open approach to jazz in the American capital. American officials wanted the Wreckers to immerse themselves in the jazz world and to meet Willis Conover, who broadcast *Music USA*, the Voice of America's jazz program, since it began in 1955. Conover had an international following. The group also planned to travel to New York, Chicago, New Orleans, and San Francisco, "regional centers of jazz music."[16]

The Wreckers performed "before 6,700 steaming persons" at the festival. They lit into the waltz "Hi-Fly" by Randy Weston as they performed in what they saw as the "land of Lincoln, Armstrong and Faulkner." Their third-stream and traditional music received the most hearty applause. During the finale, Polish, Russian, and Danish musicians jammed with American trumpeter Don Ellis, who discussed the virtues of jazz with a Russian journalist. A reporter commented that Polish jazz had become very accomplished, but "American jazz was still way out in front." The Wreckers also attended an affair at the Waldorf-Astoria, where such musicians as Gerry Mulligan and Quincy Jones, along with manager George Wein, appeared.[17] After returning home, the group performed at the 1962 Warsaw Jazz Jamboree.[18] The reporting officer exalted the band's performance, underscoring that the group's success reflected the popularity and respectability of free jazz in the Eastern bloc.[19] Most important, in a letter to Jerome F. Margolius, assistant director of the Committee on Leaders and Specialists, Roman Waschko, the Polish impresario during the tour, avowed that the Wreckers' visit had fostered a "better understanding among nations" and created unique "opportunities for . . . personal contacts."[20]

In the wake of the Wreckers' success, the two superpowers extensively negotiated the viability of a jazz tour to the Soviet Union, both still seeking to "destroy the myths about each other."[21] The official tour of the Michigan University Symphonic Band to the Soviet Union early in 1961 provided the segue for American jazz in Russia. Initially, Soviet officials did not want the group to tour Baltic cities because the region had achieved substantial cultural freedom from Moscow and had gained notoriety for its exuberant and far-reaching jazz scene.[22] Yet U.S. officials insisted that the Baltics be included in the tour, and the band performed in the region. Although the group played jazz tunes, the American ambassador decided not to identify the music too closely with jazz in formal public programs, keenly aware of official Soviet ambivalence toward the music.[23]

After this tour and in the wake of the Bay of Pigs calamity, the Soviets accepted Benny Goodman for an official jazz tour. Sol Hurok,
the American impresario, and George Avakian, Goodman's manager,
helped complete the pivotal negotiations. Hurok apparently had a
disdain for jazz.[24] Avakian recalled that Soviet officials refused Louis
Armstrong because they feared that his exuberant style of jazz might
"cause riots." When Avakian suggested Ellington, Soviet officials exclaimed, "No, no, no. He would be . . . too far out." It was only when
Avakian suggested Goodman that the Soviets agreed to jazz. They declared, he "would be best. . . . After all, our orchestras play his music,
and the public will understand his music, they've heard . . . that kind
of swing."[25]

Many hailed Goodman's tour as a rousing and inspiring turning point on both sides of the Iron Curtain. As the tour began, just
months before the Cuban missile crisis, *Time* magazine reported on
the "Rhapsody in Russia": the Benny Goodman Orchestra "blew into
Leningrad . . . pining, hot and groovy." It was "the jazz-happiest crew
the band had yet encountered."[26] The group's appeal grew as Goodman
performed in cities that included Russia's jazz capitals, Moscow and
Leningrad. He played such tunes as "Rhapsody in Blue," "Let's Dance,"
and "One-o'clock Jump," and even performed encores in his raincoat.
Goodman's musicians also became "spurred on by [a] small percentage
of Soviet jazz fans" yearning for the band's live performances.[27] Most
important, several newspapers noted that Goodman even appealed to
Khrushchev, who, although mystified, voiced sincere appreciation for
Goodman's music. The *New York Times* reported that "Benny Goodman's Concert Pleases But Puzzles Khrushchev."[28]

Importantly, Soviet jazz scholar Vladimir Feuertag recalled that in
St. Petersburg, the whole tone of the city changed when Goodman
came to town. Feuertag, who attended Goodman's concert, remembers how some young Soviet fans even risked arrest to hear and see
the Americans and their music. Soviet youth, especially those among
the *stilyiagi*—rebellious Russian youth who openly emulated Western
culture and values and also hailed the visits of American jazz artists—
even debated the organization of his band. They mused: did the bandleader, the conductor standing at the front directing the orchestra,
resemble a dictator, directing a nation? Because live American jazz in
the Soviet Union was such a unique occurrence, according to Feuertag,
the moment resonated as a high point in relations with America for
years thereafter. During the tour, many Soviet fans even expressed a

desire to hear renditions of the modern jazz avant-garde. Through their fright, ambivalence, and determination, the Soviet youth helped establish contacts, friendships, and memories that endured, reflecting the Soviet people's compelling embrace of Goodman as a symbol of mutual understanding.[29]

During Goodman's tour, jazz scholar Leonard Feather, a conservative critic, traveled to the Soviet Union to survey the jazz world and to attend some of Goodman's concerts. Like Feuertag, he observed that some Soviet fans exhibited their fervor for Goodman by shouting and whistling zealously, just as jazz fans did in the United States.[30] *Down Beat* expressed the hope that the tour would foster a more active relationship between Soviet and American jazz artists, while *Variety* declared that Goodman's band scored a "cultural coup" in Russia by helping to gain acceptance of jazz as a legitimate art form.[31] In the same vein, Russian jazz pianist Yuri Vikharieff asserted that Goodman provided a unique and critical impetus to peaceful relations.[32]

Goodman's tour, however, did not escape controversy. An editorial in *Down Beat* pointed out that the CU chose Goodman because it sought to ensure that it did not sponsor musicians who had a reputation for drug and alcohol use. This view angered many in the jazz world because it seemed to be an offhand reference to the rebellious practitioners of free jazz. The friction that increasingly arose between the jazz establishment—especially jazz critics—jazz practitioners, and the CU had become progressively more clear as "aesthetic activism" redefined the social and political role of jazz musicians in the wider world.[33] Musicians like Dizzy Gillespie and jazz pianist George Shearing criticized the government's decision to support Goodman for the first Soviet jazz tour, arguing that his musical style—1930s style swing music—was too narrow for modern audiences.[34] A policy maker pointed out, however, that the CU had initially asked Armstrong to tour the Soviet Union, a request that he had turned down.

Equally controversial, the CU reportedly specified that the band play "sanitized" versions of American jazz, not modern jazz renditions. In an article for the *New York Times*, jazz scholar John S. Wilson, who served on the CU's music selection panel in the mid-1960s, declared that Goodman's tunes were too "lackluster." The musicians in the band even characterized his choices of music in the same way that reactionaries scorned bop in the 1940s—as "moldy fig."[35] They then wrangled over the musical selections. Some Soviet audiences disliked Goodman's singer, Joya Sherill, whose rendition of "Katyushka," a Russian folk song performed in Georgia, caused audiences to boo her off the stage.[36] *Variety* reported that during the tour, Goodman "was barely able to quell a Bolshevik uprising among his own sidemen."[37] The band members had become "Miffed on [Their] Moscow Mission."[38] They wanted to introduce the Soviet people to modern American jazz music that extended beyond the conservatism and predictability of the jazz mainstream. Even many Soviet fans expressed a desire to hear renditions of the modern jazz avant-garde.[39]

Goodman's demeanor and character also evoked considerable tension. Avakian points out that the musicians' criticized Goodman as "tired and commercial" and called him "not the most articulate of men." They scoffed at his attitude, rehearsal schedules, scores, arrangements, and personality. They also claimed that the CU chose Goodman for personal reasons—because he had "campaigned" to get selected by the government for several years. Significantly, some musicians criticized Goodman because he had reportedly asked Duke Ellington, Lionel Hampton, and Jack Teagardan to accompany him as "sidemen," reports that Goodman eventually denied.[40] The members of Goodman's band also fell prey to what many have called Goodman's "ray"—the unfriendly glare that he frequently gave musicians whenever he expressed disapproval at something.[41]

To add to the fervor, Soviet officials sometimes suspected musicians of unsavory offensives. This view keenly colored attitudes toward cultural interactions. The *New York Times* alluded to a prevalent Soviet fear: that the Americans might be dispersing jazz propaganda. It proclaimed that "Izvestia Sees Cloak and Dagger in Goodman's Band's Horn Cases."[42]

After Goodman's band returned, President Kennedy praised the tour as an inspired moment in the Cold War. He expressed his support for cultural relations with the Soviet Union in a letter to Premier Khrushchev. He declared that he was honored that Khrushchev had attended Goodman's concert and wrote that he looked forward to attending a performance by the Bolshoi Ballet when it visited the United States.[43]

In the wake of Goodman's success, the Soviet Union did not diminish its trenchant anti-American propaganda, especially after the CU sent Paul Winter's Jazz Group on an official tour to Latin America in 1962, just after the Bay of Pigs. The Soviets revealed their distress when the Soviet group, the Moiseyev dancers, toured the United States. Soviet officials made a propaganda film about the visit called *Beyond the*

Footlights America: A Film Reflection of the Moiseyev Dancers in the U.S. It depicted the United States as a "huge country, complicated, rich and poor, peaceful and bellicose," and did "its best to blacken life" in the United States. Though artists prevailed in the Cold War, in New York an old man mocked American freedom. Boston was scorned for its "radioactive fish," and Cleveland as the "home of steel" where "only one smoke stack out of five" worked.[44] It was in this context that Khrushchev implemented a cultural crackdown that lasted until 1963 and that the Cuban missile crisis dramatically reshaped U.S.-Soviet cultural affairs.

Khrushchev justified the decision to deploy missiles in Cuba, professing that he sought to create a deterrent to American involvement in the Caribbean. In his memoirs, he wrote that "I remember those days vividly," and he recalled that the Soviet Union "had an obligation to do everything in [its] power to protect Cuba's existence as a Socialist country and as a working example to the other countries of Latin America." Thus losing Cuba "would have been a terrible blow to Marxism-Leninism."[45] After a series of dramatic negotiations, Kennedy persuaded Khrushchev to remove the missiles from the island, thereby eliminating the Cold War threat from American borders. The world recognized that Kennedy had achieved astounding "success"— he had protected the Western Hemisphere from the brink of nuclear war.[46]

Khrushchev had apparently underestimated Kennedy's determination and ability to manage international crises because he regarded Kennedy as a young and inexperienced president.[47] Thereafter, U.S.-Soviet cultural exchanges took a dramatic turn. American policy makers canceled several Soviet tours, including the Soviet basketball team tour of the United States. They surmised that such a tour might unsettle the public or incite protests or violence; they also attempted to ascertain "the point at which the continuance of the exchange program would worsen rather than ease tensions."[48] During a critical Interagency Meeting on Soviet and Eastern European Exchanges on October 24, 1962, Georgi Zhukov, chairman of the Council of Ministers State Committee on Cultural Relations with Foreign Countries and a a member of the Soviet mission, encouraged the continuation of cultural contacts despite Cold War disputes. Both sides planned to meet in Moscow in December to reexamine cultural affairs. In hindsight, Khrushchev acknowledged that "only a fool would think that we wanted to invade the American continent from Cuba."[49]

These pivotal U.S.-Soviet cultural negotiations continued in the wake of the missile crisis in part because Kennedy, Rusk, and Khrushchev believed that culture provided a critical bridge to understanding even at the most turbulent moments in the Cold War. As Kennedy called culture and the arts the "great democrat" among men and nations, Rusk declared that "even when the two superpowers are 'eyeball to eyeball' and locked in crisis, there are frequently solid contacts at lower levels."[50] Khrushchev, "[s]eeking to take the heat off the situation somehow," said to his "comrades": "Let's go to the Bolshoi Theater." He jested that both at home and abroad, "They'll say to themselves, 'If Khrushchev and our other leaders are able to go to the opera at a time like this, then at least tonight we can sleep peacefully.'"[51]

As the crisis subsided, President Kennedy, and later, President Johnson, debated how culture could help achieve important policy goals with the youth worldwide. Kennedy believed that in the era of "rapid and sometimes violent change" and in the midst of "ruthless" Soviet competition, "young leaders have risen and are rising to power, political change is occurring, and the events with which the traditional arts of diplomacy must deal are moving with breathtaking speed." Culture could thus "broaden . . . horizons" among the youth. Further, as Kennedy indicated in a letter to Rusk, culture could be employed in an attempt to sway their "attitudes and actions," most notably in countries that had recently become independent.[52] The youth would be the leaders of the next generation. Rusk concurred and also expressed the importance of reaching those who could potentially "frustrate" American efforts.[53]

By 1963, as jazz's international appeal dynamically redounded among young people, the Soviets remained aware that the hunger for jazz among Russian youth had intensified along with their desire for increased cultural ties with the West. *Variety* declared that the "Reds [Were] Using Jazz to Strengthen Free World Ties."[54] It seemed that the Soviet Union had begun to prepare the Soviet people for "détente" with the United States.[55] The Soviet people's long-standing interest in African American music and art became so clear that Soviet youth played American jazz standards just like the Americans.[56] Even Khrushchev affirmed, "I also like some contemporary music."[57]

In this context, the CU sought to assess both the potential for dissent and the allure of American values among young people in the Soviet bloc. In 1958 the Soviet Ministry of Culture had inaugurated a union-wide proclamation that called for the creation of recreational

and entertainment establishments for the youth. Authorities reluctantly accepted such establishments "as a useful outlet for the impulses and desires which however 'undesirable,' are realities of the local
scene."[58] The youth organization of the Soviet Union, the Komsomol,
responded to this order by opening several recreational establishments throughout the Soviet Union. The Komsomol opened jazz cafés
in Moscow and Leningrad; while conservative Russian youth had insisted on "Russian jazz or no jazz," others simply wanted jazz. Conservative jazz pronouncements became less frequent after Khrushchev
left office in 1964.[59] Popular jazz clubs in the Soviet Union flourished
in the mid-1960s, and favorable discussions about American and Russian jazz increasingly appeared in Soviet publications such as *Smena*.
The Soviets considered jazz serious music.

American officials who reported on the profusion of jazz included
Ernest G. Wiener, counselor for cultural affairs; David E. Boster, counselor for political affairs; and Ambassador Foy D. Kohler. Weiner remarked that, as the West may not have known, Russian youth cafés,
like Moscow's Blue Bird Cafe, which opened in 1964, even "had [their]
own 'call girls.'" Boster attended Jazz Night in Pyatigorsk in 1966, where
Rumanian and Yugoslavian vocalists performed a jazz concert before a
young crowd; their ebullient reactions to the singers, Mikki and Luki,
contributed to the overwhelming boisterousness of the evening. Luki
drew gasps and then cheers from the "low-cut back of her dress" and
"brought down the house with a wild, Louis Armstrong type version
of 'I Can't Give You Anything But Love.'" Similarly, Kohler observed a
Rumanian jazz sextet in Moscow, directed by Bebe Prisada. He commented on an animated "highlight" of the show: "a twisting rollicking
performance by a 270 pound swinging Bucharest hunchback in a blue
blazer and white trousers named Teodoresku Gogo who warmed up
with 'Baby Twist.'" The mid-1960s was a time when, according to some
American officials, Eastern European culture was "ultra modern."[60]

As the United States recognized the fervor for jazz in the Eastern
bloc, American involvement in Vietnam jeopardized U.S.-bloc affairs.
Poland had publicly denounced American policies in Vietnam and
consequently decreased cultural tours with the United States. In several speeches in 1965, Polish leader Wladyslaw Gomulka voiced "bit-
terness and vexation" and increased anti-Americanness, according to
an official who characterized Gomulka's pronouncements as "more
vitriolic" than those from the Soviet Union.[61] Rumania also canceled
the tour of a folk dance troupe.[62] In exchange talks, Secretary of State

Rusk indicated that he objected to the cancellation, reiterating that the two countries had signed the contract for the tour when Rumania was fully aware of the American position in Southeast Asia. He urged Rumania not to halt cultural tours because of political tensions and hoped they would continue.[63] Even youth in Rumanian adamantly clashed with American policies. The embassy in Bucharest observed that "foreign students" had protested the Gulf of Tonkin incident and subsequently presented the embassy with a protest document "signed by 209 Afro-Asian and Latin American students" studying in the country.[64]

The Vietnam War also brought about a clash of Cold War values during a meeting of the International Working Group on East-West Cultural Contacts in June 1966. The Working Group included the Soviet Union, Italy, Norway, Belgium, Denmark, the Ukraine, the Federal Republic of Germany, Canada, and the Netherlands. Andrei Zhukov, a member of the Soviet cultural delegation, supported cultural activities with the United States but urged containment of the Vietnam conflict. The Soviets considered a "freeze" on cultural relations because of the Vietnam War. Zhukov declared that in light of America's enormous power, he especially disliked U.S. aggression toward Vietnam because it was "a fraternal socialist country."[65]

Such disputes also occurred between the United States and Czechoslovakia, increasingly one of the most liberal regimes in the Soviet bloc. Like the Soviets, the Czechs canceled various tours because of U.S. involvement in Vietnam and called for a "slow down" of travels to the United States, despite the fact that reciprocal artistic visits had proven fruitful and constructive. The regime frequently encountered disaffected youth and feared the power of "all things Western—jazz, clothing . . . literature, art, and political concepts." Czech officials exhibited extreme "sensitivity" to what they saw as "pernicious Western influence."[66] A variety of American groups, including the Cleveland Orchestra, had toured Czechoslovakia, while such Czech groups as the Czech Philharmonic had toured the United States. The Czech Fialka Pantomime Theater also traveled to New York City for the World's Fair. Other Czech groups to tour the United States included Laterna Magika, the Black Scenes of Prague, and the Prague Chamber Orchestra.[67]

In 1965 the president of Columbia Artists Management met an official from the Czech concert agency who still insisted on a cultural "freeze" because of the Vietnam War.[68] American officials, however, regarded this explanation as a "pretext" and attributed the freeze to pervasive Western influence.[69] In 1966 U.S.-Czech negotiations finally took a positive turn when the Czechs accepted Woody Herman's jazz orchestra for a tour. Yale Richmond, the American negotiator, "told the [Czech] Ambassador that I did not know whether we had him to thank for these events or some supernatural power. . . . Ambassador [Karel] Duda, still smiling and looking very self satisfied, conceded modestly that he had 'a little' to do with it."[70]

Like other bloc countries, the Soviet Union in part expressed its opposition to American policy in Vietnam by thwarting the arena of cultural affairs.[71] The two countries reached an impasse when the Soviet Union refused to accept the number of American groups specified in the exchange agreement (five) ratified a year earlier. Accordingly, the Soviet Union canceled the tour of the celebrated American musical *Hello Dolly*, and the United States subsequently refused to approve a tour for the Bolshoi Ballet.

Secretary of State Rusk, nonetheless, remained adamant about maintaining détente with the Soviet Union in the cultural arena.[72] Both sides finally reached an agreement in March 1966. The two rivals had a common interest: after the Sino-Soviet split in 1963, both aimed to thwart fervent Chinese cultural and political expansion that had arisen in Asia, Africa, and Latin America.[73]

Evidently, as Yuri Saulskii, the Russian jazz advocate from Goskontsert who helped arrange Soviet jazz tours, proclaimed, from the Russian point of view, American Cold War jazz in the Soviet Union presented a keen challenge to authorities because it had become coveted cultural property for the Russian people. One of the most vocal proponents for Russian jazz in the Soviet cultural hierarchy, Saulskii pointed out that the Soviets regarded jazz as a form of Russian music. Soviet musicians identified with American jazz musicians stylistically as artists and regarded them foremost as international symbols of creativity and freedom—the issue of race had become less important than the cultural and ideological impulses that Soviet and American musicians shared.

These cultural similarities between African American and Russian jazz artists burgeoned. In this vein, in an article in the *New York Times Magazine* in April 1961, Gilbert Millstein revealed that the Soviets had finally accepted the saxophone as part of Soviet life—"The Sax Comes Up the Moskva River," he declared. Stalin had banned the saxophone in 1949 as a symbol of Western decadence and imperialism. Writing for *Down Beat*, in "The Saga of Jelly Roll Menshikov," Whitey Mitchell called the Soviet Union's acceptance of the saxophone the "latest phase of the Cold War."[74] Reflecting on such developments, Cornel West has put forth the idea that "like their Russian and Central European counterparts, the black artists grapple with madness and melancholia, doom and death, terror and horror, individuality and identity," "unknown to most in the New World."[75] Jazz writer John Tynan likewise commented on the popularity of jazz among Russian intellectuals, students, and professionals. Though a critical opponent of the American jazz avant-garde who especially regarded Coltrane's music as "anti-jazz," Tynan evocatively praised how the appeal of American jazz had grown in Eastern Europe.[76] He discussed the observations of Harold Jousen, a Hollywood manager who wrote for *Down Beat* and *Billboard* and who had surveyed the jazz scene in the West as well as in Moscow, Warsaw, Budapest, Prague, and East Berlin. Noting that the diversity and intensity of the jazz scene in Prague had become especially astonishing, he mused how Prague emerged as a center of jazz activity in the Eastern bloc. According to the *Christian Science Monitor*, "The Czechs were 'far out' in the field of jazz"—they sponsored the Czechoslovak Karolovy Vary Jazz Festival, one of the first jazz festivals in the Communist bloc. Even after the construction of the Berlin Wall, when bloc authorities attempted to restrict jazz, festivals in Eastern Europe frequently took place.[77]

As jazz flourished in the Soviet bloc, all forms of the music eventually became accepted by Soviet authorities. Leo Feigin, who later traveled in the Soviet Union, asserted that most forms of American jazz had taken hold in the country by the mid-1960s, especially in the Baltic republics. A strict yet comparatively open cultural atmosphere prevailed under Leonid Brezhnev's leadership. It was a time when "culture wars" permeated Soviet society. Folk singer Vladimir Vysotsky was quickly becoming a cultural icon, and the socially defiant *stilyagi* of the 1950s still held a prominent niche in Soviet life. Even Louis Armstrong appeared on Soviet television for the first time in 1966 as a guest on *Evening Meeting*. During the show, Armstrong performed the popular tune "Mack the Knife."[78] As astute Soviet jazz fans grew more vocal about increasing their contacts with the West, the listeners of *Jazz on VOA* suggested that the radio show play the music of modern groups from New York's trendiest places, rather than more traditional tunes that reflected Voice of America's propaganda aims.[79]

Heightening the controversy, Soviet jazz scholar Leonid Pereverzev published a series of articles in *Myzikalnaia Zhizn* (Musical Life) applauding the parallel rise of jazz in Eastern Europe and the United States. The series illuminated his view of the history of the blues, spirituals, ragtime, and New Orleans-style jazz, and closely examined the evolution of all forms of American jazz in the modern era: swing, cool, be-bop, and free jazz. As in the 1950s, Pereverzev keenly empathized with African American musicians because, like Russian jazz musicians, he asserted that their second-class status had not prevented them from creating a unique art form that was admired throughout the world.[80] Again, for the Soviets, issues of culture and class in Soviet and American jazz had become paramount over the hotly debated issue of race.

Jazz writer Gene Lees observed another important cultural dynamic that infused Soviet jazz debates. He wrote that Leonid Osipovich Utyosov, a noted jazz advocate and one of the best-known and wealthiest jazz men in the Soviet Union, admired jazz to such an extent that he claimed that Russians in Odessa, not blacks in New Orleans, had invented jazz. Utyosov's sentiments reflected an ardent Soviet desire to define a distinct Russian, rather than an American, form of modern jazz.[81] Many Soviet artists adamantly claimed that jazz was not exclusively "black intellectual property."[82] Two Russian jazz men even defected to the United States in 1964 to find more expressive freedom. As Saulskii pointed out, musicians throughout the Eastern bloc often claimed all forms of the music as their own and sponsored a variety of jazz festivals to showcase their artistry. He promoted successful jazz festivals in the Soviet sphere, especially in Czechoslovakia.

This period also saw the rise of the "New Thing" in Russia. Ornette Coleman's style of free jazz was reportedly first introduced in the Soviet Union at Leningrad's second jazz festival in 1963.[83] Soviet musicians reportedly played free jazz in their own Soviet way: without expressing sentiments of "protest or pessimism" like American jazz performers.[84] Soviet jazz scholars increasingly embraced the artistic and intellectual fervor that reinforced the idea of jazz as Soviet cultural property.[85]

In this context, Soviet officials, still ambivalent about U.S.-Soviet cultural contacts, only sometimes allowed "remarkably frank and free exchange" between American and Soviet artists. The deputy director of the USIA remained aware of the fact that suspicion of artists' activities lingered among Soviet cultural authorities after 1963 in the aftermath of Khrushchev's cultural crackdown. Consequently, some

Soviet artists continued to fear contacts with the West.[86] In 1966 *Variety* reported that Ellaine Lorillard and jazz pianist Billy Taylor encouraged the United States and the Soviet Union to cool off their rivalry by sponsoring an exchange of jazz festivals.[87] By the end of the year, jazz festivals had taken place in Moscow and Leningrad, and numerous American commentators spoke of the "rehabilitation" of Russian jazz.[88] Such festivals especially blossomed during détente and in the early 1990s after the fall of the Soviet Union.[89]

Jazz developments in the Soviet bloc, along with the Vietnam War and the declining impact of race, led the CU to decisively change its rhetorical approach to jazz. The cultural thaw between the United States and the Soviet Union that had begun with Geneva resurged in the mid-1960s. Not only did the CU acknowledge jazz as an indispensable Cold War trope that bridged cultural and ideological differences between the superpowers, but it also recognized jazz as a potent impetus for cultural internationalism. Such sentiments found a new voice in both the American and Soviet cultural hierarchies. The CU thus called upon jazz diplomacy to assuage tensions as political disputes strikingly divided the Cold War world. Aesthetic dynamics had become paramount as the United States reshaped its cultural image and as the country adjusted to a myriad of challenges arising out of new and increasingly contentious Cold War exigencies. By 1966 "jazzocracy" prominently reentered the Cold War arena as modern jazz boldly reached new global venues.

Chapter 6
Bedlam from the Decadent West, 1967–1968

The unstated democratic principles inherent in a jazz performance are abstract and subtle but certainly not lost on populations where subtetly is a large part of life. Nor does the protest of jazz go unnoticed, and protest certainly is a keystone of democracy. But perhaps more than any other characteristic, it is the music's joyful hope, sometimes encased in sorrow, that touches deepest.
—Don DeMicheal, 1963

By the late 1960s the sentiments of renowned Soviet writer Maxim Gorky, who characterized jazz as "bedlam from the decadent West" in 1928, took on a new meaning. Several prominent figures in the American jazz world turned the Soviet jazz world on its head when they visited the Soviet bloc and promoted the cause of cultural internationalism. They engagingly focused Soviet attention on the redemptive aspects of American society as the United States became more enmeshed in the quagmire of Vietnam. Not surprisingly, the American ethos at home and abroad during these years reflected the crises and contradictions of the American containment policy in Vietnam. The war continually heightened tensions between the superpowers as it shattered the Cold War liberal consensus that had shaped American policy for most of the 1950s and 1960s. President Johnson could no longer justify a foreign policy that defied the parameters of a pluralistic democracy: Alexis de Tocqueville had warned generations earlier that the foreign policy of a vibrant democracy had to be both feasible in an international context and viable enough to satisfy the wishes of the public at home.[1]

Protest against American bombing in North Vietnam became a far-reaching, worldwide phenomenon.[2] From 1965 to 1967 the United States dropped more bombs on Vietnam than all of the bombs dropped on Europe during World War II.[3] Much of the world, including America's European allies, questioned the legitimacy of American democracy and further lost faith in America's ability to uphold its professed ideals.[4] At home, many black and white activists and artists avidly opposed the war, and the counterculture overtook America's social and cultural landscape. With the Black Power movement expanding the terrain of cultural protest, widespread liberal dissent distinctly emerged, especially among America's Cold War intellectuals.[5]

In this context, when the Soviet Union broke the ice and accepted the Earl Hines New Orleans-style jazz band for an official tour in 1966, the two superpowers reached an uncanny milestone in Cold War cultural relations.[6] Hines's group became the first jazz band to tour the Soviet Union since Benny Goodman's in 1962. Before the tour, Hines professed, "I want to prove to the youngsters of this era that jazz isn't as bad as it's painted both from the musical and social point of view."[7]

In an article in *Down Beat*, Michael Zwerin, Hines's trombone player, described his experiences during his travels. He amusingly recalled that the band showed up in the Soviet Union "raggedy" and "grumbly" and pointed out that when the group visited the ambassador's residence, they "walked into the high ceilinged opulence of Spasso House looking like a dusty provincial circus." Notably, seeing the embassy staff "dressed to the nines" made him feel very "bohemian." He also remarked that American officials expressed their confidence in the band's ability to create goodwill in the Soviet Union, a country "hungry for American jazz."[8] He himself, however, felt somewhat exploited because he believed that jazz did not receive the same level of support or respect in the United States as it did abroad. He candidly recalled that Oliver Jackson, the drummer, had to perform without his own drum set during some of the initial concerts because his drum set had been misplaced. Showing zealous admiration for the band, a Soviet fan enthusiastically loaned Jackson his own drum set.[9]

The remainder of the tour made an indelible impact on the Soviet people, according to the reporting officer, who concluded that the musicians significantly helped improve images of American life.[10] The American embassy in Moscow likewise reported that the band achieved astonishing success, declaring that the musicians played before thousands of eager Soviet jazz fans in such cities as Kiev; they also mingled with some Soviet citizens and held jam sessions attended by enthusiastic admirers and musicians. Some Soviet fans even insisted on meeting with band members in secret locations, despite warnings from Soviet officials and Goskonstert—the Soviet concert agency— which historically discouraged "unofficial" contacts. Moreover, the conductor for the Georgia Philharmonic entertained the band with a "midnight dinner in a mountain-top restaurant outside Tbilisi." Hines's band visited numerous Soviet cities and performed before a total of 90,000 fans.[11] Controversy nonetheless ensued early during the tour, because Soviet officials feared rioting in Moscow and Leningrad—two of the most "hip cities" in Russia, where the "restive element," Soviet youth, especially exerted considerable influence. Officials then canceled the band's appearances in those cities, a decision that caused a major hullabaloo.[12] The *New York Times* reported that protests had arisen in the United States because the Soviets had changed the band's performance schedule. It concluded that Soviet officials changed the tour without notice in an effort to protest American involvement in Vietnam.[13]

As the Vietnam War seemingly caused a rift in jazz diplomacy and as efforts to win the Cold War in Asia met with greater futility, it became clear that by 1967, civil rights laws had not assuaged urban discontent. A thunderous riot occurred in Detroit in July 1967 resulting in many lost lives; the American image faltered, and racial conflicts consumed the country.[14] This racial and political divide fueled cultural debates and became equally cacophonous in the politics of jazz. In the midst of racial fissures that racked the jazz world, the conservative jazz establishment voiced controversial views of black and white jazz artists, some of which echoed the elitism of officials who delineated jazz policy. Both Monson and Eric Porter elaborate on a compelling issue that continued to emerge in jazz debates during these years— was jazz exclusively American, or African American, or simply the cultural property of Americans?[15]

Many renowned white jazz commentators explored this cultural quandary. George Wein, president of Festival Productions, exhibited a keen eye toward trends in the jazz world. He not only negotiated official jazz tours and managed such celebrated artists as Louis Armstrong and Duke Ellington, but he also became one of the first jazz managers to produce numerous international jazz festivals, especially in Eastern Europe. Wein viewed jazz as an American cultural product and did not deem that international difficulties wrought by the Cold War affected musicians' lives as much as more pressing, everyday issues—such as securing gigs and mere artistic survival.[16] Wein himself had become a perceptive, avid supporter of African American jazz artists and promoted them in ways similar to Norman Granz, at a time when rock and roll was eclipsing jazz as America's and the world's most popular musical art form.

Jazz aficionado Stanley Dance proclaimed that people worldwide celebrated jazz because "the music has served as an accompaniment to a good time," even though jazz proved "too demanding intellectually" for some international audiences. Most important, he referred to the music as a product of African American suffering, a struggle for equality, or the denial thereof.[17]

Contrarily, Willis Conover, who became known as "the most important man in international jazz," defended the Americanness of jazz. Since 1955 his radio show, *Music USA*, broadcast worldwide on the Voice of America, reached millions of people daily. His program, a vital expression of American values and a pivotal instrument in the cultural Cold War, represented "the main contact musicians in Communist countries" had with jazz. Conover referred to himself as "a lower case voice identified with the music that symbolized freedom."[18] Conover also published the *Friends of Music USA Newsletter*, which expounded upon trends in the jazz world. On one occasion in 1968, Conover printed a letter from a West German jazz fan who contended that Conover's show played a "narrow range of music." This listener argued that such musicians as Glenn Miller did not represent the best in American jazz. He claimed that, unlike Conover's show, an anti-American jazz program in East Berlin targeted African Americans by playing mostly "black" jazz. The German listener urged Conover to counter such an effort by playing more of the "average Negro GI" jazz on his show—the jazz that had gained a vocal following in many European cities, he claimed.[19]

In a detailed reply, Conover expressed his controversial view of jazz, and like jazz policy makers, he adamantly defended the older generation of jazz musicians. He declared that he did not like to broadcast "immature" musicians, nor did he like what he saw as the teenage new-age hype music, the music that said, "Yeah, the world's in a mess, so let's make the music ugly too." He lamented the fact that groups like the Beatles and other rock and roll bands had a negative commercial influence on jazz. Simultaneously, Conover dismissed the issue of race when he retorted that "the whole issue of listening to skin instead of to music is simply irrational."[20] He went on to proclaim that he made an effort to play music by both white and black jazz musicians. Yet he did not find it necessary to change one for the other.

In a subsequent letter, the German critic admitted that the German show was "specifically propagandistic for the sake of negroes." Yet he still advocated that Conover make an effort to "present the plight" of African American jazz artists. Conover, however, asserted that he did not believe that he had a responsibility to bring attention to the "plight" of African Americans on his music program. He commented that "a program should play music not talk about it." For him, jazz remained an arena of American life in which blacks and whites worked together "without strain." The race question, he alleged, had emerged in debates about American tours to Africa only because the State Department surmised that the arts in Africa existed in an "early stage of development," thus making cultural collaboration with Americans critical to the growth of the continent's cultural life.[21]

Such controversies progressed as Soviet foreign policy makers reassessed national security policies and cultural exchanges. The Soviet Union increasingly lost hold of its sphere of influence and aimed to subdue rising nationalist movements that eventually contributed to the fall of the Soviet Union in the 1990s. Soviet officials intently focused on gaining economic support from the West to help their declining economy, recognizing that cultural exchanges had become an important source of revenue.[22] Sol Hurok, the spirited American impresario who negotiated numerous Soviet-American tours, arranged reciprocal tours for the Bolshoi Stars and such noted American groups as the Minnesota Band.[23] Other American artists who toured the Soviet Union included the Boston Players; on one occasion they received a "thunderous ovation." The American Circus sold out in Tbilisi. And Stanley Kunitz, the established modern American poet, recited Goethe's poetry to a rapt Soviet audience; he professed that "a poet is like an eagle, who flies so high that he recognizes no boundaries."[24]

Surprisingly, in mid-1967 U.S.-Soviet cultural affairs came to an impasse when American officials urged Hurok to prevent Baltic groups from performing in the Russian Festival of Stars, which was scheduled to perform in New York City.[25] Vocal anti-Soviet protests occurred in New York, and American officials feared that the group would encounter opposition, especially from members of the Jewish community who remained aware of the Soviet's history of repression of Jews. Consequently, the Soviets canceled all of their artists' performances in the festival and initially gave no reason for the decision.[26]

After the cancellation of the performance, which had included 200 Soviet artists, Hurok expressed keen disappointment at the cultural and financial loss. *Variety* explained the incident by claiming that Soviet hard-liners exhibited a "coolness toward the Yanks" resulting

from American actions in Vietnam. Despite the fact that some Soviet officials had recently traveled to the United States to attend a film
festival, some American officials believed that the Soviets clearly expressed their overall displeasure with global affairs by thwarting cultural exchanges.[27] The Soviets surmised: "How can our boys and girls
sing and dance happily in a country which is waging war?"[28]

   Variety further speculated that Soviet cultural policies had vacil-
lated because of a reported shake-up at the Soviet Ministry of Culture.
The Soviet Ministry of Culture attempted to reduce the power of a
pivotal cultural group—the Shelepin Group. Alexander Shelepin, after Stalin's death, had served as head of the Soviet Secret Police until
1961, when he became the secretary of the Central Committee. He had
sharply criticized Khrushchev's foreign policy initiatives in the 1960s
and, with several Soviet colleagues, including Sergei Romanovsky,
who served as the chairman of the State Committee for Cultural Relations with Foreign Countries, plotted to overthrow him.[29]

   In an article, "Impugning American Motives in Cultural Exchanges," Romanovsky declared that cultural relations with the United
States proved harmful to international cooperation. He boldly characterized American culture as "corrupt, degenerate, [and] anti-dem-
ocratic." Romanovsky then claimed that the United States sought to
penetrate socialist countries with subversive Western culture. Critical
of bourgeois society and its "'parallel' culture," he asserted that cultural contacts with the West led to "'ideological subversion' in socialist
countries, accompanied by a tainted ideology, internal interference,
and 'anti-Communism.'" Soviet scholars and officials had come under
attack by Romanovsky for encouraging these "offenses." Overall, he
vehemently criticized the "fruitlessness of the American effort" and
portrayed Cold War cultural competition as the "contraband of pu-
trid ideological wares."[30] The American embassy in Moscow believed
that such political jockeying occurred because of the "fallout" after
Khrushchev's demise late in 1964. Cultural disagreements emanated
from a "struggle . . . on [the] highest levels" of power.[31]

   As the Soviets briefly balked on cultural exchanges, America's
deepening quandary in Vietnam continued to impel countercultural
expressions in the jazz world. Such musicians as Miles Davis disdained the tragedy of the war, while John Coltrane saw his music as
the best way to "change" thinking about the war.[32] Archie Schepp abhorred what he saw as the racial hypocrisy emanating from the war
in Vietnam.[33] In a letter to a soldier in Vietnam who admired his jazz,

Louis Armstrong wrote:

> I'd like to 'step in here for a 'Minute or 'so' to "tell you how much—I 'feel
> to know that 'you are a 'Jazz *fan*, and 'Dig' 'that 'Jive—the 'same as 'we 'do,
> "yeah." "*Man*—I carry an 'Album, 'loaded with '*Records*—'Long playing
> 'that is."
>   I said "All of that to Keep 'Music in your 'heart the 'same as 'you're 'doing.
> And '*Daddy*—you '*Can't 'go 'wrong*."[34]

In his endearing farewell, he remarked:

> Give my regards to the fellows that's in your company. And the other fel-
> lows too. And now I'll do you 'Just like the 'Farmer did the 'Potato—I'll
> 'Plant you 'Now and 'Dig you 'later. I'll 'Close now. It's a *real 'Pleasure*
> 'Writing—'You."
>   . . . Satchmo[35]

In the wake of the Vietnam War, jazz fans worldwide continued to
embrace many of the modernist tendencies of free jazz. Given impetus by such avant-garde American jazz musicians as Anthony Braxton, free jazz increasingly became part of the global movement toward
youth rebellion during these years.[36] In the Soviet Union, "Once Degenerate Jazz [Continued to] Swing Past [the] Iron Curtain," popular jazz festivals took place in several cities, and jazz records became
readily available. Like Yuri Saulskii, many Soviet officials increasingly
recognized that the "bedlam" from the West had become a central
"part of Iron Curtain life."[37] The proliferation of modern jazz symbolized Soviet youth's unyielding embrace of Western ideas of prosperity,
freedom, and civilization.

Charles Lloyd's gripping performance at the Tallin Jazz Festival in
May 1967 strikingly illuminated the links between modern jazz and
the rising tide of cultural nationalism in the Soviet bloc that expanded
during the early Brezhnev years. In the spirit of "jazzocracy," Lloyd imparted a message of hope and solidarity and represented the first step
toward an "exchange" of jazz festivals in the Soviet Union and Eastern Europe. Such festivals took place in the 1970s when the Bureau of
Educational and Cultural Affairs (CU) collaborated with George Wein
and Festival Productions to bring jazz to Eastern Europe and other
regions.[38] When manager George Avakian arranged Lloyd's visit with
Estonian officials, Avakian encountered so much resistance that his

dream of "making history" nearly went "up in smoke."[39] Estonia remained one of the Baltics' jazz capitals.

Nonetheless, Avakian overcame official Soviet objections, and Lloyd performed stunningly for Estonian audiences. They received him so enthusiastically that Soviet officials attempted to prevent him from finishing his gig.[40] In an official report, an American official who exhibited considerable knowledge of jazz aptly compared the Soviet jazz musicians who performed at the festival to some of the most accomplished American jazz artists of the day—including John Coltrane, Ornette Coleman, and Sonny Rollins. He commended Lloyd for creating lasting cultural bonds between the citizens of rivaling superpowers.[41] The young, accomplished Soviet writer Vasily Aksenov similarly extolled the fact that Lloyd portrayed a refreshing picture of America: he noted that Lloyd's distinctive Afro, his bobbing saxophone, his effusive expressiveness, and his "soft, lyric, tender" music evoked impassioned cheers and zealous ovations from the crowds.[42]

Yuri Saulskii, who also directed jazz bands in Moscow and helped organize festivals, alluded to another important factor that contributed to the zeal for such performances. Although the Soviets acknowledged the complex dynamics of America's racial ideology, what remained important for the Soviet youth was that American jazz represented both the freedom of expression and the spirit of rebellion against authority that Soviet youth so fervently sought to emulate. Saulskii also underscored that Soviet jazz artists embraced the openness and improvisatory nature of free jazz because it reflected the distinctive theoretical features of a free, open, democratic society, which they genuinely esteemed.[43]

Shortly after Lloyd's astounding success, another jazz great, Gerry Mulligan, traveled to the Soviet bloc on a private tour. His trip to Moscow in July 1967 represented another windfall for American jazz in Russia. The Soviet Youth Council, the Komsomol, helped arrange evening performances for the group. During a jam session, Russia's "best jazz" musicians flocked to hear Mulligan play, and at a "jazz café" the Komsomol agreed that musicians and officials could socialize with Mulligan. Yet the Komsomol did not want the Soviets and Americans to speak among themselves in private, thereby requesting that an official "police musician" remain among the group. He helped approve the music for the jam sessions and sought to ensure that the Soviet musicians did not "play like Coltrane." One jam session took place at the apartment of a Moscow architect, where Soviet musicians posed numerous questions about jazz and, contrary to official Soviet con-vention, even continued to speak with Mulligan as they escorted him "to his car."[44]

Some Soviet jazz musicians enthusiastically avowed that Mulligan's influence had made them more adept, technically and musically. Mul-ligan appeared equally "impressed" by the Soviet group the KM Quar-tet, which participated in a jam session, and he was sincerely flattered by how well they knew his music and arrangements. Mulligan also enjoyed his discussions with Soviet jazz connoisseurs. According to a reporting officer, such a "once in a lifetime experience" became invalu-able for Soviet youth because they successfully mingled with Ameri-can musicians and avoided official trouble.[45] Soviet jazz scholar Vladi-mir Feuertag emphasized that such experiences impelled Russian jazz intellectuals to further identify jazz not only as an American but also as a Russian art form.[46]

Shortly thereafter, Willis Conover's visit to Estonia and Rumania became another boon for American jazz in the Soviet bloc. In Ru-mania, Conover received avid praise from young jazz fans as he at-tended an "evening of jazz" at the ambassador's residence as well as a recording session for a local Rumanian jazz quintet. Upon meeting jazz musician Janchi Korossy, whom he called the "best jazz pianist in Eastern Europe," Conover, exuding charm and charisma, interacted with "local jazz buffs." According to an official, Conover and his wife both exhibited "outgoing" and "warm" personalities and helped make many new friends.[47]

In the wake of the momentous travels of Lloyd, Mulligan, and Con-over, another pivotal event ignited the jazz fervor in the Eastern bloc: the death of John Coltrane. Because he remained a dynamic symbol of the jazz avant-garde at home and abroad, his death represented a set-back for jazz and world culture. In the eyes of such outspoken Ameri-can critics as Amiri Baraka, black cultural activism suffered a great loss. Although Miles Davis disdained the links between political militancy, black power, and jazz activism, he succinctly depicted the shock and sadness that arose thereafter. He declared that Coltrane "was express-ing through his music what H. Rap Brown and Stokely Carmichael and the Black Panthers and Huey Newton were saying with their words, what the Last Poets and Amiri Baraka were saying with their words in poetry. He was their torchbearer in jazz, now ahead of me. He played what they felt inside and were expressing through riots—'burn, baby, burn.'"[48] Similarly, jazz scholar Waldo E. Martin has implied that Coltrane's death was a setback for the aesthetic development of jazz that was inspired by the delicate relationship between jazz and Cold War politics.[49] Jazz fans in the Eastern bloc likewise wept for Coltrane in their own way.[50]

Apparently, the persistent jazz fervor continually caused alarm among Soviet officials and overwhelmed the Soviet hierarchy. When American and Soviet negotiators discussed cultural tours in 1968, the Soviets adamantly refused jazz as a matter of "quality and artistic tendency." Free jazz seemed to represent the end of civilization for policy makers on both sides of the Iron Curtain. Political hedging quickly ensued—the American embassy in Moscow asserted that dancers from the United States might not perform at a 1969 Soviet ballet festival if the Soviet Union did not accept an American jazz band for a tour.[51]

The CU continued its efforts to disseminate jazz among Soviet people because it remained keenly aware that jazz practitioners provided Soviet youth with coveted contact with influential American artists who could personally inspire them with America's unique cultural accomplishments. Recognizing the poignant interest in all things Western among Soviet youth, policy makers even attempted to increase the Soviets' knowledge of and support for American Cold War policies, particularly in Vietnam. Cultural contacts remained valuable in this way, the embassy surmised, because American and Soviet students could converse with one another about many diverse topics while increasing understanding, imparting common values, and bridging differences across a vast ideological divide.[52]

In this vein, President Johnson continued efforts to increase cultural openness in the Soviet bloc and reiterated his belief that culture should not simply serve as a political tool. He insisted that the United States regard culture as a means to bring about peaceful relations as political interactions faltered. Still echoing the sentiments of avid cultural internationalists, he asserted that culture could help ameliorate breaches caused by international tensions. Johnson had expressed such views at a meeting with Soviet officials at Glassboro College in New Jersey in June 1967.[53] Johnson, however, implied that he recognized the difficulty of achieving such aims amid the havoc of racial conflicts and the war in Vietnam. He asserted, "I know that we could never break down the distrust between the United States and the Soviet Union if the Iron Curtain survived as an unnatural barrier between East and West. The Soviets had lowered the Iron Curtain against the West, of course. But I felt that we had unwittingly helped strengthen it by some of our policies."[54]

Most unspeakably, in 1968 the world witnessed the assassinations of Martin Luther King Jr. and Robert F. Kennedy, tragic events that exposed the alarming persistence of the racial dimension of Cold War battles in the United States.[55] Adding to the complex evolution of jazz and internationalism, by 1968 rock and roll replaced jazz as the favorite musical pastime at home and abroad. Even in the Soviet Union, where the southern republics most vociferously challenged Moscow's authority, rock and roll markedly took hold.[56]

Two additional Cold War battles in 1968 brought jazz diplomacy and superpower relations to yet another bleak impasse: the Tet Offensive in January and the Soviet invasion of Czechoslovakia in August. The Tet Offensive occurred when the North Vietnamese launched a surprise attack during Tet, a Vietnamese holiday, killing and injuring thousands of American soldiers. Although the Americans subsequently routed the Vietnamese, Tet impaled the American image in several ways: it sharply damaged American prestige and credibility; it significantly underscored that, despite its claims, the United States was not winning the war in Vietnam; and it exposed the inherent weaknesses of the American containment policy. As Johnson suspected that Soviet spies worked to thwart his foreign policies, he addressed the country, expressing his hopes to bring an end to the war.[57]

In the wake of Tet, the Soviet Union again curtailed cultural exchanges. It asserted that before cultural relations could completely resume, the United States would have to show "demonstrable evidence" that it had pursued peaceful policies in Vietnam, worked toward settling the conflict, and discontinued its backing for South Vietnam's struggle against the Viet Cong.[58] The United States nonetheless continued to employ jazz in other Cold War arenas. The CU sponsored Charles Lloyd's integrated group on an official tour to Southeast Asia. Still praised for their triumph at Tallin, these jazz diplomats reflected jazz's enormous symbolic value in the most turbulent regions of the Cold War world. An American reporter observed that "Charles Lloyd's Quartet [Is] Jazzing through [the] Orient in U.S. State Dept. Tour." Lloyd's group performed in Okinawa, Hong Kong, Bangkok, South Vietnam, Kuala Lampur, Penyang, Singapore, Manila, Tokyo, Nagoya, and Osaka.[59]

As American jazz made inroads in Asia, an American official recognized significant distinctions in Soviet bloc and American approaches to cultural affairs. He argued that while some American officials attempted to relegate cultural relations to a separate domain in international affairs, because of the Vietnam War, the Soviets increasingly deemed that cultural affairs remain intertwined with politics—"The better the relations, the better the exchange program."[60] Reflecting similar sentiments, as Polish protests against American involvement in Vietnam increased, Polish officials declared that they did not want to accept "hostile" American artists whom they had to clear "politically" before a tour. Poland maintained that tours should continue only after the political climate improved.[61] The United States responded in kind, for "even before Czechoslovakia," it refused visas for a Polish dance group.[62]

Notably, however, the conundrum of Vietnam had not decreased the fervor for American jazz in Soviet bloc countries, especially in Czechoslovakia during the period of flourishing cultural and political openness—the "Prague Spring." In March 1968, as Tet ensued, such celebrated jazz artists as Ella Fitzgerald and Count Basie performed in the country in the midst of preparations for an international jazz festival.[63] Jazz gained further notoriety when Bradford Graves, a sculptor from New York, constructed a monument to John Coltrane in Czechoslovakia's Carpathian Mountains.[64] Significantly, the Soviet jazz fervor blossomed as the Soviet Union increasingly lost hold of it sphere of influence. The "Prague Spring" had become such a dynamic movement that it "frightened" much of Eastern Europe, and, consequently, the Soviet Union quickly repressed it.[65] The Soviet invasion of Czechoslovakia profoundly altered the course of cultural affairs, belying a Soviet commitment to more peaceful, open relations with the West. It led American Cold Warriors to promptly suspend performing arts tours to and from the countries that had participated in the invasion.[66]

Not all members of the CU agreed with this policy. Some did not want to "nullify" the effects of the boycott by resuming cultural contacts too quickly and emphatically resolved that tours would remain "low key" and "gradual."[67] Yet Guy Coriden, of the CU, questioned the soundness of the decision to cancel tours, fearing that the United States might imperil its long-range goal of increasing cultural openness with the Communist bloc.[68] Robert Landry, writing for *Variety*, later warned that in times of deep international tensions, culture should not fall prey to politics, because artists' independence collapses. Such a development represented a threat to America's international prestige. Landry asserted that "in the politics of cultural exchange, Vietnam is Czech-mated and Tchaikovsky is forgiven."[69]

By the time cultural negotiations took place in November 1968, political tensions had subsided, and the United States resumed U.S.-Soviet cultural tours. The CU scheduled groups, including the U.S. hockey team, for a Soviet exchange, but the team canceled the tour, citing high travel costs as the reason.[70] Seeking to ensure that the United States did not appear insensitive to the people of the invaded country, the CU approved a tour to Czechoslovakia for the University of Illinois Jazz Band.[71] At the same time, Czechoslovakia considered allowing American Dixieland bands to perform in the country.[72] In Prague, an enthralling concert showcasing Czechoslovak jazz occurred at the end of year, while in Moscow, the momentous 1968 jazz festival took place. Even as rock and roll began to permeate Soviet society, the festival evoked heated discussions about the popularity of jazz, the styles of jazz, and the role Russian jazz played in Soviet life.[73] The volatility of Cold War cultural affairs led Secretary of State Rusk to express the view that, in the arena of culture, "we must act with a balance of restraint and firmness, remain true to our values, yet be tolerant of diversity."[74]

As Vietnam and Czechoslovakia checkmated the U.S.-Soviet cultural rivalry, diversity became a more prominent benchmark for the CU, in part because of the increasing cultural solidarity among black intellectuals and activists worldwide. Moreover, the CU still competed for the allegiance of new nations as the Communist bloc effectively used cultural products to gain significant sympathy and support for its Marxist programs.[75] During his trip to Africa late in 1967 and early 1968, Vice President Hubert Humphrey reiterated that it remained critical to reach the youth—future leaders—in what he called Africa's rapidly changing "new" environment.[76] Likewise, Rusk believed that the interests of blacks abroad could not be ignored in the late 1960s. He contended that "we had to recognize that the breakup of the old colonial empires and the emergence of newly independent nations were one of the epochal developments of our time."[77]

Echoing this "epochal development," black intellectuals reexamined African-centered views of culture and history as they attempted to define what Elliot Skinner has characterized as "Africanity"—a view of the world emanating from an African perspective.[78] Thus, although Africa remained a low priority in cultural affairs, the CU recognized the need to acknowledge the transnational racial and cultural move-ment that burgeoned among black intellectuals in the face of Com-munist competition. Accordingly, the CU approved Randy Weston's all-black jazz sextet for an African tour in 1967; it became the first all-black jazz band to travel on an official tour to Africa since 1962.

Weston's tour symbolized a new American approach to cultural affairs. Previously, in the 1950s, American cultural policies had rein-forced the traditional Western approach to Africa, which historically denied Africa's contribution to world civilization. Yet in 1967 Weston's tour revealed an American awareness of the importance of Africanity and also highlighted the CU's appreciation of the idea of "transcultural continuity": jazz was not only America's cultural product, but it also was, in part, Africa's contribution to world civilization. Another criti-cal shift in jazz diplomacy had occurred.[79]

Nevertheless, the factious nature of race relations and the Vietnam War that had vexed cultural affairs still caused suspicion of Ameri-can cultural activities among global audiences.[80] Langston Hughes expressed the skepticism toward race, cultural tours, and democracy that often surfaced in the jazz world at home and abroad. In his poem "Envoy to Africa," he wrote:

My name is Lord Piggly-Wiggly Wigglesfoot Brown.
I was born in a quaint old English manor town.
I now find myself engaged in diplomatic chore
That looks as though it might turn into a bit of a bore.
I was sent to inform the natives of this dark place
that the Atlantic Charter will eventually apply to their race.
Of course, at the moment, we could hardly afford
To stretch the Atlantic Charter that broad.
But I will say this to each native race:
  Some day you's be equal—
  If you'll just stay in your place.[81]

Simultaneously, American attempts to liberate Vietnam through Americanization further damaged the American image and under-mined the world's confidence in American leadership.[82] The tragic assassination of Martin Luther King in Memphis, Tennessee, added to the world's fury. President Johnson remembered that "on the day that Hanoi made an agreement with the United States to begin peace talks," he heard that "King has been shot." He beckoned the country to "reject the blind violence," asserting that "it's only by joining together and only by working together that we can continue to move toward equality and fulfillment for all our people." He recalled the "strain of the day."[83] The rueful events of 1968 strikingly incensed the youth at home and abroad who looked to a future of peaceful global relations; because of American involvement in Vietnam, the race question in the United States remained a heated issue but lost its "strategic importance."[84]

With the election of Richard Nixon as president in 1968, the intense backlash to the civil rights movement and Black Power, and the country's return to an era of conservatism that echoed the 1950s, Johnson recognized the limitations of American democracy. He declared that the country "had come a long way," yet he knew that "the American struggle for justice was just beginning."[85] The "world stage of diplomacy" toward the end of 1960s remained a complicated and tumultuous arena.

The redefinition of America's cultural mission in the midst of the Vietnam War heightened the significance of jazz as a Cold War trope. The CU expressly acknowledged that racial equality had become integral to the idea of both democracy and world civilization and called on jazz as a fervent symbol of this dynamic. Jazz diplomacy transformed Cold War affairs and played a role in the globalization of black culture. Jazz tours reflected how cultural relations existed in a domain that remained separate from world affairs. Even for the Soviets, the profusion of jazz in part gave impetus to a new cultural critique of the Cold War.

As jazz played out on the "world stage of diplomacy" in the late 1960s, it symbolized American attempts to resurrect its besmirched image as American power declined. Jazz tours exemplified a unique domain in world affairs in which diplomats amicably interacted and conveyed hopes for peaceful relations even at the height of international tension. Jazz indeed was a global music. As the world remained engulfed in the flames of the Cold War, Louis Armstrong alluded to the enduring global appeal of the jazz ethos. He avowed that

in 1947 I organized my All Stars Band. . . . Another tour of all America, 1953. We made our first trip to Germany. Were the first attraction there, after the war. I was fifty-three years old. We toured all over Italy. We went everywhere in Africa. . . . 1960s we toured overseas again. This time we went to all of the countries. We returned to the States and played Las Vegas—Reno—Lake Tahoe—in California we made more movies. We went to England, 1967. Back home in 1969 still doing the things that I love, playing music and singing. . . . Just wanted to say that music has no age. Most of your great composers—musicians—are elderly people, way up there in age—they will live forever.[86]

Conclusion

It was not until the era of détente that American jazz policy makers became bold enough to embrace both internationalism and the movement toward free jazz that had reshaped the jazz world of the 1960s and which they had deemed "too far out" for jazz tours during height of the Cold War.[1] Only then did the paragons of free jazz from the 1960s and 1970s become icons in the jazz policy of the Bureau of Educational and Cultural Affairs (CU) at home and abroad. This exemplified the primacy of the U.S.-Soviet rivalry in shaping jazz diplomacy. Jazz as an instrument of containment symbolized anti-Communism and fell within conservative parameters. But by the 1970s, as the space race depleted the Soviet economy and Soviet power sharply began to decline, the United States, still enmeshed in Vietnam, sought to create more stable, open relations with Communist countries. Both sides aimed to compromise.

The evolution of racial and cultural events in the post-World War II era had reshaped the course of American foreign affairs. In 1954, when President Eisenhower beseeched policy makers to embark upon a new path in foreign affairs by employing the performing arts to create a more positive image of the United States worldwide, he feared that the United States was under a state of Cold War cultural siege by Communist nations. Abroad, prevailing notions of American materialism, militarism, and cultural desolation fueled this belief. In the midst of dichotomous Cold War events, American performers helped to fight Communism—they created a new international language, broke down cultural barriers, and engendered mutual understanding among nations.

Yet by the end of the 1960s Cold War cultural policy had shown its vulnerabilities. Cultural affairs could not avoid clashing with the broad social and political issues of the day, both at home and abroad. Efforts to implement containment, spurred on by American involvement in Vietnam, impelled significant changes in cultural policy. Additionally, as events in Little Rock in 1957, Birmingham in 1963, Selma in 1965, and Detroit in 1967 revealed, the paradox of American race relations distinctly influenced attitudes abroad of American life, and the image of the nation remained enigmatic.

Thus, although State Department officials aspired to buttress the image of American race relations and to maintain effective contacts with newly emerging nations—as well as with countries in the Soviet bloc—jazz tours did not always improve the image of the United States. This occurred because, as nationalist movements developed at home and abroad, some nations, though they recognized the appeal of American culture, often did not seek to emulate American values. Moreover, American officials sometimes expressed elitist views toward the cultures with which they sought to improve relations. And, as several jazz tours demonstrated, some officials did not endorse the explicit cultural and political goals of jazz diplomacy. Many factors consequently undermined cultural efforts. Also, because of the frequent emphasis on race and containment rather than on culture and internationalism, many observers at home and abroad remained skeptical about cultural policy, and some objected to official jazz tours. Consequently, in its attempts to promote the idea of "jazzocracy," the president's program sometimes lost its effectiveness and meaning.

Such attitudes, however, did not diminish the symbolic importance of jazz diplomacy. In May 1969 President Richard Nixon bestowed the Medal of Freedom on bandleader Duke Ellington, and in the *Saturday Review*, jazz commentator Stanley Dance reported that during the ceremony at the White House, President Nixon proclaimed that "in the royalty of American music, no man swings more or stands higher than the Duke."[2] The United States Information Agency (USIA) made the event into a film and presented it at Moscow's International Film Festival in July 1969. Both Willis Conover and Leonard Garment, the latter a recent special assistant to Nixon, served as members of the U.S. delegation.[3]

Despite a variety of successful tours, jazz diplomacy often illuminated the dichotomies that had emerged between blacks and whites in the cultural and political arenas. It was a time when a new black aesthetic emerged on the international stage. The resulting "aesthetic activism" sometimes reflected artists' "commitment to revolutionary change" and validated black survival; it sometimes affirmed black rights in the United States; and at times it symbolized racial harmony and integration. It even represented what Cornel West has characterized as a "barometer of freedom," or "a form of affirmation."[4] At other times this "aesthetic activism" reflected DuBois's notion of sorrow and the blues, which he alluded to throughout his lifetime. In 1962 DuBois stated, "I have lived in the land of black folk and under a culture which they created. . . . I am thrilled and hopeful from all this which I have seen."[5]

Although a conservative critic, Don DeMicheal, an editor of *Down Beat* in the 1960s, also alluded to links between democracy, culture, and "aesthetic activism" when describing the jazz ethos during this era. He observed: "Jazz is democracy, that is freedom of expression of self, sometimes angry, sometimes exclamatory, within a social (the group members) and judicial (limit imposed by music "laws") structure."[6]

As the United States propelled the black aesthetic onto the world stage and embraced jazz as a unique American contribution to world culture, a deep ideological divide persisted in the CU and in the jazz world. Although many different musicians—such as Miles Davis, Archie Schepp, Ornette Coleman, Charles Mingus, and John Coltrane—represented many different styles of jazz, mainstream "sanitized" jazz performed by the older generation of black and white jazz musicians prevailed in cultural policy. Jazz tours thus heightened the friction among black and white artists in the jazz world at home and abroad. In this context, such critics as DeMicheal lamented the fact that State Department jazz programs remained "encrusted in conservativism." From 1954 to 1968, despite the popularity of modern jazz, the State Department's lack of interest in modern and free jazz groups "smack[ed] of a fear of boat-rocking." Moreover, the State Department often underwent criticism for using race as an obvious ploy; sometimes jazz policy resulted in the perpetuation of stereotypes.[7] In the 1950s and 1960s jazz and jazz diplomacy came to represent the soul of a divided people.

In employing jazz as a central element of the American containment policy, the United States capitalized on the idea that jazz could help dispel beliefs in Communism and foster liberalization. In many regions of the world, the U.S. government sometimes employed jazz to acknowledge power shifts and to appeal to new and emerging nations, as it used jazz to help provide a bulwark against the expansion of Soviet cultural influence. Yet in the wake of the Vietnam War, jazz diplomacy often amplified the dichotomy between theory and practice in foreign affairs. Jazz diplomacy evolved as American expatriates became more alienated from American society. In addition, although the United States took note of the world's cultural diversity, in the wake of the expansion of cultural internationalism in the postwar era, it often did not embrace the divergent worldviews of foreign peoples. Thus, as multiculturalism and Americanization extended throughout the world, jazz diplomacy underscored the contradictions of American democracy even as American policy makers aimed to exhibit American exceptionalism on the world stage. Such dynamics called for a new definition of international relations, which the CU did not offer until the 1970s. Culture itself became a measure of a nation's wealth and power.[8]

Importantly, an ideology of whiteness and anti-Communism pervaded the discourse that shaped jazz diplomacy, even during the era of détente, as jazz continued to play an important role in bringing democratic values to the Soviet bloc.[9] Many groups, including the Minnesota Band in 1969, Duke Ellington in 1971, and the Thad Jones, Mel Lewis Jazz Orchestra in 1972, traveled to the Soviet Union; and avid Soviet jazz fans came from many parts of the country to hear the bands' energetic jazz renditions, which sparked praise worldwide. Many other bands followed. Although the jazz fervor in the late 1960s gave way to the popularity of rock and roll in the 1970s and 1980s and hip-hop in the 1990s, jazz musicians made remarkable inroads in the Eastern bloc, personally and culturally, through both private and official efforts.[10]

U.S.-Soviet cultural relations took a dramatic turn in 1979 when the two countries suspended cultural tours after the Soviet invasion of Afghanistan and the defection of several top Soviet artists to the United States. The United States also boycotted the Olympics the next year. The U.S.-Soviet cultural program resumed during the Gorbachev era—the era of glasnost and perestroika.[11] As Western cultural values permeated Soviet culture, jazz and the influx of American culture contributed to the Soviet Union's loss of cultural and political credibility among the Soviet people.

Thus, as various scholars have pointed out, the end of the Cold War in part came about not only because of recurrent challenges to the Soviet Union's political and economic leadership but also because of the allure and diffusion of modern jazz and Western cultural values. The appropriation of black cultural products thereby played a critical role in the lessening of Cold War tensions and gave significant impetus to what Walter Hixson characterizes as "parting the curtain."[12] Jazz in the 1990s gained even greater respectability in many regions of the former Soviet Union. Post-Soviet jazz acquired a new, distinct voice, and many Soviet and Eastern European jazz musicians gained international prominence, often recording and performing with renowned American jazz musicians.

Jazz's international popularity, particularly among the youth, grew powerful and undeniable during the "Americanized Century." The State Department had become keenly aware of this from 1954 to 1968 as it employed jazz as an instrument of Cold War containment. Jazz diplomacy thus also contributed to the globalization of African American culture in the twentieth century. In the post-9/11 era, with the unyielding preponderance of American cultural products abroad, it remains especially important for cultural policy makers to acknowledge the significance of the cultural diversity and plurality of U.S. and world cultures. African Americans' involvement in official cultural efforts led artists and others to wrestle with an important issue regarding the essence of American culture: jazz was not only an American and African American cultural product, but it was also, in the eyes of many cultures of the world, a global music. In this way, musicians, artists, and politicians worldwide elevated jazz and culture above the contentious realm of Cold War politics.

Most important, jazz diplomacy illuminated the unequivocal limitations of a democracy in the conduct of foreign affairs. At a time when the struggle for freedom at home and abroad continued to shape international culture and politics, the development of jazz and world events had a profound influence on the evolution of American democracy. As the Cold War challenged America's evolving democratic system, it also obscured the plurality of American culture that made the country unique. Ultimately, because conservative jazz was used to thwart Soviet propaganda worldwide, many of the innovators of jazz who became well known at home and abroad were excluded from cultural tours. Thus jazz diplomacy, especially in the midst of the war in Vietnam, did not reflect the ideals of a pluralistic republican democracy. Moreover, jazz tours during these years never had the unwavering support of the American people. Ultimately, echoing de Tocqueville, Cold War jazz diplomacy obscured America's cultural and political pluralism from 1954 to 1968. When jazz policy embraced internationalism and expanded to include a wider array of jazz musicians and jazz styles in the 1970s, it attempted to adjust to the newly emerging world order; only then did it gain both credibility and viability at home and abroad. Through the tribulations of the Cold War, America redefined its beliefs, its ethos, and its political system, as it continued to wrestle with its identity as a member of a global artistic community.

Notes

Introduction

1. Ernest G. Wiener, Counselor for Cultural Affairs, Embassy Moscow to Department of State, Airgam #A-819, "Jazz Night at the Blue Bird Café," January 18, 1965, 3, University of Arkansas Libraries, Special Collections Division, Fulbright Papers, Manuscript Collection (MC) 468, Bureau of Educational and Cultural Affairs (CU), Group 2, "Cultural Presentations Program," Series 1, "General and Historical Files, boxes 47–52 (hereafter cited as CU, Series 1; when all documents are from the same file, the file is listed at the end of the note). For more on jazz in Russia, see Michael May, "Swinging Under Stalin: Russian Jazz during the Cold War and Beyond," in *Here, There, and Everywhere: The Foreign Politics of American Popular Culture*, ed. Reinhold Wagnleitner and Elaine Tyler May (Hanover, N.H.: University Press of New England, 2000), 179–191; Reinhold Wagnleitner, "The Empire of Fun, or Talkin' Soviet Blues: The Sound of Freedom and U.S. Cultural Hegemony in Europe," *Diplomatic History* 23 (Summer 1999): 499–524; S. Frederick Starr, *Red and Hot: The Fate of Jazz in the Soviet Union* (New York: Oxford University Press, 1983).

2. For more on cultural relations during the Cold War, see Wagnleitner and May, *Here, There and Everywhere*; David Caute, *The Dancer Defects: The Struggle for Cultural Supremacy during the Cold War* (Oxford: Oxford University Press, 2005); Robert A. Haddow, *Pavilions of Plenty: Exhibiting American Culture Abroad in the 1950s* (Washington, D.C.: Smithsonian Institution Press, 1997); Walter Hixson, *The Myth of American Diplomacy: Identity and U.S. Foreign Policy* (New Haven, Conn.: Yale University Press, 2008).

3. Nicholas J. Cull, *The Cold War and the United States Information Agency: American Propaganda and Public Diplomacy, 1945–1989* (Cambridge: Cambridge University Press, 2008), 81.

4. Ibid., xiv–xvi.

5. A pivotal work on the *Brown* decision is Richard Kluger, *Simple Justice: The History of* Brown v. Board of Education *and Black America's Struggle for Equality* (New York: Vintage Books, 1977), 749. See also Mary L. Dudziak, "Josephine Baker, Racial Protest and the Cold War," *Journal of American History* 81, no. 2 (September 1994): 543–570.

6. Walter L. Hixson, *Parting the Curtain: Propaganda, Culture, and the Cold War, 1945–1961* (New York: St. Martin's Press, 1997); Penny M. Von Eschen, *Satchmo Blows Up the World: Jazz Ambassadors Play the Cold War* (Cambridge, Mass.: Harvard University Press, 2004), 1–57, 92–120, 185–222. For a compelling discussion on changing ideas of race and democracy, see Manning Marable, *The Great Wells of Democracy: The Meaning of Race in American Life* (New York: Basic Civitas Books, 2002), 23–25, 29.

7. In *Freedom Sounds: Civil Rights Call Out to Jazz and Africa* (New York: Oxford University Press, 2007), Ingrid Monson offers a definitive and compelling account of jazz activism and aesthetic agency during the Cold War years as well as the cultural and racial paradoxes that this activism created.

8. Akira Iriye, "The Americanized Century," *Reviews in American History* (March 1983): 124–128; W. E. B. DuBois, *The Souls of Black Folk*, ed. Brent Hayes Edward (New York: Oxford, 2007), 1.

9. Cull, *Cold War and the United States Information Agency*, 1–21.

10. Allison Blakely, "European Dimensions of the African Diaspora: The Definition of Black Racial Identity," in *Crossing Boundaries: Comparative History of Black People in Diaspora*, ed. Darlene Clark Hine and Jacqueline McCleod (Bloomington: Indiana University Press, 1999), 91; John Hope Franklin, "The Two Worlds of Race: A Historical View," in *Race and History: Selected Essays* (Baton Rouge: Louisiana State University Press, 1989), 132–152. See also Michael Hunt, *Ideology and U.S. Foreign Policy* (New Haven, Conn.: Yale University Press, 1983).

11. Franklin, "Two Worlds of Race," 132–140. See also Reginald Horsemann, *Race and Manifest Destiny: The Origins of American Racial Anglo-Saxonism* (Cambridge, Mass.: Harvard University Press, 1981), 1–6, 298–303. George Fredrickson offers a critical perspective on these issues in *The Black Image in the White Mind: The Debate on Afro-American Character and Destiny, 1817–1914* (New York: Harper and Row, 1971).

12. Franklin, "Two Worlds of Race," 141–152.

13. A definitive examination of soft power is Joseph S. Nye Jr., *Soft Power: The Means to Success in World Politics* (New York: Public Affairs, 2004). For perspectives on race and the Cold War, see Brenda Gayle Plummer, *Rising Wind: Black Americans and U.S. Foreign Affairs, 1935–1960* (Chapel Hill: University of North Carolina Press, 1997); Brenda Gayle Plummer, ed., *Window on Freedom* (Chapel Hill: University of North Carolina Press, 2003); Paul Gordon Laurel, *Power and Prejudice: The Politics and Diplomacy of Racial Discrimination* (1988; reprint, Boulder, Colo.: Westview Press, 1996); Mary L. Dudziak, *Cold War Civil Rights: Race and the Image of American Democracy* (Princeton, N.J.: Princeton University Press, 2000); Penny M. Von Eschen, *Race against Empire: Black Americans and Anti-Colonialism, 1937–1957* (Ithaca, N.Y.: Cornell University Press, 1997); Thomas Borstelmann, *The Cold War and the Color Line: American Race Relations in the Global Arena* (Cambridge, Mass.: Harvard University Press, 2001); Michael Krenn, *The Color of Empire: Race and American Foreign Relations* (Washington, D.C.: Potomac Books, 2006). Notably, Borstelmann argues that "it was during the Cold War that one of the central tensions of American history was largely resolved, at least in the public sphere: the conflict between an older vision of an America founded on hierarchies such as race and gender, and a newer ideal of a society free of legalized discrimination and enforced inequality" (*Cold War and the Color Line*, x).

14. Plummer, *Rising Wind*, 233, 235, 257–298.

15. Cull, *Cold War and the United States Information Agency*, 1-21.

16. David Levering Lewis, "Introduction," in *W. E. B. DuBois: A Reader* (New York: Henry Holt, 1995), 2; Henry Louis Gates Jr., "W. E. B. DuBois, and the Talented Tenth," in Henry Louis Gates Jr. and Cornel West, *The Future of the Race* (New York: Alfred A. Knopf, 1996), 132. See also David Levering Lewis, *W. E. B. DuBois: The Fight for Equality and the American Century, 1919–1963* (New York: Henry Holt, 2000), 37–152.

17. Paul Robeson, "Pesni Moego Naroda," *Sovetskaia Muzyka* 7 (July 1949): 100–104.

18. Elliot P. Skinner, "Hegemonic Paradigms and the African World: Striving to Be Free," in Hine and McLeod, *Crossing Boundaries*, 64. See also Lewis, *W. E. B. DuBois*, 395–396.

19. Plummer, *Rising Wind*, 37–216; see also Plummer, *Window on Freedom*, introduction.

20. Quoted in Gates, "W. E. B. DuBois and the Talented Tenth," 131; see also 123–125, 132. Gates is referring to DuBois's speech in 1948, "The Talented Tenth Memorial Address," in ibid., 159–177. DuBois also stated that race is "not simply a physical entity. . . . It was what all races really are, a cultural group" (ibid., 163). DuBois spoke to the concept of race in many of his writings. See, for example, W. E. B. DuBois, "The Negro Problems," in Lewis, *DuBois: A Reader*, 48–53.

21. Alain Leroy Locke, *Race Contacts and Interracial Relations: Lectures on the Theory and Practice of Race* (reprint, Washington, D.C.: Howard University Press, 1992), 12. For Gobineau, see Arthur Comte de Gobineau, *The Inequality of the Human Races* (reprint, New York: H. Fertig, 1967).

22. Locke, *Race Contacts*, 12–13.

23. Ibid., 13.

24. Ibid., iii.

25. Elazar Barkan, *The Retreat of Scientific Racism: Changing Concepts of Race in Britain and the United States between the World Wars* (Cambridge: Cambridge University Press, 1992), 2–3, 8, 11; Stephen Steinberg, *Turning Back: The Retreat from Racial Justice in American Thought and Policy* (Boston: Beacon Press, 1995), 44–45; Gunnar Myrdal, *An American Dilemma: The Negro Problem and Modern Democracy* (New York: Harper and Brothers, 1944).

26. Clifford Geertz, *The Interpretation of Cultures* (New York: Basic Books, 1973), 127.

27. Akira Iriye, *Cultural Internationalism and World Order* (Baltimore: Johns Hopkins University Press, 1977), 3. Iriye offers a definition of culture as the "structures of meaning," which constitute "memory, ideology, emotions, life styles, scholarly, and artistic works, and other symbols" (ibid., 3). Anthropologist Clifford Geertz has defined

culture as the "webs of significance" in which man is "suspended" and which "he himself has spun." This includes the "meanings . . . construing social expression on their surface enigmatical" (Geertz, *Interpretation of Cultures*, 5).

28. Iriye, *Cultural Internationalism*, 130, 147, 160–168.

29. Cull, *Cold War and the United States Information Agency*, 52.

30. Frederick Charles Barghoorn, *The Soviet Cultural Offensive: The Role of Cultural Diplomacy in Soviet Foreign Policy* (Princeton, N.J.: Princeton University Press, 1960). See also Dudziak, "Josephine Baker." For this view of jazz, see Starr, *Red and Hot*, 203–234.

31. Steven J. Whitfield, *The Culture of the Cold War*, 2nd ed. (Baltimore: Johns Hopkins University Press, 1996), 1–14, 20–25; Paul Boyer, *By the Bomb's Early Light: American Thought and Culture and the Dawn of the Atomic Age* (Chapel Hill: University of North Carolina Press, 1985).

32. Whitfield, *Culture of the Cold War*, 7.

33. For more on the lives of these significant figures, see Martin Bauml Duberman, *Paul Robeson* (New York: Alfred A. Knopf, 1989); Lewis, *W. E. B. DuBois*; Phyllis Rose, *Jazz Cleopatra: Josephine Baker in Her Time* (New York: Doubleday, 1989). See also Lewis, *DuBois: A Reader*, 10.

34. Emily Rosenberg, *Spreading the American Dream: American Economic and Cultural Expansion, 1890–1945* (New York: Hill and Wang, 1982), 7.

35. Ibid.

36. Frank Ninkovich, *The Diplomacy of Ideas: U.S. Foreign Policy and Cultural Relations, 1938–1950* (Cambridge: Cambridge University Press, 1981), 125–127.

37. Ibid., 8; see also 113–183. Their ideological differences often arose at the meetings of the United Nations Educational, Scientific, and Cultural Organization (UNESCO).

38. Ibid., 182–183.

39. Cull, *Cold War and the United States Information Agency*, 101; see also 136–144.

40. Dudziak, "Josephine Baker," 543–570.

41. Dudziak, *Cold War Civil Rights*, 249–254.

42. Lawrence W. Levine, *Black Culture and Black Consciousness: Afro-American Folk Thought from Slavery to Freedom* (Oxford: Oxford University Press, 1977), 291.

43. Cornel West, "Black Strivings in a Twilight Civilization," in Gates and West, *Future of the Race*, 79–80, 88–89.

44. Ibid., 102–103.

45. Cull, *Cold War and the United States Information Agency*, 101; see also 136–144.

46. Gunther Schuller, *Early Jazz: Its Roots and Musical Development* (New York: Oxford University Press, 1968), 8. For a critical perspective on culture and resistance, see Edward Said, *Culture and Imperialism* (New York: Vintage Books, 1993).

47. For the emergence of the Black Arts Movement in the mid-1960s, see Eric Porter,

What Is This Thing Called Jazz: African American Musicians as Artists, Critics, and Activists (Berkeley: University of California Press, 2002), 191–239. Baraka espoused ideas of black nationalism.

48. DuBois, *Souls of Black Folk*, 8–9.

49. Monson, *Freedom Sounds*, 4-12; Morroe Berger, "Jazz: Resistance to the Diffusion of a Culture Pattern," *Journal of Negro History* 32 (1947): 461–494. Marshall Stearns, in *The Story of Jazz* (New York: Sidgwick and Jackson, 1957), attempted to identify the forces that reflected the increasing cultural unity of the jazz art form.

50. Monson, *Freedom Sounds*, 6.

51. Scott Saul, *Freedom Is, Freedom Ain't: Jazz and the Making of the Sixties* (Cambridge, Mass.: Harvard University Press, 2003), 2. Controversies about the suitability of mainstream jazz in cultural tours will be explored in succeeding chapters.

52. Eric Porter, "It's About That Time," in *Miles Davis and American Culture*, ed. Gerald Early (St. Louis: Missouri Historical Society Press, 2001), 139.

53. Saul, *Freedom Is, Freedom Ain't*, 4–5. For an eloquent account of the civil rights movement, see David J. Garrow, *Bearing the Cross: Martin Luther King, Jr., and the Southern Christian Leadership Conference* (New York: Vintage Books, 1986).

54. George Hutchinson, *The Harlem Renaissance in Black and White* (Cambridge, Mass.: Harvard University Press, 1995), 31; see also 29–30, 221–222, 308. Many influential African American intellectuals became prominent during this era: Alain Locke, W. E. B. DuBois, Langston Hughes, Claude McKay, James Weldon Johnson, Countee Cullen, and countless others.

55. Nathan Irvin Huggins, *The Harlem Renaissance* (London: Oxford University Press, 1971), 199, 201. See also Hutchinson, *Harlem Renaissance*, 397–398. Black artists wanted to prove their own civility and "worth" in the face of a society that degraded their humanity and branded them as socially barbaric. Simultaneously, black jazz musicians saw white musicians grasping to imitate the music they created.

56. Huggins, *Harlem Renaissance*, 195.

57. Ibid., 201. See also Olly Wilson, "Black Music as an Art Form," in *The Jazz Cadence of American Culture*, ed. Robert O' Meally (New York: Columbia University Press, 1998), 82–101.

58. Huggins, *Harlem Renaissance*, 159, 204. See also Porter, *What Is This Thing Called Jazz*, 17–18; Hutchinson, *Harlem Renaissance*, 221–223.

59. Huggins, *Harlem Renaissance*, 137–243; Hutchinson, *Harlem Renaissance*, 178, 289–312.

60. Wilson Record, *The Negro and the Communist Party* (New York: Antheneum, 1971), 15, 55.

61. David Stowe, *Swing Changes: Big Band Jazz in New Deal America* (Cambridge, Mass.: Harvard University Press, 1994), 70–72. See also Huggins, *Harlem Renaissance*,

209–213. Many blacks also joined the American Communist Party in the 1930s, where they could express nationalist ideas despite the fact that the party officially opposed expressions of black nationalism. See Record, *Negro and the Communist Party.*

62. Stowe, *Swing Changes,* 70–72. See also Robin D. G. Kelley, *Race Rebels: Culture, Politics, and the Black Working Class* (New York: Free Press, 1994), 105, 123–158; Brent Edwards, *The Practice of Diaspora: Literature, Translation and the Rise of Black Internationalism* (Cambridge, Mass.: Harvard University Press, 2003), 3; Michael Denning, *The Cultural Front: The Laboring of American Culture in the 20th Century* (New York: Verso, 1996), 362–402, 423–462. Many blacks joined in response to the aftermath of the Great Depression, a cataclysmic event that influenced blacks more than other ethnic groups.

63. Edwards, *Practice of Diaspora,* 3. For "black Marxism," see ibid., 276–282.

64. Porter, *What Is This Thing Called Jazz,* 15–16. For a profound portrayal of Hurston's life, see Zora Neal Hurston, *Dust Tracks on a Road* (Thorndike, Me.: G. K. Hall, 1997).

65. Porter, *What Is This Thing Called Jazz,* 47, 48.

66. Laurence Bergreen, *Louis Armstrong: An Extravagant Life* (New York: Broadway Books, 1997), 437–474; Ted Gioia, *The History of Jazz* (New York: Oxford University Press, 1997), 216, 220–234. Many categories of jazz overlap, and jazz practitioners often played several different styles of the music. Jam sessions also became an important component of jazz tours. A jam session was either a spontaneous, unrehearsed performance by a group of musicians or an impromptu display of musical improvisation among several musicians. The jam session remained at the center of jazz performance.

67. Ron M. Radano, *New Musical Figurations: Anthony Braxton's Cultural Critique* (Chicago: University of Chicago Press, 1993), 13–14, 17. See also Stowe, *Swing Changes,* 141–179.

68. Porter, *What Is This Thing Called Jazz,* 83–84; Stowe, *Swing Changes,* 141–179, esp. 145–167.

69. Porter, *What Is This Thing Called Jazz,* 83–84.

70. Radano, *New Musical Figurations,* 13–14, 17. See also Stowe, *Swing Changes,* 141–179.

71. Leroi Jones [Amiri Baraka], *Blues People: Negro Music in White America* (Westport, Conn.: Greenwood Press, 1980), 229, 230–231.

72. Gioia, *History of Jazz,* 273–278.

73. Ibid., 281–289.

74. Ibid., 313–330.

75. Monson, *Freedom Sounds,* 172.

76. Ibid., 330.

77. Charles Mingus, interview by Sy Johnson, Oral History–Smithsonian Institu-

tion, February 19–22, 1978, cassettes 1–2, transcript, 3, Rutgers University Institute of Jazz Studies, Rutgers University, Newark, N.J.

78. Cozy Cole, interview by Bill Kirchner, April 1980, Jazz Oral History Project, cassette 1, transcript, 8, 35 Rutgers University Institute of Jazz Studies.

79. Monson, *Freedom Sounds*, 12, 171, 259–261.

80. Radano, *New Musical Figurations*, 68, 82–83; Porter, *What Is This Thing Called Jazz*, 191.

81. Franz Fanon, *The Wretched of the Earth* (New York: Grove Press, 1963), 211. See also Porter, *What Is This Thing Called Jazz*, 203.

82. Duke Ellington, *Music Is My Mistress* (Garden City, N.Y.: Doubleday, 1973), 192.

83. Stuart Nicholson, *Reminiscing in Tempo: Duke Ellington in Portrait* (Boston: Northeastern University Press, 1999), 344–350.

84. Toni Morrison, *Jazz* (New York: Alfred A. Knopf, 1992), 65.

85. J. C. Thomas, *Coltrane: Chasin' the Trane: The Music and Mystique of John Coltrane* (1975; reprint, New York: Da Capo Press, 1976), 57.

86. W. E. B. DuBois, "Criteria of Negro Art," in Lewis, *DuBois: A Reader*, 513–514. One of the first uses of the term "Cold War jazz" was by Frank Thompson Jr. in *American Jazz Annual*, Newport edition, 1956 (New York: Hemisphere Press, 1956), 27–28, 86–88, cited in Saul, *Freedom Is, Freedom Ain't*, 15.

87. For an illuminating discussion of the many aspects of the jazz paradox, see Porter, *What Is This Thing Called Jazz*, 1–53.

88. Burton Peretti, *The Creation of Jazz: Music, Race and Culture in Urban America* (Urbana: University of Illinois Press, 1993), 2–25; Porter, *What Is This Thing Called Jazz*, 18. For an earlier view of race and jazz, see Leonard Neil, *Jazz and the White Americans: The Acceptance of a New Art Form* (Chicago: University of Chicago Press, 1962).

89. For a discussion of native symbolic forms, see Herbert Applebaum, *Perspectives in Cultural Anthropology* (Albany: State University of New York Press, 1987), 485.

90. Frank Kofsky, *Black Nationalism and the Revolution in Music* (New York: Pathfinder, 1970), 125–144; Gates and West, *Future of the Race*, 84. Porter also elaborates on these cultural distinctions in *What Is This Thing Called Jazz* (7–11).

91. Gates and West, *Future of the Race*, 56, 64.

92. West, "Black Strivings," 77–78. Porter elaborates on the creation of an intellectual discourse among jazz artists in *What Is This Thing Called Jazz* (xiii–xiv, 101–148).

93. A comprehensive study on youth dissidence in the 1960s is Jeremi Suri, *Power and Protest: Global Revolution and the Rise of Détente* (Cambridge, Mass.: Harvard University Press, 2003). Suri reveals how the global youth movement of the 1960s embraced a myriad of cultural forms—including plays, music, and literature—to express dissent against authority. These forms became "the language of dissent" among the youth of Asia, Europe, the United States, and Latin America. Although he does not discuss

specific examples of jazz and global dissent, he refers to music as a component of this movement, thus implying that jazz also contributed to the "language of dissent" in societies beyond the United States and the Eastern bloc (Suri, *Power and Protest*, 88).

94. Levine, *Black Culture and Black Consciousness*, 297.

Chapter 1. Battling the Reds

1. Borstelmann, *Cold War and the Color Line*, 8. See also Von Eschen, *Race against Empire*, 126, 130; Dudziak, *Cold War Civil Rights*, 86. For Soviet initiatives, see Caute, *Dancer Defects*.

2. W. E. B. DuBois, "What Is the Meaning of 'All Deliberate Speed?'" in Lewis, *DuBois: A Reader*, 423.

3. Morrell Heald and Lawrence S. Kaplan, *Culture and Diplomacy: The American Experience* (Westport, Conn.: Greenwood Press, 1977), 16.

4. Plummer, *Rising Wind*, 168–169.

5. Michael T. Bertrand, *Race, Rock, and Elvis* (Urbana: University of Illinois Press, 2000), 41–43.

6. Heald and Kaplan, *Culture and Diplomacy*, 3–16.

7. Ibid., 16. See also Hixson, *Parting the Curtain*, 129–133.

8. Howard A. Cook, Chief Public Services Division, to Markus, January 3, 1955, b 81, National Archives and Records Administration (NARA), Records of the Department of State, College Park, Md., RG-59, Decimal File 032, 1955–1959 (hereafter cited as DF 032, 1955–1959; when all records are from the same file, the file is listed at the end of the note).

9. Cook to Rubin, August 17, 1955, b 82, DF 032, 1955–1959. See also Cook to Rubin, September 1, 1955, b 82, DF 032, 1955–1959; *Foreign Relations of the United States* [*FRUS*], 1955–1957, Vol. 24, *Soviet Union; Eastern Mediterranean*, #98, "Memorandum of Conversation, Washington," September 20, 1955. The United States and the Soviet Union also discussed opening a USIS office in Moscow. Walter Hixson offers an astute account of the Geneva Summit in *Parting the Curtain*, 97–101.

10. DOS Memo of Conversation (MOC), "HEW Exchange with USSR," September 16, 1955; DOS MOC, "Exchange of NY and Moscow Mayors," October 21, 1955, b 83; DOS MOC, "U.S. Artists to USSR," July 19, 1955, b 82; U.S. Government (USG) Office Memo, "Visit of Soviet Artists to the U.S.," b 85; Anatole Heller to Moscow, November 10, 1955; and USG MOC, "Isaac Stern to Soviet Union," December 15, 1955, b 84, DF 032, 1955–1959; Arthur Bronson, "U.S. Steps Up Cultural Front War: $2,250,000 'Seed Coin Aids Show Biz,'" *Variety*, March 23, 1955, 1.

11. Strobe Talbott, ed., *Khrushchev Remembers* (Boston: Little, Brown, 1970), 394–400.

12. Richard S. Stites, *Russian Popular Culture: Entertainment and Society since 1900* (Cambridge: Cambridge University Press, 1992), 118–119, 123–135.

13. *FRUS*, 1955–1957, *Soviet Union*, #104, "National Security Council Report," June 29, 1956, 244.

14. Stoessel to Ryan, April 7, 1955, b 81, reply to Francis Ryan, to DOS, March 23, 1955, DF 032, 1955–1959.

15. Letter cited in Alexander Bisno to Walter J. Stoessel Jr., Acting Officer in Charge, European Affairs, March 1955, b 81. Stoessel replied in Stoessel to Bisno, October 3, 1955, b 87. Soviet exchanges are also justified in Department of State Instruction (DOS Instr.) 1449, March 3, 1955, b 81, DF 032, 1955–1959.

16. Bohlen to SOS, Department of State Incoming Telegram (DOS Incom.) 1620, "Pravda Article re: Exchange Contacts," January 24, 1956, b 85; DOS Instr. 1735 to SOS, February 3, 1956, b 85; Department of State Outgoing Telegram (DOS Out.) 19, October 1, 1956, b 87; and Stoessel to Director, Nyherald Tribune, February 7, 1956, b 85, DF 032, 1955–1959.

17. Paul Kapp, Manager, Delta Rhythm Boys, to Walter Stoessel, July 16, 1955, 1–2, b 82, DF 032, 1955–1959.

18. Irving R. Levine, "U.S.S.R. May Cite 'Porgy' as Evidence There's No Iron Curtain for Arts," *Variety*, December 28, 1955, 1, 63.

19. Foreign Service Despatch (FSD) 883, Athens, to DOS, April 24, 1956, b 86, DF 032, 1955–1959. See also *FRUS*, Vol. 24, #110, "Memorandum of Conversation," Department of State, Washington, D.C., February 28, 1957, 256–257.

20. Talbott, *Khrushchev Remembers*, 343.

21. Cull, *Cold War and the United States Information Agency*, 121.

22. Dwight D. Eisenhower to Eugene Holman, July 18, 1956, in *The Papers of Dwight David Eisenhower*, ed. Louis Galambos and Duan Van Ee, Vol. 17 (Baltimore: Johns Hopkins University Press, 1996), 2208.

23. Bronson, "U.S. Steps Up Cultural Front War," 1; "Culture for Export," *Time*, June 6, 1955, 78. The Cultural Presentations Program will be explored in greater depth in chapter 3.

24. Talbott, *Khrushchev Remembers*, 343.

25. Plummer, *Rising Wind*, 261.

26. Cull, *Cold War and the United States Information Agency*.

27. MOC, Fred Schang, Columbia Artists, and Robert O. Blake, Eastern Europe, February 11, 1957, b 88, DF 032, 1955–1959.

28. Dulles, [stamp], to Clarence B. Randall, Special Assistant to the President, February 12, 1957, b 88. See also Hoover, Acting, to Budapest, DOS Instr., A-72, November 19, 1956, b 87, DF 032, 1955–1959.

29. Eisenhower to Nikolai Aleksandrovich Bulganin, November 4, 1956, Cable Secret, in Galambos and Van Ee, *Papers of Dwight D. Eisenhower*, 2362.

30. Hoover, Acting, to Budapest, DOS Instr., A-72, November 19, 1956, b 87, DF 032, 1955–1959.

31. Harold C. Vedeler, Counselor of Embassy, Hungary, to DOS, FSD-199, November 9, 1956, b 87, DF 032, 1955–1959.

32. Henry P. Leverich, Official in Charge, Balkan Affairs, to Martens, n.d., b 85, reply to Andre Martens, Columbia Artists Management, to DOS, January 30, 1956, and attach; see also Beam to SOS, DOS Incom. 1356, April 20, 1959; Macomber to Rep. Leslie C. Arends, n.d., b 91, DF 032, 1955–1959. Vedeler recommended classical musicians as well as jazz groups such as Louis Armstrong's.

33. John C. Guthrie, First Secretary of Embassy, Moscow, to DOS, FSD-252, "Educational Exchange: President's Fund," October 30, 1956, b 87, DF 032, 1955–1959.

34. Albert W. Sherer, First Secretary of Embassy, Prague, to DOS, FSD-323, "Visit of Mr. Robert Dowling, Chairman of the Board of the American National Theater Academy (ANTA)," February 13, 1957, b 97, DF 032, 1955–1959.

35. Llewellyn E. Thompson, Moscow, to DOS, FSD-703, "Reception of Mr. Robert Dowling by Khrushchev," June 2, 1958, b 97. See also DOS MOC, "Columbia Artist Management Team to Moscow and Prague," August 14, 1958, b 89; and Albert W. Sherer, First Secretary of Embassy, Prague, to DOS, FSD-323, "Visit of Mr. Robert Dowling, Chairman of the Board of the American National Theater Academy (ANTA)," February 13, 1957, b 97, DF 032, 1955–1959.

36. M. Tsouvalas and J. E. Magdanz, DOS Instr. CA-3349, to Moscow, Prague, Warsaw, "President's Fund: Cultural Attractions to Soviet Bloc Countries," October 17, 1956, b 87, DF 032, 1955–1959.

37. Joseph C. Kolarek, Country Public Affairs Officer, Belgrade, to USIS, FSD-Tousi 9, July 25, 1956, b 86. This perspective also arises in Tsouvalas and Magdanz, DOS Instr. CA-3349; Dulles to Moscow, DOS Out., May 13, 1958; Dulles, F. T. Merrill, DOS, to Ambassador Lacy, May 20, 1958, b 87, DF 032, 1955–1959.

38. Richard H. Davies, Moscow, to DOS, FSD-406, "Visit to the Soviet Union by American Artists' Delegation," January 16, 1959, b 90, DF 032, 1955–1959.

39. "Radio Moscow in Switch to Jazz," *Variety*, June 29, 1955, 43. See also "Jazz Around the World," *Time*, June 25, 1956. For a discussion of the Voice of America and U.S. radio propaganda in the Soviet Union in the 1950s, see Hixson, *Parting the Curtain*, 29–55.

40. "Muscovite Ramblers: For Jazz, There's Nothing–in Russia–Like Utysov's Gosudarstvennyi Estradnyi Orkestr," *New York Times Magazine*, April 17, 1955, 25.

41. "Chto Vi Dumaete o Dzhaze i Legkoi Muzyke?" *Sovetskaia Muzyka* (November 1956): 98–108. Richard Stites discusses this era of jazz in the Soviet Union in *Russian Popular Culture*, 130–135.

42. "Muscovite Ramblers."

43. Maxim Gorky, "The Music of the Gross," trans. Marie Budberg, *Dial* 85 (December 1928): 480–484.

44. Stites, *Russian Popular Culture*, 118–119, 123–135.

45. Dillon, Acting, to Tokyo, DOS Instr. A-449, "CP: President's Program: Soviet Cultural Competition in Japan," April 20, 1959, b 91. See also DOS Instr. A-65, "CP: President's Program: Communist Entertainers in Cambodia," February 6, 1959, b 90, DF 032, 1955–1959.

46. Wallner, Rio, to SOS, DOS Incom. 328, "Chicom Culture in AA," August 29, 1958, b 90; Herter to Lapaz, DOS Out., "Chicom Cultural Efforts," December 19, 1958, b 90; R. N. Phillips, DOS Out. to Santiago and ARA, "Chicom Delegation in Caracas," November 10, 1958, b 90; DOS Out. 129 to All ARA Diplomatic Posts, August 15, 1956, b 87; Alberto M. Vasquez, First Secretary of Embassy, Mexico, to DOS, FSD-312, September 26, 1958, b 90, DF 032, 1955–1959.

47. Phillips, "Chicom Delegation in Caracas."

48. DOS Out. 639 to Taipei, February 8, 1957, b 88, DF 032, 1955–1959.

49. Joseph S. Evans Jr., Counselor of Embassy for Public Affairs, Tokyo, to DOS, FSD-169, "U.S. Is Losing Cultural Cold War in Japan," August 6, 1958, b 89; George M. Hellyer, Counselor of Embassy for Public Affairs, Tokyo, to DOS, FSD-998, "President's Program," March 6, 1959, b 91, DF 032, 1955–1959.

50. Von Eschen, *Race against Empire*, 151.

51. Miles Davis and Quincy Troupe, *Miles: The Autobiography* (New York: Simon and Schuster, 1989), 194.

52. Dudziak, *Cold War Civil Rights*, 113–114.

53. Von Eschen, *Race against Empire*, 155–160.

54. Ibid., 125; Borstelmann, *Cold War and the Color Line*, 5. The West relied on Africa to provide important natural resources and raw materials; these included uranium from South Africa, cobalt and copper from the Belgian Congo, iron ore and coal from Bechuanaland, cocoa from Ghana, rubber from Liberia, and bauxite from Guinea.

55. Borstelmann, *Cold War and the Color Line*, 5.

56. Von Eschen, *Race against Empire*, 169–175.

57. Ibid. For an additional perspective on Bandung, see *FRUS*, Vol. 18, *Africa*, 1955–1957, #128, "Memorandum from the Assistant Secretary of State for Congressional Relations (Hill) to the Vice President," February 18, 1957 (Washington, D.C.: USGPO, 1989), 372.

58. Dudziak, *Cold War Civil Rights*, 49–54; Von Eschen, *Race against Empire*, 169–175.

59. Arnold Manoff to DOS, February 23, 1955, b 81, DF 032, 1955–1959.

60. Richard Straus, Office of German Affairs, Bureau of European Affairs, to Carl Ditton, National Association of Negro Musicians, Inc., March 16, 1955, b 81, DF 032, 1955–1959.

61. Edward A. Symans, Attaché, Warsaw, FSD-198, November 19, 1956, 2, b 87, DF 032, 1955–1959.

Chapter 2. Jazz Diplomacy at Home and Abroad

1. Borstelmann, *Cold War and the Color Line*, 4.

2. W. E. B. DuBois to Sylvia Pankhurst, February 16, 1954, in *The Correspondence of W. E. B. DuBois*, Vol. 3, *1944–1963*, ed. Herbert Aptheker, 356 (Amherst: University of Massachusetts Press, 1978). DuBois also discussed the impending trip of Ethiopian emperor Haile Selassie to the United States.

3. Dudziak, *Cold War Civil Rights*, 54; see also 107–114. For an engrossing discussion of the *Brown* decision, see Kluger, *Simple Justice*.

4. Lisa E. Davenport, "Jazz and the Cold War: Black Culture as an Instrument of American Foreign Policy," in Hine and McLeod, *Crossing Boundaries*, 286.

5. Ibid., 286–287.

6. Minutes of Music Advisory Panel, International Exchange Program of the American National Theater Academy, March 20, 1957, University of Arkansas Libraries, Special Collections Division, Fulbright Papers, MC 468, CU, Group 2: "Cultural Presentations Program," Series 5: "Committees and Panels for the Performing Arts," Box 100: Folder 2, November 1954–December 1956; Folder 3, January 1957–December 1958; Folders 4 and 5, 1959–1960; Folders 6 and 7, 1961–1963 (hereafter cited as CU, Series 5; when all documents are from the same file, the file is listed at the end of the note). The music panel consisted of prestigious individuals from prominent American universities and performing arts centers. It also included leading music critics and eminent American musicians, conductors, and composers.

7. Minutes of Music Advisory Panel Meeting, International Exchange Service of ANTA, April 20, 1960; Minutes of Music Advisory Panel Meeting, International Cultural Exchange Service of ANTA, December 20, 1961, CU, Series 5.

8. For an account of USIS cultural efforts in the Soviet Union in the 1950s, see Hixson, *Parting the Curtain*, 121–150. The USIS was also responsible for ticket sales, sending invitations, and advertising.

9. Operations Coordinating Board, "Terms of Reference for OCB Cultural Presentation Committee," August 16, 1955, CU, Series 1.

10. William Chafe, *The Unfinished Journey: America since World War II* (New York: Oxford University Press, 1995), 136. This occurred at a time when new Cold War alliances, including the North Atlantic Treaty Organization (1949), the South East Asian Treaty Organization (1954), the Warsaw Pact (1955), and the Organization of American States (1948), had been or were being formed.

11. Monson, *Freedom Sounds*.

12. "Takes More'n Tenn. Bomb to Stop Satchmo," *New York Post*, February 20, 1957, f Louis Armstrong, 1955–1958, Rutgers University Institute of Jazz Studies. See also Bergreen, *Louis Armstrong*, 446, 465, 473.

13. Louis Armstrong to Joe Glaser, August 2, 1955, in Thomas Brothers, ed. *Louis Armstrong, In His Own Words: Selected Writings* (New York: Oxford University Press, 1999), 160, 162.

14. Duke Ellington, *Music Is My Mistress* (Garden City, N.Y.: Doubleday, 1973), 235–236. See also Michael Cogswell, *Louis Armstrong: The Offstage Story of Satchmo* (Portland, Ore.: Collectors Press, 2003), 168–174.

15. Duke Ellington, "Ellington: The Race for Space," in *The Duke Ellington Reader*, ed. Mark Tucker (New York: Oxford University Press, 1993), 293; for the entire excerpt, see 293–296.

16. Dizzy Gillespie, *To Be or Not to Bop: Memoirs* (Garden City, N.Y.: Doubleday, 1978), 405–412.

17. Gene Lees, *Oscar Peterson: The Will to Swing* (Rocklin, Calif.: Prima Publishing and Communications, 1990), 123–125.

18. Ellington, *Music Is My Mistress*, 236.

19. Gillespie, *To Be or Not to Bop*, 407.

20. Ibid., 407, 408.

21. George Wein, President, Festival Productions, and Bob Jones, interview by author, January 17, 1999, New York, tape recording, Festival Productions, New York; George Avakian, interview by author, July 3, 1993, Riverdale, N.Y., transcript, 9–10.

22. Louis Armstrong and His All Stars, "King for a Day," from *The Real Ambassador*, Columbia, CL5850 and OL5850, 1961, cassette.

23. Ross Firestone, *Swing, Swing, Swing: The Life and Times of Benny Goodman* (New York: W. W. Norton, 1993), 17. He began playing as a sideman and eventually worked with such celebrated artists as Art Blakey, Leonard Bernstein, and Lionel Hampton.

24. Minutes of Music Advisory Panel, International Exchange Program, May 3, 1955, 4. See also Minutes of Music Advisory Panel, International Exchange Program, December 20, 1955, 3, CU, Series 5. The panel suggested Duke Ellington's racially mixed group for an African tour, but Ellington could not tour because of logistical reasons. It was reported that Ellington refused to fly.

25. R. G. Johnson to Budapest, DOS Instr. A-23, September 23, 1955, b 83, 2, NARA, Records of the Department of State, RG-59, DF 032, 1955–1959. The term "America's classical music" appears in Grover Sales, *Jazz: America's Classical Music* (New York: Da Capo Press, 1992).

26. FSD-41, "Czech Orchestra Plays American Jazz in Hungary," July 23, 1955, 1–2, b 82, DF 032, 1955–1959.

27. Ibid.

28. Ibid., 2.

29. Ibid.

30. N. Spencer Barnes, Chargé d'affaires, ad interim, Budapest, to DOS, FSD-150, October 16, 1956, b 87, DF 032, 1955–1959.

31. "United States Has Secret Sonic Weapon, Jazz," *New York Times*, November 6, 1955.

32. "Jazz Around the World," 52. For a discussion of *Music USA* in the Soviet Union, see Hixson, *Parting the Curtain*, 29–55.

33. Barry Ulanov, *Down Beat*, January 11, 1956, 14.

34. Adam Clayton Powell Jr. to Robinson McIlvaine, January 10, 1956, b 85, DF 032, 1955–1959. For Powell, see also Plummer, *Rising Wind*, 249–253.

35. Department of State, *Sixth Quarterly Report: President's Emergency Fund for Participation in International Affairs, October 1–December 31, 1955*, 18, USIA Historical Collection, USIA Library, Washington, D.C. See also Davenport, "Jazz and the Cold War," 287.

36. John F. Von Gelder, J. D. MacLaury, to DOS, March 1956, attach. to: Senator John F. Kennedy, Massachusetts, to John Leahy, Congressional Liaison Officer, April 15, 1957, b 88, DF 032, 1955–1959.

37. Harwood Keaton to CU, February 11, 1956, b 88, DF 032, 1955–1959.

38. Gillespie, *To Be or Not to Bop*, 413, 414.

39. David B. Bittan, "Gillespie Trumpet Would Blow 'Iron Curtain' Down," *Philadelphia News*, February 10, 1956, f Dizzy Gillespie, 1956–Nov. 24, VII, 161–203, Rutgers University Institute of Jazz Studies.

40. Conflict had ensued in Guatemala in 1954 when the United States helped overthrow its government, which had nationalized the United Fruit Company and other significant U.S. holdings.

41. Murray Robinson, "Culture Rolls On," May 12, 1956, f Dizzy Gillespie, 1956–Nov. 24, VII, 161–203, Rutgers University Institute of Jazz Studies.

42. William L. S. Williams, American Consul General, Dacca, to DOS, FSD-266, "President's Fund: Dizzy Accounting," May 18, 1956. For more on his perspective, see Williams to DOS, FSD–106, "Educational Exchange: President's Fund," November 16, 1956, b 88, f Dizzy Gillespie, DF 032, 1955–1959. The band did not have enough publicity to draw larger audiences. Although audiences in Dacca responded coolly to Stearn's *History of Jazz Program*, they revealed an avid appreciation for Gillespie's music.

43. Williams, "Educational Exchange."

44. Ibid.

45. Ibid.

46. Ibid. See also Marshall Stearns, "Is Jazz Good Propaganda: The Dizzy Gillespie Tour," *Saturday Review*, July 14, 1956, 29, 30. Comments also appear in "Dizzy's Troupe Casts Spell Over Mideast Audiences," *Down Beat*, June 13, 1956, 17.

47. Stearns, "Is Jazz Good Propaganda," 28–31; Williams, "Educational Exchange."

48. Gillespie, *To Be or Not to Bop*, 421.

49. Stearns, "Is Jazz Good Propaganda," 30.

50. "Dizzy's Troupe Casts Spell," 17. After some initial official reservations, Stearns also lectured for the political science faculty at the University of Ankara.

51. C. Edward Wells, Country PAO, Ankara, to DOS, FSD-593, "Visit of Dizzy Gillespie and His Band to Turkey," June 1, 1956, b 88, DF 032, 1955–1959.

52. Wells to DOS, FSD-78, "President's Fund: Visit to Turkey of Dizzy Gillespie Orchestra," August 8, 1956, b 88, DF 032, 1955–1959.

53. Stearns, "Is Jazz Good Propaganda," 30. See also "Gillespie in Ankara: Resounding Applause in Turkey, a Critical Essay," *Metronome*, July 3, 1956, 15–16.

54. Stearns, "Is Jazz Good Propaganda," 30.

55. Robinson, "Culture Rolls On," 161–203.

56. *New York Post*, May 28, 1956, f Dizzy Gillespie, 1956–Nov. 24, VII, 161–203, Rutgers University Institute of Jazz Studies. Women played a significant role in revolutionizing jazz in the Cold War era.

57. Stearns, "Is Jazz Good Propaganda," 31.

58. "Gillespie's Glory in Greece: Athenian Kids Salvo Him with 'Bravo, Deezie' After Scary Start–Trumpeter's Reaction to Frisco Ban," *Variety*, January 30, 1957, 43.

59. Duncan Emrich, Acting PAO, Athens, to DOS, "Dizzy Gillespie," June 4, 1956, b 88, DF 032, 1955–1959.

60. Ibid.

61. Ibid.

62. Stearns, "Is Jazz Good Propaganda," 31.

63. Joseph C. Kolarek, Country PAO, Belgrade, to DOS, FSD-Tousi 12, "Educational Exchange," August 1, 1956, 6–11, b 88, DF 032, 1955–1959.

64. Ibid., 7.

65. Ibid.

66. Ibid., 7, 11.

67. Stearns, "Is Jazz Good Propaganda," 30.

68. Ibid., 31.

69. Dwight D. Eisenhower to Josip Broz Tito, November 12, 1956, in Galambos and Van Ee, *Papers of Dwight David Eisenhower*, 2382, 2384.

70. Walter M. Batson Jr., PAO, Quito, FSD-51, "IES, PF: Dizzy Gillespie Orchestra in Quito," July 26, 1956, attach.: USIS Pamphlet, *What You Should Know about Jazz and Dizzy Gillespie*, b 88; Henry B. Lee, PAO, Quayaquil, FSD-14, "Educational Exchange: Visit of Dizzy Gillespie's Orchestra to Quayaguil, July 26 and 27," August 1, 1956, b 88; and James H. Webb Jr., PAO, Montevideo, "The Performance of the Dizzy Gillespie Orchestra, Sunday August Fifth," August 7, 1956, 1, b 89, DF 032, 1955–1959.

71. *What You Should Know about Jazz and Dizzy Gillespie.*

72. Clary Thompson, PAO, Athens, to DOS, FSD-876, May 20, 1958, "IES: Request for Visit to Greece of Harry Belafonte and/or Outstanding Dance or Jazz Orchestra," b 94, f Harry Belafonte, DF 032, 1955–1959.

73. Mrs. Lawrence C. Fuller, of Ardmore, Pa., to McConnell, n.d., attach. to: McConnell to Dulles, May 9, 1957, b 88, DF 032, 1955–1959.

74. John A. Williamson, Veneers, Foreign and Domestic Woods and Lumber, to John Marshall Butler, DOS, April 12, 1957, b 88, DF 032, 1955–1959.

75. William L. McGlocklin, American United Life Insurance Company, to Christian Herter, Assistant Secretary of Cultural Affairs, May 10, 1957, b 88, DF 032, 1955–1959.

76. Jean Scheinfeld, to Christian A. Herter, Asst. Sec., May 5, 1957, b 88, DF 032, 1955–1959.

77. Maurice S. Rice, Deputy Chief, Public Services Division, to Ray Stringham, Supreme Court Library, Salem, Ore., August 19, 1957; Stringham to Dulles, April 29, 1957, b 88, DF 032, 1955–1959.

78. John P. Meagher, Chief, Public Services Division, to William L. McGlocklin, American United Life Insurance Company, July 19, 1957, b 88, DF 032, 1955–1959.

79. James F. Magdanz, Director, Cultural Presentations Staff, to Terry Love, August 14, 1958, b 88, f Dizzy Gillespie, DF 032, 1955–1959.

80. "Gillespie in Bid to Defend State Dept. Jazz Program Before Senate Critics," *Variety*, May 15, 1957, 59.

81. Stearns, "Is Jazz Good Propaganda," 30, 31.

82. Gillespie, *To Be or Not to Bop*, 427.

83. Ibid., 434.

84. "Armstrong to Lead Way in Musical Cultural Invasion?" *Down Beat*, January 11, 1956, 7; "Near East Click Cues Woo of Dizzy in Latin Lands; Satchmo's O'Seas Coin," *Variety*, May 30, 1956, 43. *Variety* claimed that Armstrong's requested fee of $1,500 per week was too high for the State Department. See also Robert G. Hill, Assistant Secretary, to Senator Frank Carlson, June 10, 1957, b 88, DF 032, 1955–1959.

85. "Near East Click Cues Woo of Dizzy," 43.

86. "Just Very," *Time*, June 4, 1956, 63.

87. Louis Armstrong to Joe Glaser, February 11, 1957, Special Collections, "Louis Armstrong Correspondence," Music Division, Library of Congress, Washington, D.C. Armstrong, however, was not able to attend the independence celebration in 1957.

88. William Glover, "Satch a Real Cool, Warm-Hearted Envoy," *New York Times*, February 10, 1957, f Louis Armstrong, 1955–1958, Rutgers University Institute of Jazz Studies. The second quotation appears in Interview of Louis Armstrong by Edward Morrow, 1956, "Louis Armstrong in Africa," Reel #78, Service #38, cassette, Louis Armstrong Archive, Rosenthal Library, Queens College, Flushing, N.Y.

89. Wilson C. Flake, Ambassador, Ghana, to Robert H. Thayer, August 27, 1959, b 1, f Country Background (cb) Accra, NARA, Lot Files, RG-306, United States Information Agency, Country Project Files, 1951–1964, "Africa" (hereafter cited as USIA/Africa).

90. Davenport, "Jazz and the Cold War," 283. For a viewpoint on the racial divide in

the jazz world, see Charley Gerard, *Jazz in Black and White: Race, Culture, and Identity in the Jazz Community* (Westport, Conn.: Greenwood Press, 1998).

91. Davenport, "Jazz and the Cold War," 283. For a theoretical discussion of cultural containment, see Ninkovich, *Diplomacy of Ideas*, 139–141.

92. Firestone, *Swing, Swing, Swing*, 393–394.

93. "BG Set Crew; Goodwill Swing through Far East," *Variety*, October 31, 1956, 1. See also "BG Band to Take 6-Week Far East State Dept. Tour," *Down Beat*, November 28, 1956, 9.

94. John M. Anspacher, Country, PAO, Cambodia, to DOS, FSD-36, "Goodman, Westminster Choir and Tom Tom-Arrow, to Phnom Penh," January 3, 1957, 1, 2, b 88, DF 032, 1955–1959. He also remarked that when Goodman arrived, he appeared at the same time as the Westminster Singers, resulting in the presentation of "two sharply divergent art forms" (ibid.)

95. Ibid.

96. John P. McKnight, PAO, Seoul, to DOS, USIS, FSD-302, January 1957, 1–3, b 88, DF 032, 1955–1959. Such problems as a lack of publicity, schedule changes, and flight delays hampered the visit. On one occasion, Koreans stood out in the snow for hours for a sold-out concert, but Goodman's flight arrived so late that the concert had to be canceled.

97. "Benny Goodman Sways Thailand," *New York Times*, December 23, 1956.

98. "BG Swing-Ding in Singapore," *Variety*, January 9, 1957, 8.

99. Starr, *Red and Hot*, 271.

100. J. B. Webster and A. A. Boahen, *The Revolutionary Years: West Africa since 1800* (Essex, England: Longman Group, 1980), 282; Von Eschen, *Satchmo Blows Up the World*, 59–71. For more on U.S.-Africa relations, see Joseph Harris, *Perspectives on the Changing Relationship between Afro-Americans and Africans* (Khartoum, Sudan: Institute of African and Asian Studies, University of Khartoum, 1976).

101. Webster and Boahen, *Revolutionary Years*, 296–297, 382–385.

102. Kwame Nkrumah, *Africa Must Unite* (New York: International, 1963). Nkrumah helped organize a series of conferences that helped other nations move toward independence. His book *Africa Must Unite*, although written years later, put forth his philosophy of Pan-Africanism and the African personality. These ideas caused concern among some American officials, but appealed to blacks in the United States and throughout the diaspora.

103. Porter, *What Is This Thing Called Jazz*, 167–169; Saul, *Freedom Is, Freedom Ain't*, 209–210, 213–224.

104. Donald W. Laum, Chargé d'affaires, Accra, to DOS, FSD–249, "Educational Exchange: President's Fund, Wilbur De Paris Jazz Band, 12 Day Tour of Accra and Kumasi," March 14, 1957, 2, b 100, f Wilbur De Paris, DF 032, 1955–1959. See also *Sunday Mirror*,

February 24, 1957, b 100, f Wilbur De Paris, DF 032, 1955–1959; Dulles, J. J. Jova, L. J. LeClair, Algiers, April 25, 1957, USIA/Africa.

105. Dwight Eisenhower, Diary, November 21, 1956, in Galambos and Van Ee, *Papers of Dwight David Eisenhower*, 2404.

106. Lloyd V. Steere, American Consul General, Southern Rhodesia, FSD-276, "President's Fund Tour for Wilbur De Paris," January 18, 1957, b 100, f Wilbur De Paris, DF 032, 1955–1959.

107. Greene, Leopoldville, to SOS, DOS Incom. 95, February 19, 1957. See also DOS Instr. CA-7092, "Educational Exchange: President's Fund: Wilbur De Paris Jazz Band," March 5, 1957; Ruth J. Torrence, American Consul, Leopoldville, to DOS, FSD-230, "Visit of Wilbur De Paris Jazz Orchestra," April 26, 1957; and DOS Incom. 77, January 28, 1957, 2, b 100, f Wilbur De Paris, DF 032, 1955–1959.

108. John Anderson Naunda, Jazz Club's Federation, to American Consul, Dar Es Salaam, April 27, 1957, b 100, f Wilbur De Paris, DF 032, 1955–1959.

109. Cushman C. Reynolds, PAO, Khartoum, to DOS, FSD-288, May 2, 1957, b 100, f Wilbur De Paris, DF 032, 1955–1959.

110. G. Lewis Johns, Ambassador, Tunis, to DOS, FSD-465, "Tunisian Tour of WDP Orchestra," May 9, 1957, 1. See also Kones, Tunis, to SOS, DOS Incom. 615, May 7, 1957, b 100, f Wilbur De Paris, DF 032, 1955–1959.

111. Paul B. Taylor, Chargé d'affaires, Addis Ababa, to DOS, FSD-240, "CP: Wilbur De Paris Visit, April 20–25," May 20, 1957, b 100, f Wilbur De Paris, DF 032, 1955–1959.

112. Davenport, "Jazz and the Cold War," 291.

113. Ibid. Moreover, at the African Stadium, a small crowd attended. The embassy believed that only Armstrong could have drawn the desired audiences.

114. Richard S. Leach, American Consul, Nairobi, to DOS, FSD-19, "Educational Exchange: Report on Visit of Wilbur De Paris Jazz Band to East Africa," July 15, 1957, b 100, f Wilbur De Paris, DF 032, 1955–1959.

115. Ibid. Illuminating comments also appear in Edmund J. Dorsz, American Consul General, Nairobi, "Report on Tanganyika, Nairobi," July 1957, b 100, f Wilbur De Paris, DF 032, 1955–1959. The musicians even impressed an Englishman, who expressed amazement at their "trim business-like appearance" when the band first stepped on stage. To him, they resembled a "board of directors" getting ready for a meeting (ibid.).

116. *FRUS*, Vol. 18, *Africa*, 1955–1957, #7, "Memorandum from the Assistant Secretary of State for Near Eastern, South Asian, and African Affairs, (Allen) to the Secretary of State," August 12, 1955, 20.

117. Edmund J. Dorsz, American Consul General, to DOS, FSD-180, January 28, 1957; Ralph H. Hunt, American Consul General, Lagos, to DOS, FSD-241, "IES, ANTA Project for Nigeria," June 24, 1957, b 88, DF 032, 1955–1959.

118. Saul, *Freedom Is, Freedom Ain't*, 6.

119. Monson, *Freedom Sounds*.

120. Roy E. Larson and Glenn G. Wolfe, "U.S. Cultural Presentations: A World of Promise," in *Cultural Presentations USA*, July 1, 1963–June 30, 1964, 7–8, USIA Historical Collection, Washington, D.C.

121. Robert G. Hill, Assistant Secretary, to Hon. Walt Horan, March 19, 1957, b 100, f Wilbur De Paris, DF 032, 1955–1959.

122. Davis and Troupe, *Miles*, 220.

Chapter 3. Jazz Means Freedom

1. Warsaw, DOS Incom. 1435, April 12, 1957, b 88, DF 032, 1955–1959.

2. Dudziak, *Cold War Civil Rights*, 118–119, 123, 151; Plummer, *Rising Wind*, 278; Plummer, *Window on Freedom*.

3. Thomas C. Holt, "Slavery and Freedom in the Atlantic World: Reflections on the Diasporan Framework," in Hine and McLeod, *Crossing Boundaries*, 37.

4. Dudziak, *Cold War Civil Rights*, 151.

5. Ibid., 147.

6. Cary Fraser, "Crossing the Color Line: The Eisenhower Administration and the Dilemma of Race for United States Foreign Policy," *Diplomatic History* 24 (Spring 2000): 233–234.

7. "Ellington: The Race For Space," in Tucker, *Duke Ellington Reader*, 295.

8. Saul, *Freedom Is, Freedom Ain't*, 2, 182, 201–205.

9. "State Dept. Pipes Up with 'Satchmo, for the Soviets,'" *Variety*, July 31, 1957, 1, 7; "Ike Swipe May Cost Satchmo Edsel Spec; Others 'Penalized,'" *Variety*, September 25, 1957, 1.

10. "Louis Armstrong, Barring Soviet Tour, Denounces Eisenhower and Gov. Faubus," *New York Times*, September 19, 1957, f Louis Armstrong, 1955–1958, Rutgers University Institute of Jazz Studies. See also "Satch Speaks Twice," *Down Beat*, October 31, 1957, 10.

11. *Pittsburgh Courier*, September 28, 1957, in Brothers, *Louis Armstrong*, 193–194.

12. "Satch Speaks Twice."

13. "Louis Armstrong, Barring Soviet Tour."

14. Congressman George Grant, HOR, Committee on Agriculture, to Dulles, September 24, 1957; and Hoghland to Grant, n.d., b 93, f Louis Armstrong, DF 032, 1955–1959.

15. *Gazette and Daily*, September 1957, attach. to: Hoghland, to Lester Hill, Committee on Labor and Public Welfare, U.S. Senate, October 11, 1957, b 93, f Louis Armstrong, DF 032, 1955–1959. See also Gerald Early, *This Is Where I Came In: Black America in the 1960s* (Lincoln: University of Nebraska Press, 2003), 48.

16. Bergreen, *Louis Armstrong*, 437–474.

17. Richard Zieglar to Sirs, September 22, 1957, b 89, DF 032, 1955–1959.

18. Sarah E. Williamson to DOS, November 29, 1957; see also enclosure: poem by Oliver Allstrom, b 89, DF 032, 1955–1959.

19. *Miami Herald*, October 9, 1957, attach. to: John F. Meagher, Chief, Public Services Division, to Zieglar, October 30, 1957, b 89, DF 032, 1955–1959.

20. Williamson to DOS, November 29, 1957.

21. Ralph Gleason, "Perspectives," *Down Beat*, February 6, 1958, 33.

22. "Eisenhower's Action Lauded by Satchmo," *New York Times*, September 26, 1957, f Louis Armstrong, 1955–1958, Rutgers University Institute of Jazz Studies.

23. *Pittsburgh Courier*, September 28, 1957, in Brothers, *Louis Armstrong*, 194.

24. "Ambassador Satch Sounds Off: Jazzman Wants Wider Exchange of Artists to Lessen World Tensions," *Variety*, January 29, 1958, 1.

25. Erling E. Ayars, Penn Mutual Life Insurance Company, to Herman Adams, attach. to: John F. Meagher, Chief, Public Services Division, to Ayers, October 18, 1957, b 89, DF 032, 1955–1959.

26. See, for example, DOS Instr. A-021, "President's Program Musical Group," September 5, 1958, b 90, f Louis Armstrong, DF 032, 1955–1959. For more on Africa, see Webster and Boahen, *Revolutionary Years*, 375–383.

27. Glenn L. Smith, Acting PAO, Ankara, to DOS, June 10, 1957, b 88, DF 032, 1955–1959. Many new and emerging leaders on the African continent leaned toward socialism or declared neutrality in the Cold War. Most significant, Kwame Nkrumah, the most powerful leader on the continent, continually espoused his policy of world peace, Pan-Africanism, and nonalignment.

28. Dan Hendrickson to J. F. Dulles, September 9, 1957, attach.: AP Wirephoto. See also Dulles to Embassy Ceylon, Colombo, DOS Instr. A-56, November 15, 1957, b 89, DF 032, 1955–1959.

29. Richard M. McCarthy, Country PAO, Bangkok, IES, FSD-534, "Evidence of Effectiveness, President's Fund: Marian Anderson," January 20, 1958, b 93, f Marian Anderson, DF 032, 1955–1959.

30. Richard M. McCarthy, Country PAO, Bangkok, to DOS, FSD–385, "President's Fund Program, Visit of Marian Anderson," November 19, 1957, 2, 4, b 93, DF 032, 1955–1959.

31. Jean M. Dery, Attaché of Embassy, Rangoon, to DOS, FSD-941, "Visit of Marian Anderson to Rangoon, 10/21/57," April 30, 1958, b 93, f Marian Anderson, DF 032, 1955–1959. Likewise, Anderson also received praise in Dacca and Bombay, although qualified. See William L. S. Williams, American Consul General, Dacca, to DOS, FSD-125, December 27, 1957; and John V. Lund, PAO, Bombay, to DOS, FSD-469, January 21, 1958, b 93, f Marian Anderson, DF 032, 1955–1959.

32. Thomas D. Bowie, Counselor of Embassy for Political Affairs, Saigon, to DOS,

FSD-14, "Educational Exchange: Marian Anderson Visit," November 18, 1957, 4–5, b 93, DF 032, 1955–1959.

33. Walter LaFeber, *The American Age: U.S. Foreign Policy at Home and Abroad*, Vol. 2, 2nd ed. (New York: W. W. Norton, 1994), 552.

34. Thomas D. Bowie, Counselor of Embassy for Political Affairs, Saigon, to DOS, FSD-14, "Educational Exchange: Marian Anderson Visit," November 18, 1957, 4–5, b 93, DF 032, 1955–1959.

35. Ibid.

36. Ibid.

37. *Hindu*, November 12, 1957, b 93, f Marian Anderson, DF 032, 1955–1959

38. Richard S. Barnsley, Acting Chief PAO, Manila, to DOS, FSD-502, "Educational Exchange: President's Fund: Visit to Manila of Marian Anderson," December 6, 1957, b 93, f Marian Anderson, DF 032, 1955–1959.

39. Quoted in ibid., 2.

40. Ibid., 3.

41. Ibid.

42. Representative Charles O. Porter to Dulles, January 2, 1958; [attach. to:] Andrew H. Berding, Assistant Secretary, to Porter, January 9, 1958, b 93, f Marian Anderson, DF 032, 1955–1959.

43. Robert Lewis Shayon, "The Lady from Philadelphia," *Saturday Review*, January 18, 1958, 57.

44. Stephen W. Baldanza, Country PAO, Addis Ababa, to DOS, FSD-162, "Visit of the Florida A&M Players," December 1, 1958. See also Bliss, Addis Ababa, to SOS, DOS Incom. 274, September 4, 1958, b 102, f Florida A&M University Players, DF 032, 1955–1959.

45. Burt F. McKee Jr., PAO, Cairo, to DOS, FSD-422, "Educational Exchange: Cultural Presentations: Florida A&M Players," December 16, 1958, b 102, f Florida A&M University Players, DF 032, 1955–1959.

46. Ibid.

47. Henry A. Dunlap, PAO, Ghana, to DOS, "CP: PP: Florida A&M Players," December 29, 1958, b 102, f Florida A&M University Players, DF 032, 1955–1959.

48. Wilson C. Flake, Ambassador, Ghana, to DOS, DOS Incom., 1958, b 1, f Country Programs Accra, b 201, NARA, Lot Files, RG-306, USIA/Africa.

49. Cushman C. Reynolds, PAO, Khartoum, to DOS, "Tour of the Florida A&M University Players," April 10, 1958, b 102, f Florida A&M University Players, DF 032, 1955–1959.

50. Ibid.

51. Dudziak, "Josephine Baker"; Dudziak, *Cold War Civil Rights*, 62–63, 67–77.

52. Dulles to Embassy, Paris, DOS Instr. A-201, "Josephine Baker," November 4, 1958, b 94, f Josephine Baker, DF 032, 1955–1959.

53. Borstelmann, *Cold War and the Color Line*, 85; Dudziak, *Cold War Civil Rights*, 62–63.

54. Lewis, *W. E. B. DuBois*, 309–312.

55. W. E. B. DuBois, "The Souls of White Folk," in Lewis, *W. E. B. DuBois: A Reader*, 464.

56. W. E. B. DuBois to the Foreign Editor of the *Literary Gazette*, September 26, 1957, in Aptheker, *Correspondence of W. E. B. DuBois*, 412–414.

57. Lewis, *W. E. B. DuBois*, 309, 310–312. DuBois did not believe that socialism could work in the United States, a capitalist society, and "disdained" the American Communist Party.

58. Fales, Hague, to SOS, DOS Incom. 466, "American Negro, William Edward Burghardt DuBois Delivers Strongly Anti-United States Speech at the Hague–Last Event Before an Estimated Audience of 180," September 12, 1958, b 101, f W. E. B. DuBois, DF 032, 1955–1959.

59. Lewis, *W. E. B. DuBois*, 560. "The DuBoises bore up under one week of bad films, badly dubbed, and badly written literature, better left untranslated, until the Soviet Writers Union flew them out of Central Asia to Moscow" (ibid.).

60. John M. Dennis, American Consul, Prague, to DOS, FSD–158, "W. E. B. DuBois in Prague," October 10, 1958, b 101, f W. E. B. DuBois, DF 032, 1955–1959. The official criticized DuBois when he publicly condemned the racial segregation of 1895–1905–an era of racial violence led by the Ku Klux Klan. See also Lewis, *W. E. B. DuBois*, 309, 310–312.

61. John W. Piercey, Labor Attaché, Oslo, FSD–555, "Ruth Reese, American Negro Singer, Speaks on U.S. Racial Policies," February 10, 1960, 1, b 29, f Samuel Reber, 2-1462, NARA, Records of the Department of State, Record Group-59, Decimal File 032, Foreign Policy File, 1960–1963 (hereafter cited as DF 032, 1960–1963; when all documents are from the same file, the file is listed at the end of the note). Though she praised whites who fought racism and proclaimed that blacks must also fight to achieve their goals, she believed that "prosperous whites disdain[ed] blacks' material success" and that they derided ambitious blacks by using the term "a proud Negro" as "a term of abuse" (ibid.).

62. Duberman, *Paul Robeson*, 381–464. Allison Blakely provides an astute critique of Robeson's activities in the Soviet Union in *Russia and the Negro: Blacks in Russian History and Thought* (Washington, D.C.: Howard University Press, 1986), 147–155.

63. Lightner, Berlin, to DOS, "Robeson for Berlin Cultural Festival," 1960; see also and Dillon, Acting [Assistant Secretary], to Wellington, DOS Out., "Robeson's Statements and Actions Abroad," 1960, 1–2, b 40, f Paul Robeson, 1-2260, DF 032, 1960–1963.

64. Howard Trivers, Chief, Eastern European Affairs, to DOS, FSD-782, June 23, 1960; and James P. Parker, American Consul, Aukland, FSD-11, "Paul Robeson Gives

Three Concerts in Aukland," November 7, 1960, 1–2, b 40, f Paul Robeson, 1-2260, DF 032, 1960–1963.

65. Lightner, "Robeson for Berlin Cultural Festival."

66. Trivers to DOS, FSD-782.

67. Boris H. Klosson, Counselor for Political Affairs, Moscow, FSD-457, February 18, 1960, b 40, f Paul Robeson, 1-2260, DF 032, 1960–1963.

68. [Ambassador] Llewellyn E. Thompson, Moscow, to DOS, DOS Incom. G-825, "Paul Robeson in Moscow," April 28, 1961, 1–2, attach: Translated newspaper articles from *Trud* and the *Literary Gazette.*

69. Ibid.

70. FSD-15, James A. Elliot, PAO, Singapore, to USIA, December 1, 1958, 2, b 90, DF 032, 1955–1959.

71. W. K. Bunce, Counselor for Public Affairs, New Delhi, to DOS, FSD-963, February 28, 1958, b 89, DF 032, 1955–1959.

72. Briggs, Rio, to SOS, DOS Incom. 1187, March 18, 1958; and Johnson, Prague, to SOS, #279, b 89, DF 032, 1955–1959.

73. Warsaw, DOS Incom. 1435, April 12, 1957. See also J. Magdanz and Herter, DOS Out. 778 to Warsaw, April 10, 1957, and March 26, 1957, b 88, DF 032, 1955–1959.

74. See, for example, DOS Instr. A-021, "President's Program Musical Group," September 5, 1958, b 90, f Louis Armstrong, DF 032, 1955–1959.

75. Porter, *What Is This Thing Called Jazz,* 119–124.

76. Frank J. Lewand, Cultural Attaché, Warsaw, to DOS, FSD–355, "Report on Dave Brubeck Jazz Quartet Concerts in Poland," March 24, 1958; and Edward A. Symans, Press Attaché, Warsaw, to DOS, FSD-399, April 17, 1958, b 97, f Dave Brubeck, DF 032, 1955–1959.

77. W. K. Bunce, Consul for Public Affairs, Bombay, New Delhi, FSD-1512, "Combined Report on Brubeck in India," 3, June 6, 1958, 1, b 97, f Dave Brubeck, DF 032, 1955–1959.

78. W. E. B. DuBois, "Criteria of Negro Art," in Lewis, *W. E. B. DuBois,* 514.

79. Lewand, "Report on Dave Brubeck," 1.

80. Ibid., 3.

81. Ibid., 2.

82. Ibid.

83. C. Edward Wells, Country PAO, Ankara, FSD-363, "CP: PP: Dave Brubeck in Turkey, Ankara, Istanbul, Izmar, March '58," December 12, 1958, 3, b 97, f Dave Brubeck, DF 032, 1955–1959.

84. Ibid.

85. W. K. Bunce, Consul for Public Affairs, Bombay, New Delhi, FSD-1512, "Combined Report on Brubeck in India," June 6, 1958, 1, b 97, f Dave Brubeck, DF 032, 1955–1959.

86. Ibid., 2–3.

87. Ibid.

88. Ibid.

89. John T. Reid to DOS, FSD-1451, "CP: President's Program," June 16, 1959, 1; see also John T. Reid, Cultural Attaché, New Delhi, FSD-104, "Cultural Presentations, President's Program: Conditions Affecting CP," July 28, 1959, 1, b 91, DF 032, 1955–1959. In New Delhi, where some audiences sometimes mistook jazz for rock and roll and others even considered the music "vulgar and noisy," Indian audiences–from young rock and rollers to classical devotees–praised his performances and became new fans.

90. Bunce, "Combined Report on Brubeck," 4.

91. "U. of Ga. Nixes Brubeck (Bassist a Negro) but OK at Atlanta Race Spot," *Variety*, March 4, 1959, 49. For more on this story, see "Brubeck's 'No Play Sans Negro Bassist,' Cues Shoutout at Dixie U.; Buck Ram, in U.K. Hits U.S. 'Bigotry,'" *Variety*, January 20, 1960, 63; Ralph Gleason, "An Appeal from Dave Brubeck," *Down Beat*, February 18, 1960, 12–13.

92. "U. of Ga. Nixes Brubeck."

93. Ralph Gleason, "Perspectives," *Down Beat*, March 17, 1960, 43; Norman Granz, "The Brubeck Stand," *Down Beat*, July 14, 1960, 24.

94. "AFM, Agencies Back Granz Plan for Jazzmen's Non-Segregation Clause," *Variety*, November 8, 1961, 55. Granz continued to fight for nonsegregation clauses in musicians' contracts. See "Strong Action against Jim Crow," *Down Beat*, December 7, 1961, 13.

95. Gleason, "Appeal from Dave Brubeck," 12–13.

96. George Hoefer, "The Change in Big T: From Footloose Jazzman to Musical Statesman," *Down Beat*, November 26, 1959, 18–21.

97. Ibid., 18.

98. Ibid., 19. For Phnom Pehn, see Edmund H. Kellogg, Chargé d'affaires, ad interim, Phnom Pehn, to DOS, FSD-367, "Problems of Cultural Presentations in Cambodia," April 6, 1959, 7, b 91, DF 032, 1955–1959. Previously, such American artists as the Westminster Singers and Benny Goodman had performed there with mixed results. Thomas D. Bowie, Saigon Counselor of Embassy for Political Affairs, to DOS, FSD-373, "Proposed Tours of American Folk Singer," April 19, 1958, b 91, DF 032, 1955–1959.

99. Walter M. Oden, Vice Consul, Hue, to DOS, FSD-8, "Conditions Affecting Cultural Presentations," March 16, 1959, b 91, DF 032, 1955–1959.

100. Hoefer, "Change in Big T," 20–21.

101. Ibid., 19.

102. Howard Elting Jr., Counselor of Embassy, Saigon, to DOS, FSD-385, "CP: The Program in Vietnam during the Winter of 1958–1959 and Program Recs.," May 25, 1959, b 91, DF 032, 1955–1959.

103. Cairo, "Cultural Presentations: President's Program: Red Nichols Jazz Band,"

February 19, 1960. See also Leonard R. Greenup, Acting PAO, Athens, "Cultural Presentations: President's Program," March 3, 1960; Calcutta, to New Delhi, "Red Nichols Jazz Band Performs in Calcutta," April 7, 1960, b 36, f Korin Maazal, 6-462, DF 032, 1960–1963.

104. Daniel P. Oleksiew, PAO, Bombay, FSD-560, "Cultural Presentations, President's Program, Red Nichols in Bombay City," April 22, 1960, 1–2, b 36, f Korin Maazal, 6-462, DF 032, 1960–1963.

105. New Delhi, "Cultural Presentations: President's Program: Red Nichols Jazz Band," September 2, 1960, b 36, f Korin Maazal, 6-462, DF 032, 1960–1963.

106. Colombo, FSD-59, "Cultural Presentations: President's Program: Red Nichols Jazz Band," November 12, 1960, b 36, f Korin Maazal, 6-462, DF 032, 1960–1963.

107. Ibid.

108. H. S. Hudson, PAO Khartoum, FSD-310, "President's Fund Programs: Herbie Mann Jazz Group, Holiday on Ice," May 14, 1960, 1–2, b 36, f Korin Maazal, 6-462, DF 032, 1960–1963.

109. Articles are attachments to ibid.

110. Saul, *Freedom Is, Freedom Ain't*, 2–33.

111. NAACP Release, "Jazz Stars," b A40, f "Awards: Spingarn Medal," Papers of the National Association for the Advancement of Colored People (NAACP), Manuscript Division, Library of Congress, Washington, D.C. (hereafter cited as NAACP Papers). See also John Swed, *So What: The Life of Miles Davis* (New York: Simon and Schuster, 2002), 179–182.

112. NAACP Press Release, September 3, 1959, "Goodman to Present Spingarn Medal to Duke Ellington Aboard Steamer," b A40, f "Awards: Spingarn Medal," NAACP Papers.

113. "Draft of Remarks by Benny Goodman in Presentation of Spingarn Medal to Duke Ellington aboard the Liner, S.S. U*nited States*, 10:15 A.M., Friday, Sept. 11, 1959," b A40, f "Awards: Spingarn Medal," NAACP Papers.

114. "Statement of Duke Ellington On Board the S.S. *United States*, On Receiving the Spingarn Award, 1959," b A40, f "Awards: Spingarn Medal," NAACP Papers.

115. Martha Boyles, "Miles Davis and the Double Audience," in Early, *Miles Davis and American Culture*, 158.

116. Saul, *Freedom Is, Freedom Ain't*, 271–273; Boyles, "Miles Davis and the Double Audience," 154–156.

117. Gary Giddins, *Visions of Jazz: The First Century* (New York: Oxford University Press, 1998), 471.

118. Ekkehard Jost, *Free Jazz* (New York: Da Capo Press, 1981), 107, 3; Saul, *Freedom Is, Freedom Ain't*, 7, 222–233. See also John Litweiler, *Ornette Coleman: A Harmolodic Life* (New York: William Morrow, 1992).

119. Lewis Porter, *John Coltrane: His Life and Music* (Ann Arbor: University of Mich-

igan Press, 1998), 133. A significant work on Coltrane is Frank Kofsky, *John Coltrane and the Jazz Revolution of the 1960s*, rev. ed. (New York: Pathfinder, 1998).

120. Porter, *John Coltrane*, 1; Thomas, *Chasin' the Trane*, 224–229.

121. Saul, *Freedom Is, Freedom Ain't*, 3. See also Porter, *John Coltrane*, 202–292; Gioia, *History of Jazz*, 46–48, 307. Coltrane played with Dizzy Gillespie's band in the late 1940s and early 1950s. Such musicians as tenor saxophonist Yusef Latif introduced Coltrane to Eastern philosophy–Coltrane remained an avid reader. Coltrane also met Indian musician Ravi Shankar in the 1960s. It was at time when Coltrane incorporated the music of India, Africa, and Latin America into his music.

122. Gioia, *History of Jazz*, 234, 350, 353, 354–362.

123. Jost, *Free Jazz*, 107. See also Porter, *What Is This Thing Called Jazz*, 191–198, 200–207.

124. James Bakst, *A History of Russian and Soviet Music* (New York: Oxford University Press, 1966), 243–245.

125. Davis and Troupe, *Miles*, 249. See also Waldo E. Martin, "Miles Davis and the 1960s Avant-Garde," in Early, *Miles Davis and America Culture*, 109–111.

126. Gioia, *History of Jazz*, 355.

127. George Fredrickson, "Reform and Revolution in American and South African Freedom Struggles," in Hine and McLeod, *Crossing Boundaries*, 72.

128. Skinner, "Hegemonic Paradigms," 65. See also Lauren, *Power and Prejudice*.

129. Garrow, *Bearing the Cross*, 127–172. See also Dudziak, *Cold War Civil Rights*, 153–154.

130. Dudziak, *Cold War Civil Rights*, 157–161.

131. Ibid.

132. Arnold Rampersad, ed., with assoc. ed. David Roessel, *The Collected Poems of Langston Hughes* (New York: Vintage Books, 1994), 562, 572.

133. The term "jazzocracy" appears in Robert G. O'Meally, ed., *The Jazz Cadence of American Culture* (New York: Columbia University Press, 1998), 117–122.

134. For more on these Cold War developments, see Walter LaFeber, *America, Russia, and the Cold War, 1945–2002* (New York: McGraw Hill, 2003). In the midst of these events, an American conducted the Moscow Symphony in Moscow to promote cultural openness in the Soviet sphere, while Francis W. Bakonyi, an African American singer, performed in Poland. See DOS Instr. 1480, "Soviet Bloc Travel of Mrs. Francis W. Bakonyi, American Negro," August 17, 1961, b 29, f Gladys Badeau, 7-262, DF 032, 1960–1963.

135. Dillon, to AE, NE, and AFE, DOS Instr. CA-1851, "CP, President's Special International Program: Cultural Presentations," August 24, 1960, 1–4, b 24, f 8-160, DF 032, 1960–1963. For African developments, see Webster and Boahen, *Revolutionary Years*, 282. For a discussion of domestic core values in the United States, see Conrad

Arensberg and Arthur Niehoff, *Introducing Social Change: A Manual for Community Development*, 2nd ed. (New York: Aldine Atherton, 1971), 226–231.

136. Joseph Palmer 2nd, American Consul General, Salisbury, FSD-616, "President's Program: Visit of Herbie Mann Jazz Group," April 8, 1960, b 36, f Korin Maazal, 6-462; Dorros, FSD-490; and Palmer, Salisbury, to SOS, August 12, 1960, G-24, f David Apter, 3-1760, DF 032, 1960–1963.

137. For the conservatism of the Eisenhower administration, see, for example, *FRUS*, Vol. 14, *Africa, 1958–1960*, #332, "Memorandum of Conversation," October 27, 1959, 699. For a pivotal perspective on Western views toward culture, see Ruth Benedict, *Patterns of Culture* (Boston: Houghton Mifflin, 1934).

138. Saul, *Freedom Is, Freedom Ain't*, 12, 13, 16–18.

139. Ibid., 20.

140. Porter, *What Is This Thing Called Jazz*, 192. He discusses the American move in this direction.

141. Scott's comments appear in George Hoefer, "Mann in Africa," *Down Beat*, July 7, 1960, 16–17.

142. Ibid. See also Davenport, "Jazz and the Cold War," 282–315.

143. *FRUS*, Vol. 19, *Africa, 1958–1960*, #30, "Report of the Conference of Principal Diplomatic and Consular Officers of North and West Africa, Tangier, May 30–June 2, 1960," 136–141, esp. 140.

144. Reel #126, service #50, cassette, Louis Armstrong Archive, Rosenthal Library, Queens College; Palmer, "President's Program: Visit of Herbie Mann Jazz Group"; Dorros, FSD-490; Palmer, Salisbury, to SOS, August 12, 1960; "Satchmo Is Real Cool About S. Africa Ban," *New York Post*, October 12, 1960, f Louis Armstrong, 1960–1961, Rutgers University Institute of Jazz Studies.

145. "Pepsi Calls Satchmo African Safari Big Booster for Sales," *Advertising Age*, October 31, 1960, f Louis Armstrong, 1960–1961, Rutgers University Institute of Jazz Studies.

146. "Satchmo to Hit Spots in Africa for Pepsi-Cola; State Dept. Rep. in Congo," *Variety*, September 21, 1960, 1. See also Edmund John Collins, "Jazz Feedback to Africa," *American Music*, 5, no. 2 (Summer 1987): 176–193.

147. Richard Berstein, PAO, Accra, to DOS, FSD-263, "Cultural Presentations: Pepsi-Cola Brought US LA," October 19, 1960, b 28, f Louis Armstrong, DF 032, 1960–1963.

148. "Armstrong's Akwaaba in Ghana," *Down Beat*, November 24, 1960, 12, f Louis Armstrong, 1960–1961, Rutgers University Institute of Jazz Studies.

149. *New York Times Magazine*, untitled article, f Louis Armstrong, 1960–1961, Rutgers University Institute of Jazz Studies.

150. Leonard Ingalls, "Armstrong Horn Wins Nairobi, Too," *New York Times*, November 7, 1960, f Louis Armstrong, 1960–1961, Rutgers University Institute of Jazz Studies.

151. "Good-Will Asset," *Journal American*, December 27, 1960, f Louis Armstrong, 1960–1961, Rutgers University Institute of Jazz Studies.

152. ["Report on Cultural Exchange, 1960"], b 1, LS CU.

153. Laurence J. Hall, Country PAO, Rabat, (Casablanca, Marrakech, Rabat, Fes), FSD-465, "Cultural Presentations: President's Program: Herbie Mann Jazz Group," April 20, 1960. Comments also appear in Laurence J. Hall, FSD-3, "Performance of Holiday on Ice in Casablanca," June 22, 1960, b 36, f Korin Maazal, 6-462, DF 032, 1960–1963.

154. Robert C. Schnitzer, quoted in Hoefer, "Change in Big T," 21. It followed that the United States did not send jazz to allied countries in Western Europe, where jazz already had considerable patronage and was well known and where artists could easily travel on their own. For a discussion regarding the resistance of a minority group to a dominant power, see Said, *Culture and Imperialism*.

155. See Henry F. Arnold, Country PAO, Seoul, to DOS, FSD-591, April 15, 1959, b 91; Robert MacClintock, Beirut, to DOS, FSD-605, "CP: PP: Conditions Affecting Cultural Presentations," April 22, 1959, b 91; J. Raymond Ylitalo, American Consul, Cebu, Manila, to DOS, "Conditions Affecting Cultural Presentations in Cebu," March 6, 1959, b 91; and Theodore B. Olson, Counselor of Embassy, Reykjavik, to DOS, FSD-125, b 90, DF 032, 1955–1959.

156. Schnitzer, quoted in Hoefer, "Change in Big T," 21.

157. Stearns, "Is Jazz Good Propaganda," 31.

Chapter 4. The Paradox of Jazz Diplomacy

1. John F. Kennedy declared his support for the arts just weeks after the Cuban missile crisis. See John F. Kennedy, National Cultural Center Dinner, November 29, 1962, in *Let the Word Go Forth: The Speeches, Statements, and Writings of John F. Kennedy*, ed. Theodore Sorensen (New York: Delacorte Press, 1988), 206–207. Porter discuss the paradoxical nature of jazz as a facet of American culture in *What Is This Thing Called Jazz*, 1–53, esp. 2–4, 52–53.

2. Clayborne Carson, *In Struggle: SNCC and the Black Awakening of the 1960s* (Cambridge, Mass.: Harvard University Press, 1994), 1.

3. Goodling to Keifl, August 2, 1961, b 25, f 8-161, DF 032, 1960–1963. For a discussion of diplomacy and cultural values, see Heald and Kaplan, *Culture and Diplomacy*, 1. For cultural affluence, see Burton Peretti, *Jazz in American Culture* (Chicago: Ivan R. Dee, 1997), 109.

4. Louis Armstrong to Leonard Feather, (1961:48), in Brothers, *Louis Armstrong*, 210.

5. Ibid.

6. For more on race and jazz during these years, see Gerard, *Jazz in Black and White*, 1–37, 67; Peretti, *Jazz in American Culture*, 109–154.

7. For a discussion of this theoretical dichotomy, see Herbert J. Ganz, *Popular Culture and High Culture: An Analysis and Evaluation of Taste* (New York: Basic Books, 1975).

8. Early, *Miles Davis and American Culture*, ix, 5.

9. Black music as art is explored in Wilson, "Black Music as an Art Form," 87.

10. FSD-105, "Educational and Cultural Exchange, Kampala, Annual Report for FY 1961," November 3, 1961, b 2, f Kampala, annual report (ar), USIA/Africa.

11. Gordon R. Arneson, Director, Office of Cultural Exchange, "Current Report on Cultural Presentations Program, 11 January 1961," 2–7, CU, Series 1.

12. Robert Beninder, ["Culture and Cold War Diplomacy"], 1963, CU, Series 1.

13. Plummer, *Rising Wind*, 269–270.

14. James Dennis Akumu to President John F. Kennedy, May 1962, CU, Series 1.

15. Borstelmann, *Cold War and the Color Line*, 169.

16. Vladislav Zubok and Constantine Pleshakov discuss the construction of the Berlin Wall in *Inside the Kremlin's Cold War: From Stalin to Khrushchev* (Cambridge, Mass.: Harvard University Press, 1996), 255–258, esp. 256.

17. Plummer, *Rising Wind*, 300–304.

18. *FRUS*, Vol. 21, *Africa*, 1961–1963, #198, "National Intelligence Estimate," August 31, 1961 (Washington, D.C.: USGPO, 1995), 299.

19. Minutes of Music Advisory Panel Meeting, International Cultural Exchange Service of ANTA, May 19, 1961, 1–2, CU, Series 5.

20. Madelaine Kalb, *The Congo Cables: The Cold War in Africa–From Eisenhower to Kennedy* (New York: Macmillan, 1982), 205; Cull, *Cold War and the United States Information Agency*.

21. Harold G. Tufty, PAO, Conakry, Message #4, "USIS Country Plan for Guinea," July 28, 1960, 5, 7, b 2, f cb Conakry USIS/Africa.

22. "U.S. Presence in Guinea," *Wall Street Journal*, 1961, b 2, f cb Conakry USIS/Africa. See also Roger Hilsman to Acting Secretary, DOS Research Memo, REF-56, October 5, 1962, "Where Guinea Stands Today," 1–3, 4, 5, b 2, f cb Conakry, USIA/Africa. Still, Guinea maintained trade relations with Russia, Czechoslovakia, Poland, and France. It also traded iron ore, gold, diamonds, and bauxite with the United States.

23. W. E. Weld Jr., FSD-373, "Stepped Up Communist Cultural Program in Morocco," January 22, 1962, b 2, f cb Rabat, USIA/Africa.

24. Dudziak, *Cold War Civil Rights*, 162–165.

25. Cull, *Cold War and the United States Information Agency*.

26. Davenport, "Jazz and the Cold War," 238, 284–286.

27. James Baldwin, *Nobody Knows My Name* (New York: Dial Press, 1961), 79–81.

28. Davenport, "Jazz and the Cold War," 293.

29. Ibid., 293–294.

30. "Cozy Cole's African Tour Drumming Up 'Top Cultural Diplomacy' for U.S.," *Va-*

riety, November 28, 1962, 2. See also Bangui to SOS, DOS Incom., November 28, 1962; and Melone, Bangui, to SOS, DOS Incom. 75, November 30, 1962, b 27, f 11-162, DF 032, 1960–1963.

31. Davenport, "Jazz and the Cold War," 294.

32. John F. Kennedy, "Special Message to the Congress on Civil Rights, 28 February 1963," in John Hope Franklin and Alfred A. Moss Jr., *From Slavery to Freedom: A History of Afro-Americans*, 7th ed. (New York: McGraw Hill, 1993), 623.

33. Garrow, *Bearing the Cross*, 283, 284; for an account of the events surrounding the march, see 231–286.

34. The Paris group delivered petitions to the international press, to the U.S. embassy in Paris, and to other U.S. embassies in Europe.

35. Maya Angelou, *All God's Children Need Traveling Shoes* (New York: Random House, 1986).

36. John W. L. Russell Jr., PAO, Fort Lamay, Chad, USIS #3, "Evidence of Effectiveness: Special Showing of Film 'Press Conference USA,'" April 16, 1963, b 1, f Freetown ar, USIA/Africa.

37. Ibid.

38. Dudziak, *Cold War Civil Rights*, 165.

39. Lewis, *W. E. B. DuBois*, 570–571.

40. Ibid., 474.

41. Dudziak, *Cold War Civil Rights*, 170–171; Joseph E. Harris, *Africans and Their History*, rev. ed. (New York: Penguin Books, 1987), 171–175, 178, 248–253. In the wake of civil rights events, the Organization of African Unity debated whether it should advocate a complete break in relations with the United States.

42. Mark B. Lewis, PAO, USIS Accra, Message #91, "Birmingham," May 22, 1963, 1, b 1, f cb Accra, USIS/Africa.

43. John F. Kennedy, "Radio and Television Report to the American People on Civil Rights," June 11, 1963, *Public Papers of the Presidents of the United States Containing the Public Messages, Speeches, and Statements of the President: John F. Kennedy*, January 1–November 22, 1963 (Washington, D.C.: USGPO, 1964), 469; for the entire speech, see 468–471. Comments also appear in Dudziak, *Cold War Civil Rights*, 179–180.

44. Dudziak, *Cold War Civil Rights*, 181–182.

45. Dean Rusk, *As I Saw It*, ed. Daniel S. Papp (New York: W. W. Norton, 1990), 587, 588. See also Dudziak, *Cold War Civil Rights*, 186–187.

46. Rusk, *As I Saw It*, 588.

47. Ibid.

48. Dudziak, *Cold War Civil Rights*, 198–199. For Kennedy's response, see John F. Kennedy, "Statement by the President on the Sunday Bombing in Birmingham," September 16, 1963, *Public Papers of the Presidents: Kennedy*, January 1–November 22, 1963, 681.

49. "'Musicians' Musician' to Tour Near East, South Asia," Regional Feature, IPS, Near East Branch, 1–7, USIA Information Agency Library, Washington, D.C. For press comments from the Middle East regarding Ellington's tour, see f Duke Ellington (2), USIA Library.

50. Ellington, *Music Is My Mistress*, 301–303.

51. Jewell Fenzi and Carl L. Nelson, "The Duke in Baghdad," *Foreign Service Journal* (August 1991): 24–26, f Duke Ellington (2), USIA Library.

52. "State Department Alters Program Affecting Jazz," *Down Beat*, February 14, 1963, 15; "Bump ANTA from Overseas Touring; State Dept. Will Have Own Panels," *Variety*, January 2, 1963, 47.

53. Minutes of Music Advisory Panel Meeting, International Cultural Exchange Service of ANTA, May 19, 1961, 1–2; Minutes of Music Advisory Panel Meeting, International Cultural Exchange Service of ANTA, February 15, 1961, 6, CU, Series 5; "Bump ANTA."

54. Embassy Tunis to DOS, Operations Memorandum, "Educational and Cultural Exchange: Special Examination of the Department's Cultural Presentations Program," November 15, 1962, 1–2; Embassy Lagos, to Department of State, Department of State Airgram A-434, "Educational and Cultural Exchange: Special Examination of the Department's Cultural Presentations Program," January 17, 1963, 1, CU, Series 1.

55. Minutes of U.S. Department of State, Bureau of Educational and Cultural Affairs, Office of Cultural Presentations, Music Panel Meeting, April 24, 1963, 2–7, CU, Series 5.

56. Minutes of Music Advisory Panel Meeting, International Cultural Exchange Service of ANTA, March 26, 1963, 4, CU, Series 5.

57. Minutes of U.S. Department of State, Bureau of Educational and Cultural Affairs, Office of Cultural Presentations, Music Panel Meeting, July 24, 1963, 8, CU, Series 5.

58. Harris, *Africans and Their History*, 249.

59. Minutes of U.S. Department of State, Music Panel Meeting, April 24, 1963, 3; Minutes of U.S. Department of State, Music Panel Meeting, July 24, 1963, 7–9, 12–13.

60. Embassy Tunis to DOS, "Educational and Cultural Exchange"; Embassy Lagos to DOS, "Educational and Cultural Exchange."

61. Minutes, September 19, 1962, and October 17, 1962, 6, CU, Series 5.

62. Ibid. For Battle's view, see "Talking Paper for Mr. Battle. . . ," attach. to: Glenn G. Wolfe, Advisory Committee on the Arts, to Mr. [Lucius] Battle, "Talking Paper for Meeting with Panels, January 17," January 14, 1963, 1–9, CU, Series 1.

63. This discussion on Larsen and Wolfe is based on Roy E. Larson and Glenn G. Wolfe, "U.S. Cultural Presentations–A World of Promise," Report of the Subcommittee of the U.S. Advisory Commission on International Educational and Cultural Affairs, Department of State, Bureau of Educational and Cultural Affairs, in *Cultural Presentations USA: Cultural Presentations Program of the U.S. Department of State, July 1,*

1963–June 30, 1964, A Report to the Congress and the Public by the Advisory Committee on the Arts, 77–99, USIA Historical Collection, Washington, D.C.

64. John F. Kennedy, Amherst College, October 26, 1963, in Sorensen, *Let the Word Go Forth,* 209–211.

65. Baldwin, *Nobody Knows My Name,* 116.

66. Nancy Bernkopf Tucker, "Lyndon Johnson: A Final Reckoning," in *Lyndon Johnson Confronts the World: American Foreign Policy, 1963–1968,* ed. Warren I. Cohen and Nancy Bernkopf Tucker (Cambridge: Cambridge University Press, 1994), 311–320. For civil rights and foreign affairs during these years, see also Plummer, *Window on Freedom.*

67. Dudziak, *Cold War Civil Rights,* 204, 207; Michael R. Beschloss, ed. *Taking Charge: The Johnson White House Tapes, 1963–1964* (New York: Simon and Schuster, 1997), 28–30, 446–450.

68. Carson, *In Struggle,* 134–136, 164–165, 208–209, 272. For the links between jazz and black power, see, for example, Porter, *What Is This Thing Called Jazz,* 244–248, 303–305. SNCC had the support of groups abroad in such countries as Cuba, North Vietnam, and the Soviet Union. SNCC members often went abroad to meet with their supporters; their travels included a visit to Africa in 1964 and the Soviet Union in 1966. Saul discusses the links between the riots, jazz, and emerging black power in the 1960s (*Freedom Is, Freedom Ain't,* 302–336).

69. Rusk, *As I Saw It,* 586, 588.

70. Fredrickson, "Reform and Revolution," 80.

71. Blakely, *Russia and the Negro,* 116. See also Dudziak, *Cold War Civil Rights,* 210–211. Some African reactions in 1964 are discussed in *FRUS,* Vol. 24, *Africa, 1964–1968,* #187, "Memorandum from the Director of the United States Information Agency, (Rowan) to President Johnson," July 17, 1964 (Washington, D.C.: USGPO, 1999), 283–284.

72. Lyndon B. Johnson, *The Vantage Point: Perspectives of the Presidency, 1963–1969* (New York: Holt, Rinehart and Winston, 1971), 157, 164, 167.

73. Garrow, *Bearing the Cross,* 242–244, 354–355. Shortly thereafter, King also wrote *Why We Can't Wait* (New York: New American Library, 1964), the work that espoused his philosophy of nonviolence.

74. Claude G. Ross, Bangui, A-176, January 27, 1964, b 2, f cb Bangui, RG 306, 1951–1964, USIA/Africa. For an account of African political affairs during these years, see Harris, *Africans and Their History,* 208–241.

75. Conakry to DOS, A-207, February 24, 1964, b 2, f cb Conakry, USIA/Africa; Arthur A. Bardos, PAO Conakry, to USIA, Message #9, "African-American Exhibit (Negro Centennial Exhibition, Chicago, 1963)," February 24, 1964, b 2, f cb Conakry, USIA/Africa.

76. "USIS Country Plan for Uganda," May 22, 1964, 5, 8, 10, b 2, f Country Plan, Kampala, USIA/Africa; Mark B. Lewis, PAO, Accra, USIS-108, June 17, 1964, b 1, f cb Accra, USIA/Africa.

77. The *Ghanaian Times* article is cited in Lewis, PAO, Accra, USIS-108, June 17, 1964; the *Time* and *Newsweek* articles are also cited in ibid.

78. Dudziak, *Cold War Civil Rights*, 221, 226–227.

79. Brewster H. Morris, Ambassador, Chad, to DOS, "ECE: American Specialist Lecturer, Dr. Raleigh Morgan," July 22, 1964, b 2, f Freetown ar, USIA/Africa.

80. Carl T. Rowan, USIA Memo for Hon. George Ball, Under Secretary of State, "Attitudes of North African Students in France: A Preliminary Report," USIS Research and Reference Service, December 10, 1964, Africa-A, NARA, Records of the Department of State, Record Group-59, Central Files 1964–1966, Culture and Information, Educational and Cultural Exchange, b 387, f EDX 32 CPP, 1164 (hereafter cited as CF-EDX, 1964–1966; when all documents are from the same file, the file is listed at the end of the note). The report measured opinions according to the "length of residence in France."

81. Josiah W. Bennett, Acting Deputy Chief of Mission, Lagos, to DOS, DOS A-162, "Article Refuting 'Look' Magazine Story Appeared in Lagos Newspaper," August 26, 1964, b 387 f EDX, Educational and Cultural Exchange (ECE), Africa-A, 1164, CF-EDX, 1964–1966.

82. Moscow to DOS, A-192, "Izvestia, 8/7 Article by Joseph A. Fondem, Cameroonian at Lumumba," August 14, 1964, b 387, f EDX, ECE, Afr.-USSR, 1164, CF-EDX, 1964–1966.

83. USIA Research and Reference Service, "East African University Student Views on International and Continental Issues, April 1965," 5, 8–9, b 1, f Area Background (ab) Africa, 1963, USIA/Africa.

84. Robert H. McBride, Minister Attaché, Paris, DOS A-1733, "Embassy Youth Program," February 4, 1965. Other activities are outlined in McBride, Coordinator Youth Program, to Members of Embassy Youth Committee, "Embassy Youth Committee," February 3, 1965, b 395, f ECE, France, 1164, CF-EDX, 1964–1966.

85. Garrow, *Bearing the Cross*, 399.

86. Johnson, *Vantage Point*, 164.

87. Lyndon B. Johnson, "Remarks of the President to a Joint Session of Congress: The American Promise" (Special Message to the Congress), March 15, 1965, in *Lyndon B. Johnson, Public Papers of the President, 1965*, Vol. 1, January 1, 1965, to May 31, 1965 (Washington, D.C.: USGPO, 1966), 281–282, 284. For the text of the entire speech, see 281–287.

88. Dudziak, *Cold War Civil Rights*, 227.

89. "Armstrong Speaks Out On Racial Injustice," *Down Beat*, April 22, 1965, 14, 15. Armstrong was on a private trip to Europe.

90. Archie Schepp, "An Artist Speaks Bluntly," *Down Beat*, December 16, 1965, 11.

91. Carson, *In Struggle*, 273; Porter, *What Is This Thing Called Jazz*, 305, 318. See also Gioia, *History of Jazz*, 354.

92. LaFeber, *American Age*, 619.

93. Plummer, *Rising Wind*, 231.

94. Thomas Noer, *The Cold War and Black Liberation: The United States and White Rule in Africa, 1948–1968* (Columbia: University of Missouri Press, 1985), 155–184; Fredrickson, "Reform and Revolution," 80–81. The United States maintained trade in South African diamonds and uranium, a prime commodity used in building the atomic bomb. Though such groups as CORE and SNCC vehemently objected to American business dealings with South Africa, many American business leaders remained actively engaged in the South African economy and pressured Johnson to reject employing economic sanctions. Strategic and economic interests frequently prevailed over securing human rights in the region.

95. Plummer, *Rising Wind*, 232.

96. Davis and Troupe, *Miles*, 405.

97. G. Edward Clark, Counselor of Embassy, Capetown, to DOS, DOS A-114, "Joint State-USIA Report: Embassy Youth Activities in South Africa," June 8, 1964, f Educational Exchange (EE), South Africa, 1164, b 400, CF–EDX, 1964–1966.

98. American Consul General, Salisbury, A-636, "Warning Letter Addressed to Nat 'King' Cole and Chubby Checker," January 7, 1964, b 401, f EE, Rhod.-S 1164, CF-EDX, 1964–1966. For a fascinating portrait of jazz in South Africa, see David Coplan, *In Township Tonight! South Africa's Black City Music and Theatre* (London: Longman, 1985).

99. Salisbury, A-636, "Warning Letter," 2. They also referred to the musicians as "enemies of this struggle for human dignity" who might fall to the "venomous wrath of all the black people in the country" (ibid.).

100. Livingston D. Watrous, American Consul General, Capetown, to DOS, DOS A-170, "Segregated Audience: Minister's Political Statement Results in All-White Theater in Coloured Area," February 9, 1965, b 402, f ECE, S-Afr., 1-364, CF–EDX, 1964–1966.

101. Thomas L. Hughes, DOS, to the Secretary of State, "Problems and Prospects for Africa," March 23, 1965, 2–8, 18–19, 22–23, 35–36; Bureau of Educational and Cultural Affairs, "Summary of African Program FY 1965, Kenya," b 1, f Africa, ab-1963, USIA/Africa; and Thomas H. Walsh, Second Secretary of Embassy, Accra, DOS A-29, "Emphasis on Youth," July 22, 1965, 1–3, b 386, f EDX 12 Youth Programs, 1165, CF-EDX, 1964–1966.

102. William H. Harben, Chargé d'affaires ad interim, Kigali, to DOS, A-31, "Emphasis on Youth, Report on Mission's Youth Program," August 26, 1965, esp. 7, 11, 12, b 400, f EE, Rwanda 1164, CF-EDX, 1964–1966; and L. Rood, Chargé d'affaires ad interim, A-40, June 26, 1965, encl. 1, b 393, f The Congo, 1164, CF-EDX, 1964–1968. See also Borstelmann, *Cold War and the Color Line*, 182.

103. Cotonou, "Emphasis on Youth," July 9, 1965, 4, 7, b 394, f EDX, ECE, Dahomey, CF-EDX, 1964–1966.

104. Nat Hentoff, "This Cat Needs No Pulitzer Prize, (1965)," in Tucker, *Duke Ellington Reader*, 366–367.

NOTES **185**

105. Gene Lees, *Cats of Any Color: Jazz, Black and White* (New York: Oxford University Press, 1995), 242.

106. Ralph Ellison, "Homage to Duke Ellington on His Birthday (1969)," in Lees, *Cats of Any Color*, 395.

107. "Duke and the Pulitzer," *Down Beat*, June 17, 1965, 12; Nicholson, *Reminiscing in Tempo*, 362. Ellington worded this sentiment in different ways.

108. George Herring, *America's Longest War: The United States and Vietnam, 1950–1975*, 3rd ed. (New York: McGraw Hill, 1996), 133–137.

109. Johnson, *Vantage Point*, 95.

110. Dudziak, *Cold War Civil Rights*, 208.

111. Herring, *America's Longest War*, 120–201.

112. #208, "Memorandum from President's Deputy Special Assistant for National Security Affairs (Komer) to President Johnson," March 10, 1966, *FRUS, Africa, 1964–1968*, 322–323. See also Dudziak, *Cold War Civil Rights*, 223.

113. Porter, *What Is This Thing Called Jazz*, 201–207. See also Saul, *Freedom Is, Freedom Ain't*, 271–336.

114. Porter, *What Is This Thing Called Jazz*, 203–207. See also Davis and Troupe, *Miles*, 271.

115. Nicholson, *Reminiscing in Tempo*, 249, 375; Ellington even had "grandma groupies" (ibid., 366).

116. Porter, *John Coltrane*, 231–249, 260–261. For more on the links between music and protest, see Margaret Reid, *Black Protest Poetry: Polemics from the Harlem Renaissance and the Sixties* (New York: P. Lang, 2001); Suzanne Smith, *Dancing in the Streets: Motown and the Cultural Politics of Detroit* (Cambridge, Mass.: Harvard University Press, 1999). For a discussion of these disaporic links, see Monson, *Freedom Sounds*, 264–265.

117. Foley to DOS, DOS A-77, August 25, 1966, b 396, f ECE Ghana, 1164, CF-EDX, 1964–1966.

118. DOS, A-140, October 30, 1966, b 396, f ECE Ghana, 1164, CF-EDX, 1964–1966.

119. William B. King, Counselor for Political Affairs, London, to DOS, A-2369, April 1, 1966, 1, encl. 1, b 404, f EDX, ECE UK 1164, CF-EDX, 1964–1966.

120. Harror, Lumbumbashi, to DOS, DOS A-45, "Youth Activities," November 7, 1966, b 403, f EDX, ECE The Congo, CF-EDX, 1964–1966.

121. Davis and Troupe, *Miles*, 272. Jazz's decline in the mid and late 1960s is discussed in several important studies, including Saul, *Freedom Is, Freedom Ain't*, 272–301; Waldo E. Martin, "Miles Davis and the 1960s Avant-Garde," in Early, *Miles Davis and American Culture*, 110. David Margolick recounts the allure of 1950s jazz in *Strange Fruit: Billie Holiday, Café Society, and an Early Cry for Civil Rights* (London: Running Press, 2000).

122. Nicholson, *Reminiscing in Tempo*, 359, 374; Porter, *What Is This Thing Called Jazz*, 303.

123. Paris to DOS, A-1913, "Emphasis on Youth, Third Country Students," March 31, 1966, b 395, f (ECE) France, 1164, CF-EDX, 1964–1966.

124. "Speech Made by Josephine Baker in Paris on the Evening of 30 October 1964 at Rally Given at Eiffel Tower Restaurant at 8 p.m. by a Committee Called 'Americans Abroad for Johnson,' 16 Place Vendome, Paris, Under the Chairmanship of Alfred E. Davidson," b A43, f Josephine Baker, 1963–1964, NAACP Papers.

125. Tyler Stovall, *Paris Noir: African-Americans in the City of Light* (Boston: Houghton Mifflin, 1996), xiv–xvi.

126. Department of State, Bureau of Educational and Cultural Affairs, "Paper for the Advisory Committee on the Arts on the Fiscal Year 1964, Cultural Presentations Program Planning for Africa," n.d., 1–2, CU, Series 1.

127. Department of State, Bureau of Educational and Cultural Affairs, "Jazz in the Cultural Presentations Program," n.d., 1–2, CU, Series 1; Davenport, "Jazz and the Cold War," 290.

128. Department of State, Bureau of Educational and Cultural Affairs, "Jazz in the Cultural Presentations Program," 1–2.

129. Godley, Kinshasha, to DOS, DOS A-136, September 15, 1966, b 403, f EE 1164, The Congo, CF-EDX, 1964–1968.

130. Johnson, *Vantage Point*, 467; see also 352.

131. Charles Ellison, Director, Office of Cultural Presentations, "Remarks by Charles Ellison, Director, Office of Cultural Presentations, Before 1965 Interim Meeting of Stated Presidents and Members of the Board of Directors of the Musical Educators National Conference, NEA Center, Tuesday, August 24, 1965, 'The Performing Arts and Our Foreign Relations,'" 1–12, CU, Series 1.

132. Charles Frankel, Assistant Secretary of Educational and Cultural Affairs, "The Era of Educational and Cultural Relations," reprint from the *Department of State Bulletin*, June 5, 1966, USIA Library.

133. Ibid.

134. Ellington, *Music Is My Mistress*, 337.

135. Leopold Sedar Senghor, "Blues," in *The Jazz Poetry Anthology*, ed. Sascha Feinstein and Yusef Komunyakaa (Bloomington: Indiana University Press, 1991), 192, 337–338.

136. Parsons, Stockholm, to DOS, DOS Incom., "Last Night Heard Oscar Brown, Jr. at Biggest Stockholm Night Club," May 2, 1964, b 402, f EDX, ECE Swe. 1164, CF-EDX, 1964–1966. An American official observed that his songs contained no anti-U.S. sentiments.

137. Nicholson, *Reminiscing in Tempo*, 359, 374.

138. *Variety*, February 26, 1964, 1.

139. Philip Jack, *Coda: Canada's Jazz Magazine* 7, no. 10 (November 1966), 1.

140. Stephen A. Dobrenchuk, American Consul, Chiengmai, to DOS, DOS A-16, "Student Disorder in Chiengmai," December 5, 1964. See also James M. Wilson Jr. Chargé d'affaires, Bangkok, to DOS, DOS A-687, "Mission Youth Activity Status Report," March 15, 1965, b 403, f EDX, ECE Thai. 1164, CF-EDX, 1964–1966.

141. John M. Dennis, American Consul, Poznan, to DOS, DOS A–96, "The Riotous Influence of the West," February 18, 1966. See also "Gazeta Poznanskaia, 'Three Times America,'" January 21, 1966, b 401, f EE Pol. 1164, CF-EDX, 1964–1966.

142. Martha Boyles, "Miles Davis and the Double Audience," in Early, *Miles Davis*, 149–171. See also Gerard, *Jazz in Black And White*, 1–37; Lees, *Cats of Any Color*, 3–18, 187–246.

Chapter 5. Jazz Behind the Iron Curtain

1. Walter R. Roberts, PAO, "USIS Country Plan for Yugoslavia," RG-59, Class 5, b 7, f Bucharest, Records Relating to the Evaluation of Cultural Programs and to Staff Visits Overseas, Europe, 1952–1960, NARA. (Although dated in 1962, the documents on these exchanges were found in the file dated 1952–1960.)

2. For Soviet political ideas, see Zubok and Pleshakov, *Inside the Kremlin's Cold War*, 270.

3. DOS Instr. 1480, "Soviet Bloc Travel of Mrs. Francis W. Bakonyi, American Negro," August 17, 1961, b 29, f Gladys Badeau, 7-262. The CU also proposed a tour for a black pianist, in DOS Instr. 446, CA-4168, "East West Exchanges, Proposed Czech Concert Tour for William Grant Nabors, American Negro Pianist," November 4, 1960, b 38, f William Grant Nabors, 11–460, b 38, DF 032, 1960–1963.

4. Carl R. Sharek, Second Secretary of Legation, Budapest, FSD-543, "Repeat Visit of American Negro Singer Scheduled," February 1962, b 42, f Harry Torczher, 2-662, DF 032, 1960–1963. A caveat arose, however, because it seemed that "Tynes was being groomed for a role similar to that now played by Paul Robeson. . . . She may perhaps be overdramatizing the efforts of the Hungarian propagandist and selling [her] loyalty short. She feels more at home in Europe than in the states" (ibid.). The official expressed this view because he observed her efforts to distinguish herself as Italian or Spanish, not as African American. He recommended that she be made aware of the fact that she might be helping Communist efforts.

5. Stanley B. Alpern, Press Attaché, A-305, "U.S. Opera Singer Tours Poland, Warsaw, Europe," October 18, 1962, b 7, f Warsaw, Records Relating to the Evaluation of Cultural Programs and to Staff Visits Overseas.

6. Stanley B. Alpern, Press Attaché, Warsaw, to DOS, DOS A–83, "Poles Acclaim the Platters," July 27, 1962, b 27, f 7-162; and Wallace W. Littell, First Secretary for Press and Culture, Moscow, to DOS, "Performing Arts Groups in Poland," July 5, 1962, f 2-162, b 26, DF 032, 1960–1963.

7. Earl Kennedy, Kennedy Travel Agency, to Patrick V. McNamara, December 28, 1962, b 28, f 1-362, DF 032, 1960–1963.

8. Dutton to McNamara, U.S. Senate, January 15, 1963, b 28, f 1-362, DF 032, 1960–1963.

9. DOS A-469, "Educational and Cultural Exchange, Follow-Up on Foreign Leader Grantee Emil Herbst," December 14, 1962, b 7, f Warsaw, Records Relating to the Evaluation of Cultural Programs and to Staff Visits Overseas. An official characterized him as an "old style Jewish humorist–in fact he looks like Harpo Marx without the curls." Despite the crisis, he believed in "Americans' . . . sincere desire for peace and fear of war" (b 7, f Warsaw, Records Relating to the Evaluation of Cultural Programs and to Staff Visits Overseas).

10. "Big Business Is Not against Integration," *Wall Street Journal*, [1962], b 7, f Warsaw, Records Relating to the Evaluation of Cultural Programs and to Staff Visits Overseas.

11. Starr, *Red and Hot*, 231, 232, 270; Stites, *Russian Popular Culture*, 118–119, 124–129, 130–135.

12. *FRUS*, Vol. 10, Part 2, 1958–1960, *Eastern Europe Region; Soviet Union, Cyprus*, #29, "Despatch from the Embassy in the Soviet Union to the Department of State, 18 July 1960" (Washington, D.C.: USGPO, 1993), 67–70. Freers also discussed the performances of Isaac Stern, Roberta Peters, and, most notably, Van Cliburn, who caused "riots" just like American pop singers in the United States.

13. Richard E. Johnson, Chargé de affairs, ad interim, A-248, "Betty Allen Enthusiastically Received in Bulgaria," January 4, 1964, b 390, f EDX-ECE, Bulgaria, 1164, CF-EDX, 1964–1966. For a forward-looking account of Soviet–Eastern European relations during this period, see Charles Gati, *The Bloc That Failed: Soviet-Eastern European Relations in Transition* (Bloomington: Indiana University Press, 1990), 29–64.

14. Charles G. Stephen, Chargé d'affairs, ad interim, to DOS, DOS A-27, "Cabaret Artist in Bulgaria," 1964, Records of the Department of State, RG 59, b 7, f Sofia, Records Relating to the Evaluation of Cultural Programs and to Staff Visits Overseas, 1952–1960. (Although dated in 1964, the documents were contained in this file.)

15. Wallace W. Littell, First Secretary for Press and Culture, Moscow, to DOS, "Performing Arts Groups in Poland," July 5, 1962, f 2-162, b 26, DF 032, 1960–1963.

16. Sztandar Mlodych, "Roman Waschko Writes from the USA: Why Our Boys Aren't Playing in Las Vegas," *Metronome*, August 1962, b 7, f Warsaw, Records Relating to the Evaluation of Cultural Programs and to Staff Visits Overseas. Saul discusses the festival in *Freedom Is, Freedom Ain't*, 275–276.

17. Mlodych, "Roman Waschko." See also John D. Scanlan to SOS, A-133, August 16, 1962, b 7, f Warsaw, Records Relating to the Evaluation of Cultural Programs and to Staff Visits Overseas.

18. DOS Incom. A-375, Warsaw, "ECE Follow Up Reporting: Foreign Specialists: Pol-

ish Jazz Combo," November 8, 1962, b 7, f Warsaw, Records Relating to the Evaluation of Cultural Programs and to Staff Visits Overseas.

19. Mlodych, "Roman Waschko." He also published an interview with Russian composer Aram Khachaturian, who enthusiastically voiced his intention to "write a number for Benny Goodman." Khachaturian's penchant for jazz was "reflected in [the rhythms] of his 'Sabre Dance'" (ibid.).

20. Roman Waschko to Jerome F. Margolius, Assistant Director, Committee on Leaders and Specialists, July 24, 1962, b 7, f Warsaw, Records Relating to the Evaluation of Cultural Programs and to Staff Visits Overseas. Lucjan Kydrynski also comments on the group in "Newport Jazz," *JAZZ* 1962, attach. to: Scanlan, A-133., b 7, f Warsaw, Records Relating to the Evaluation of Cultural Programs and to Staff Visits Overseas.

21. *FRUS*, Vol. 5, *Soviet Union*, 1961–1963, "Memorandum of Conversation," October 13, 1961, 304–305. A similar view regarding exchange negotiations appears in #168, "Editorial Note," 390. US.-USSR exchanges were "carried out under the provisions of the National Security Council"; see #145, "Letter from the Assistant Secretary of State for Congressional Relations (Dutton) to Senator Kenneth B. Keating," January, 24, 1962, 351, *FRUS*, Vol. 5, *Soviet Union*, 1961–1963.

22. For a brief view of Baltic culture, see Stites, *Russian Popular Culture*, 123, 130–135.

23. [Llewellyn E.] Thompson, Moscow, to SOS, DOS Incom. 1561, January 6, 1961; DOS Incom. 1597, January 10, 1961. See also DOS Incom., January 26, 1961; and DOS Incom. 1789, January 30, 1961, b 42, f Iris Ubal 6-260, DF 032, 1960–1963. Soviet audiences enjoyed the jazz selections that the band performed, and the musicians also played in informal jam sessions.

24. Monson, *Freedom Sounds*.

25. Avakian, interview, transcript, 14–15. See also Davenport, "Jazz and the Cold War," 297.

26. "Rhapsody in Russia," *Time*, June 29, 1962.

27. McSweeney, Moscow, to SOS, DOS Incom., July 6, 1962, Records Relations to the Evaluation of Cultural Programs and Staff Visits Overseas, b 7, f Moscow Pending.

28. "Benny Goodman's Concert Pleases but Puzzles Khrushchev," *New York Times*, May 31, 1962, MS 53, Benny Goodman Papers, b 155, f 42, Yale University Music Library, New Haven, Conn.

29. Vladimir Feuertag, interview by author in Russian, July 27, 1994, St. Petersburg, tape recording, Feuertag residence. See also, Davenport, "Jazz and the Cold War," 299.

30. Leonard Feather, "Moscow Diary," *Down Beat*, July 19, 1962, 17.

31. "Inside Soviet Jazz," *Down Beat*, August 16, 1962, 12–15, 37; "BG's Pioneer Jazz Junket Pierces Iron Curtain to Score Cultural Coup," *Variety*, June 27, 1962, 43.

32. Yuri Vikharieff, "Waitin' for Benny: A Report from Russia," *Down Beat*, July 5, 1962, 14.

33. Bill Coss, "Benny Goodman: On the First Steppe," *Down Beat*, May 24, 1962, 16–17. For aesthetic activism, see Porter, *What Is This Thing Called Jazz*, 173, 177–178, 207; Saul, *Freedom Is, Freedom Ain't*, 225.

34. "Goodman Russian Tour Stirs Mild Dissent," *Down Beat*, April 26, 1962, 13.

35. John S. Wilson, "Rectifying the Rumor Mills," *New York Times*, October 28, 1962.

36. "BG Band Miffed on Moscow Mission," *Variety*, July 11, 1962, 65.

37. "Goodman Men Sound Off About Soviet Tour," *Down Beat*, August 30, 1962, 13.

38. "BG Band Miffed."

39. Feuertag, interview. See also Davenport, "Jazz and the Cold War," 299.

40. "Goodman Men Sound Off," 36.

41. "BG Band Miffed," 65.

42. "Izvestia Sees Cloak and Dagger in Goodman's Band's Horn Cases," *New York Times*, August 7, 1962, CU, Series 1.

43. *FRUS, Kennedy-Khrushchev Exchanges*, 1961–1963, Vol. 6, "Letter from President Kennedy to Chairman Khrushchev," June 5, 1962.

44. [Terrence] Catherman, Moscow, DOS A-218, "Beyond the Footlights America, a Film Reflection of the Moiseyev Dancers in the U.S.," August 10, 1962, 1, b 43, f Frary Von Blumberg, DF 032, 1960–1963.

45. Talbott, *Khrushchev Remembers*, 493, 496.

46. Zubok and Pleshakov, *Inside the Kremlin's Cold War*, 258–271, 374.

47. Ibid., 252; for an overview of the Cuban missile crisis, see 258–271.

48. DOS, "Notes on Interagency Meeting on Soviet and Eastern European Exchanges," October 24, 1962, 1, b 7, f Moscow Pending, Records Relating to the Evaluation of Cultural Programs and Staff Visits Overseas.

49. Ibid., 1, 497.

50. John F. Kennedy, "National Cultural Center Dinner," in Sorensen, *Let the Word Go Forth*, 206; Rusk, *As I Saw It*, 363–364.

51. Talbott, *Khrushchev Remembers*, 497.

52. John F. Kennedy to Dean Rusk, November 20, 1963, b 2, f cb Freetown, USIA/Africa.

53. Rusk to African Posts, 1963, b 386, f ECE-EDX 12-Youth Programs, 11–65, NARA, Records of the Department of States, RG-59, Foreign Policy Files, 1964–1966, DF 032.

54. "Reds Using Jazz to Strengthen Free World Ties: Elmer Bernstein," *Variety*, August 14, 1963, 53.

55. Cull, *Cold War and the United States Information Agency*.

56. For Soviet views on African American art, see Blakely, *Russia and the Negro*, 105.

57. Talbott, *Khrushchev Remembers*, 521. For a pivotal view of jazz in Russia, see May, "Swingin' Under Stalin," 179–191.

58. Weiner, "Jazz Night at the Blue Bird Youth Café," 2.

59. Stites, *Russian Popular Culture*, 132–134.

60. Weiner, "Jazz Night at the Blue Bird Youth Café"; D[avid] E. Boster, Counselor for Political Affairs, Moscow, to DOS, DOS Airgram, #A-1524, "Jazz Night in Pyatig-orsk," March 22, 1966, 1; and Foy D. Kohler, Ambassador, Embassy, Moscow, to DOS, DOS Airgram #A-363, "Importation of Western Jazz via Eastern Europe," August 30, 1966, CU, Series 1.

61. Warsaw to DOS, A-1025, "Policy Questions in the Face of Gomulka's Recent Speeches: Increased Anti-American Propaganda and Particularly Moves to Cut Back Our Cultural Program in Poland," May 13, 1965, b 401, f EDX-ECE, Pol. 1164.

62. Rumanians discussed Vietnam and the cancellation of the tour in Davis, Bucharest, to SOS, "Rumanian Folk Tour," July 21, 1966, b 401, f EE Rom., 1164.

63. DOS MOC, "1966 U.S. Rumanian Exchange Talks," April 13, 1966, b 401, f EDX Rom., 1164.

64. John P. Shaw, Counselor of Embassy, Bucharest, to DOS, A-104, September 17, 196[6], b 401, f EE Rom., 1164. Another opposing viewpoint appears in Bucharest to SOS, September 23, 1964, CF-EDX, 1964–1966. Cultural tensions frequently arose in negotiations, as in DOS MOC, "Opening Session of 1966 United States–Rumanian Exchange Talks," April 5, 1966, b 401, f EDX Rom., 1164; and DOS MOC, "U.S.-Rumanian Exchange Talks," April 7, 1966, b 401, f EE Rom.-US, 1164, CF-EDX, 1964–1966.

65. Boris H. Klosson, London, to DOS, DOS A-739, "Seventh Meeting of the Working Group on East-West Cultural Contacts, June 28–29, 1966," September 27, 1966, 1, 13, 19, b 404, f EDX-ECE, UK, 1164. Zhukov's view also appears in Sofia-489, DOS Incom., November 1966, "Talk with Zhukov on Trade and Cultural Relations," b 390, f EDX-ECE Bulgaria, 1164, CF-EDX, 1964–1966.

66. Puterbridge Horsey, Prague, to DOS, "Emphasis on Youth," July 17, 1964, b 394, f ECE Czech, 1164. Czechoslovakia reportedly voiced further concern in Jay K. Hoffman and Yale Richmond, "Czech Performing Arts Groups Coming to U.S.," January 22, 1964, b 394, f ECE Czech, 1164, CF-EDX, 1964–1966.

67. DOS MOC, "Czechoslovak-U.S. Educational and Cultural Exchanges," December 1, 1965, b 394, f ECE, Czech-A 1164; and Prague, to DOS, DOS Out. A-417, "Czech-U.S. Cultural and Information Exchanges," February 28, 1964, b 394, f ECE Czech-A, 1164, CF-EDX, 1964–1966.

68. DOS MOC, "Czechoslovak-U.S. Educational and Cultural Exchanges."

69. Horsey, Prague, to SOS, "World Folk Council Negotiates First Club," June 19, 1965, b 394, f ECE Czech, 1164; and Ball to DOS, November 24, 1965, b 394, f Czech-A, 1164, CF-EDX, 1964–1966.

70. DOS MOC, "Czechoslovak-U.S. Exchanges, with Karel Duda of Czechoslova-kia," January 17, 1966, b 394, f ECE, Czech-A, 1164, CF-EDX, 1964–1966.

71. *FRUS*, Vol. 14, *The Soviet Union*, 1964–1968, #169, "Special National Intelligence Estimate," July 28, 1966, 408–410.

72. #153, "Memorandum from Secretary of State Rusk to President Johnson," March

3, 1966, in ibid., 378. See also #154, "Memorandum from Secretary of State Rusk to President Johnson," March 14, 1966, in ibid., 380–381; #151, "Memorandum from Secretary of State Rusk to President Johnson," February 13, 1966, in ibid., 374–375.

73. #153, "Memorandum"; #155, "Memorandum of Conversation," March 18, 1966, in ibid., 381; #157, "Paper Prepared in the Policy Planning Council," March 23, 1966, in ibid., 384–387.

74. Gene Lees, "Afterthoughts," *Down Beat*, April 13, 1961, 50; Gilbert Millstein, "The Sax Comes Up the Moskva River," *New York Times Magazine*, April 23, 1961, 47–48; Whitey Mitchell, "The Saga of Jelly Roll Menshikov," *Down Beat*, May 11, 1961, 20–21.

75. Gates and West, *Future of the Race*, 77–78. Additionally, in the early 1960s Soviet jazz scholars Valerii Semenovich Mysovskii and Vladimir Feuertag published a book entitled *Dzhaz; Kratkii Ocherk* (Leningrad: Gosydarstvennoe Muzykalnoe Izdatelstvo, 1960).

76. John Tynan, "Jazz Behind the Iron Curtain," *Down Beat*, March 15, 1962, 18–19. For Tynan's critical views toward free jazz, see Saul, *Freedom Is, Freedom Ain't*, 226–227.

77. Eric Bourne, "Jazz in the Soviet Sphere," *Christian Science Monitor*, April 3, 1962. For a description of the controversy surrounding the Berlin Wall, see Zubok and Pleshakov, *Inside the Kremlin's Cold War*, 256.

78. "USSR, Germany, Hungary, and Hollywood Focus on Armstrong," *Down Beat*, July 29, 1965, 8. Armstrong's appearance was filmed and then broadcast on the show.

79. Leo Feigin, *Soviet Jazz: New Identity* (London: Quartet Books, 1985), 4. See also Boris Schwarz, *Music and Musical Life in Soviet Russia: 1917–1981*, enl. ed. (Bloomington: Indiana University Press, 1989), 501; Stites, *Russian Popular Culture*, 146–177. Another compelling perspective is offered in Wagnleitner, "Empire of Fun."

80. Leonid Pereverzev, "Molodozhniie Dzhaze Moskvii," *Muzykalnaia Zhizn* 14 (July 1965): 22–23; Leonid Pereverzev, "Iz Istorii Dzhaza," *Muzykalnaia Zhizn* 3 (February 1966): 20–21; 5 (March 1966): 22–23; 9 (May 1966): 22–23; 12 (June 1966): 22–23.

81. Lees, "Afterthoughts," 50; Millstein, "Sax Comes Up the Moskva River," 47–48; Mitchell, "Saga of Jelly Roll Menshikov," 20–21.

82. For the concept of "black intellectual property," see Gerard, *Jazz in Black and White*, 4–5.

83. Yuri Vikharieff, "The 'New Thing' in Russia," *Down Beat*, September 10, 1964, 16–18.

84. "A Day in the New Lives of Two Russian Defector-Jazz Musicians," *Down Beat*, December 3, 1964, 12–14.

85. A. Medvedev and Yuri Saulskii, "Dzhaz-1965," *Muzykalnaia Zhizn* 2 (January 1966): 18–19, 24.

86. *FRUS*, Vol. 14, *The Soviet Union*, 1964–1968, #34, "Memorandum from the Depu-

ty Director of the United States Information Agency (Wilson) to the Director (Rowan)," June 1, 1964, 77; for the entire text, see 77–82. See also Starr, *Red and Hot*, 275–288.

87. "Propose Cooling of Cold War by U.S.-Soviet Swap of Jazz Festivals," *Variety*, May 18, 1966, 52.

88. *Down Beat*, September 8, 1966, 16–17; December 29, 1966, 13.

89. Yuri Saulskii, interview by author in Russian, July 25, 1994, Moscow, tape recording.

Chapter 6. Bedlam from the Decadent West

1. Walter LaFeber, "Johnson, Vietnam, and Tocqueville," in Cohen and Tucker, *Lyndon Johnson Confronts the World*, 31–55. The phrase "bedlam from the decadent West" appears in "Muscovite Ramblers," 25.

2. Henry Hampton and Steve Fayer, eds., *Voices of Freedom: An Oral History of the Civil Rights Movement from the 1950s through the 1980s* (New York: Bantam Books, 1990), 335–348.

3. LaFeber, *American Age*, 616. For U.S. policy in Vietnam during these years, see Herring, *America's Longest War*, 202–241.

4. Dudziak, *Cold War Civil Rights*, 246–247, 251.

5. LaFeber, "Johnson, Vietnam, and Tocqueville," 42–47.

6. Davenport, "Jazz and the Cold War," 299–301.

7. "State Dept. Sets Hines for Russian Tour," *Down Beat*, May 5, 1966, 12. For an account of black life in Russia in the 1960s, see Blakely, *Russia and the Negro*, 115–118.

8. The *New York Times* article is cited in Michael Zwerin, *Down Beat*, November 3, 1966, 18.

9. Ibid., 19.

10. [Foy D.] Kohler, Moscow, to DOS, DOS A-370, "Cultural Exchange: The Earl Hines Band in the USSR," September 6, 1966, 10, 12, CU, Series 1.

11. Ibid., 9, 13.

12. Ibid., 2.

13. The *New York Times* article is cited in Zwerin, *Down Beat*, 18.

14. Rhoda Lois Blumberg, *Civil Rights: The 1960s Freedom Struggle*, rev. ed. (New York: Twayne, 1991), 81–85, 167, 188; Dudziak, *Cold War Civil Rights*, 243, 245, 246; Garrow, *Bearing the Cross*, 527–574. For more on Detroit, see Smith, *Dancing in the Streets*. The FBI formed the Counter Intelligence Program (COINTELPRO) to investigate antiwar and civil rights activities.

15. Porter, *What Is This Thing Called Jazz*, 2–4, 14–18; Martha Bayles, "Miles Davis and the Double Audience," in Early, *Miles Davis and American Culture*, 149–171; Monson, *Freedom Sounds*.

16. George Wein, President, Festival Productions, interview by author, January 17, 1999, New York, tape recording, Festival Productions, New York.

17. Stanley Dance, "New Orleans Jazzfest '68," reprint, 1–7, CU, Series 1.

18. Willis Conover, *Music USA Newsletter* 4, no. 3, (1968): 15, CU, Series 1.

19. Ibid., 16.

20. Ibid., 16–17.

21. Ibid., 17–18.

22. For more on Brezhnev's foreign policy, see R. Craig Nation, *Black Earth, Red Star: A History of Soviet Security Policy* (Ithaca, N.Y.: Cornell University Press, 1992), 218–225, 245–260.

23. Harlow Robinson, *The Last Impresario: The Life, Times, and Legacy of Sol Hurok* (New York: Viking, 1994), 399–422.

24. Thompson to DOS, DOS A-212, "Recommendation of Boston Symphony Orchestra Chamber Players for Department's Scroll of Appreciation," August 11, 1967, b 370, f EDX 16 USSR, 8-167; Thompson, Moscow, to SOS, "American Circus Sold Out in Tbilisi," September 11, 1967, b 373, f EDX 16 USSR, 9-167; and Thompson to SOS, April 22, 1967, b 373, f EDX 16 USSR, 1-167, CF-EDX, 1967–1969.

25. Hurok's pivotal role in cultural exchanges during these years is explored in Robinson, *Last Impresario*, 399–422.

26. *FRUS*, Vol. 14, *The Soviet Union*, 1964–1968, #239, "Memorandum from Nathaniel Davis of the National Security Council Staff to the President's Special Assistant (Rostow) and the President's Deputy Special Assistant for National Security Affairs (Bator)," July 11, 1967 (Washington, D.C.: USGPO, 2001), 567–568. For more on these negotiations, see, for example, DOS MOC, "US-USSR Exchange Negotiations, Preamble, Section 1-General, Section VIII-Films," April 1967, b 371, f EDX USSR, 6–168; NARA, Records of the Department of State, RG-59, Central Files 1967–1969, CF-EDX, 1967–1969.

27. "Hurok Essays New US-USSR Rapport," *Variety*, September 27, 1967, 61.

28. Robinson, *Last Impresario*, 415–416.

29. Zubok and Pleshakov, *Inside the Kremlin's Cold War*, 272–273; Robinson, *Last Impresario*, 272–273.

30. Guthrie, A-1861, June 23, 1967, b 373, f 5-167, CF-EDX, 1967–1969. See also Thompson to SOS, Moscow 2099, 131323, "Romanovsky Committee," December 13, 1967, b 373, f 5-167, CF-EDX, 1967–1969.

31. Thompson, "Romanovsky Committee."

32. Davis and Troupe, *Miles*, 290; Porter, *John Coltrane*, 261.

33. Archie Schepp, "An Artist Speaks Bluntly," *Down Beat*, December 16, 1965, 11.

34. Brothers, *Louis Armstrong*, 169–170.

35. Ibid., 171. He also included a poem in the letter.

36. Von Eschen, *Satchmo Blows Up the World*, 189.

37. "Once 'Degenerate' Jazz Now Swings Past Iron Curtain," *Variety*, March 1, 1967, 44; "Jazz, a Key Part of Iron Curtain Life," *Variety*, July 19, 1967, 43.

38. "Charles Lloyd Set for Soviet Jazz Festival," *Down Beat*, April 20, 1967, 13; "Soviet Invites 1st Yank Jazz Crew," *Variety*, March 8, 1967. For the story of jazz festivals and CU tours in Eastern Europe during détente, see Von Eschen, *Satchmo Blows Up the World*, 185–222.

39. Avakian, interview, transcript, 11.

40. Ibid.; [Llewellyn E.] Thompson, Moscow, to DOS, DOS A-289, "The 1967 Tallin Jazz Festival, the Charles Lloyd Quartet, and the Visit of Willis Conover, May 26, 1967," CU, Series 1.

41. Thompson, "1967 Tallin Jazz Festival."

42. Thompson to DOS, DOS A-289, "Review of 1967 Tallin Jazz Festival by Vasily Aksenov," August 29, 1967, CU, Series 1.

43. Saulskii, interview.

44. DOS A-68, "Gerry Mulligan Performs in Moscow," July 18, 1967, 3–4, b 370, f USSR, 7-167, CF-EDX, 1967–1969.

45. Ibid., 4.

46. Feuertag, interview.

47. "Visit of Mr. and Mrs. Willis Conover, Director, Music USA, Voice of America, [October 21–28, 1967]," February 19, 1968, b 366, f EDX 4 Rom.-U.S., 1167, CF-EDX, 1967–1969.

48. Davis and Troupe, *Miles*, 285, 286.

49. Waldo E. Martin, "Miles Davis and the 1960s Avant-Garde," in Early, *Miles Davis and American Culture*, 112–114.

50. Davis and Troupe, *Miles*, 285.

51. DOS MOC, "US-USSR Exchange Negotiations," June 12, 1968, b 371, f EDX US-USSR, 6-168; see also DOS MOC, "US-USSR Exchange Negotiations, General," July 4, 5, 1968, b 371, f EDX 16 US-USSR, 7-168, CF-EDX, 1967–1969. For debates about the end of jazz, see Bayles, "Miles Davis," 157.

52. Thompson, DOS A-194, "Emphasis on Youth," August 1968, 1–4, b 372, f EDX 10 USSR, 8-168; and Rusk, DOS Out. to Saigon, June 10, 1968, b 373, f Vietn-S, 4-168, CF-EDX, 1967–1969.

53. *FRUS*, Vol. 14, *The Soviet Union*, 1964–1968, #234, "Memorandum of Conversation, President Lyndon B. Johnson, and Alexei Kosygin, Chairman of the Council of Ministers," June 25, 1967, 538–543, esp., 539.

54. Johnson, *Vantage Point*, 470.

55. Plummer, *Rising Wind*, 319, 325; Garrow, *Bearing the Cross*, 575–624.

56. Stites, *Russian Popular Culture*, 148–177; Davis, *Autobiography*, 271, 380, 406. Many authors discusses the rise of rock and roll; see, for example, Saul, *Freedom Is, Freedom Ain't*, 4–5, 271–273, 278–281; Martin, "Miles Davis," 110.

57. Richard H. Immerman, "A Time in the Tide of Men's Affairs: Lyndon Johnson and Vietnam," in Cohen and Tucker, *Lyndon Johnson Confronts the World*, 65, 71–88; Herring, *America's Longest War*, 202–241.

58. DOS MOC, "US-USSR Exchange Negotiations."

59. "Charles Lloyd Quartet Jazzing through Orient in U.S. State Dept. Tour," *Variety*, May 15, 1968.

60. Macomber to Robert P. Mayo, Director, Bureau of Budget, February 24, 1968, b 363, f EDX Fin, 1167, CF-EDX, 1967–1969.

61. DOS MOC, John G. Peters, Europe, SES, "Conversation with Jerzy Wojciesk, Cultural Attaché, Polish Embassy," October 27, 1967, b 366, f EDX Rom.-US 1167 CF-EDX, 1967–1969.

62. Thompson, Moscow, to DOS, DOS A-1189, "Polish-Soviet Cultural Exchanges," March 15, 1968, b 366, f EDX Rom.-US 1167, CF-EDX, 1967–1969.

63. Beam, Prague, to SOS, no. 1163, March 25, 1968, b 362, f EDX 10 Czech-U.S., 1-167; and DOS MOC, "U.S.-Czech Exchanges," Frantisek Pevlis, Attaché Embassy of Czechoslovakia, Andrew T. Falkiewicz, Europe/SES, March 14, 1968, b 362, f EDX 10 Czech-US 1-167, CF-EDX, 1967–1969.

64. Thomas, *Chasin' the Trane*, 224; see also photo between 160 and 161.

65. LaFeber, *American Age*, 623.

66. DOS MOC, "U.S.-Soviet Exchanges," August 30, 1968, b 370, f EDX US-USSR, 7-168; and DOS Out. to Warsaw, Moscow, Budapest, Prague, Bucharest, Sofia, November 1968, f EDX US-USSR, 11–68, b 370, CF-EDX, 1967–1969. See also [Protocol of Conversation], Mr. McCloskey, Goskontsert, USSR, September 5, 1968, 1–3, CU, Series 1.

67. John M. Leddy to the Secretary, Confidential Memo, "Exchange of Performing Arts Groups with the USSR and Eastern European Countries–Action Memorandum," attach. to: Guy E. Coriden, to Dr. Edward D. Re, "Exchange of Performing Arts Groups with the USSR," November 6, 1968, CU, Series 1.

68. Ibid.

69. "In Politics of Cultural Exchange, U.S. Vietrek Czech-Mated by USSR," *Variety*, February 19, 1969, 57.

70. DOS MOC, Velentin Kamenev, Boris Klosson, Edward W. Brugess, November 14, 1968, b 370, f EDX US-USSR, 11-168, CF-EDX, 1967–1969.

71. DOS MOC, Vratislav Syivat and the Secretary of the Embassy of the Czech Socialist Republic; Third Secretary of the Embassy of the Czech Republic; Mr. Harry J. Gillmore, EUR, SES, DOS, December 23, 1968, b 362, f EDX 10 Czech-US, 1-167, CF-EDX, 1967–1969.

72. Prague, 4065, October 30, 1968, b 362, f EDX 10 Czech-US 1-167, CF-EDX, 1967–1969.

73. Prague, 4263, "First Concert of Czechoslovak Jazz," 1968, b 363, f EDX 13 Czech-

US, 1-167, CF-EDX, 1967–1969. Leonid Pereverzev discusses the Moscow Festival in "Prazdniki i budni nashevo dzhaza," *Muzykalnaia Zhizn* 16 (1968): 22–23.

74. Rusk, *As I Saw It*, 616.

75. As the leadership of many African countries changed, often because of coups, Communist influence continued to be a prominent concern for American officials in Africa; see *FRUS*, Vol. 24, *Africa*, 1964–1968, #230, "Intelligence Memorandum," October 19, 1967 (Washington, D.C.: USGPO, 1999), 382–383. Comments also appear in Knox, Dahomey, DOS A-22, "Emphasis on Youth," August 18, 1967, b 363, f EDX 12 Dahomey; and Cairo to SOS, March 22, 1967, f EDX-UAR 1-167, CF-EDX, 1967–1969.

76. *FRUS*, Vol. 24, *Africa*, 1964–1968, #231, "Report from Vice President Humphrey to President Johnson," January 12, 1968, (Washington, D.C.: USGPO, 1999), 388; for the entire report, see 383–403.

77. Rusk, *As I Saw It*, 586.

78. Skinner, "Hegemonic Paradigms," 56–61.

79. Ibid., 45–65.

80. Davenport, "Jazz and the Cold War," 294–295.

81. "Envoy to Africa," in Rampersad, *Collected Poems of Langston Hughes*, 441.

82. An example of such views appears in Bane to DOS, DOS A-22, "Report on the Youth Programs in Gabon," August 12, 1967, b 363, f EDX Gabon, 1-167, CF-EDX, 1967–1969.

83. Johnson, *Vantage Point*, 179.

84. Dudziak, *Cold War Civil Rights*, 254.

85. Johnson, *Vantage Point*, 179.

86. Louis Armstrong, "Good-Bye to All of You, 1969," in Brothers, *Louis Armstrong*, 190.

Conclusion

1. This phrase appears in Minutes of U.S. Department of State, Bureau of Educational and Cultural Affairs, Office of Cultural Presentations, Subcommittee on Jazz, August 30, 1967, 3, CU, Series 5.

2. Stanley Dance, "Ellington at the White House," *Saturday Review*, May 31, 1969, 5, Records of the United States Information Agency, USIA Library.

3. Ibid.; Dan Morgenstern, "Swinging at the White House," *Down Beat*, June 12, 1969, 14; "Moscow Film Festival Triggers Jazz Action," *Down Beat*, September 4, 1969, 11.

4. Addison Gayle, *The Black Aesthetic* (Garden City, N.Y.: Doubleday, 1971); Cornel West, ed., *Restoring Hope: Conversations on the Future of Black America* (Boston: Beacon Press, 1997), 117, 121.

5. W. E. B. DuBois, "Whites in Africa after Negro Autonomy," in Lewis, *DuBois: A Reader*, 692.

6. Don DeMicheal, "Jazz in Government," part 2, *Down Beat*, January 31, 1963, 20.

7. Ibid.

8. Michael Krenn, *Black Diplomats* (New York: M. E. Sharpe, [1999]); Iriye, *Cultural Internationalism*, 175. For more on theory and practice in U.S. foreign affairs, see Hunt, *Ideology and U.S. Foreign Policy*.

9. Jon Panish, *The Color of Jazz: Race and Representation in Postwar American Culture* (Jackson: University Press of Mississippi, 1997), 1–22.

10. Richmond to USIA, April 3, 1969, "Minnesota Band Opens Tour and Is Received Enthusiastically," NARA, Records of the Department of State, RG-59, Central Files 1967–1969, EDX, b 371, f EDX 16-US-USSR, 5-169. See also Wagnleitner, "Empire of Fun."

11. Robinson, *Last Impresario*, xiii–xiv.

12. Hixson, *Parting the Curtain*.

Bibliography

PRIMARY SOURCES

Unpublished U.S. Government Documents

Records of the Bureau of Educational and Cultural Affairs of the Department of State, Special Collections Division, University of Arkansas Library, Fayetteville.
Records of the President's Special International Program of the Department of State, and the Cultural Presentations Program of the Department of State, Historical Collection, United States Information Agency Library, Washington, D.C.
Records of the United States Department of State, Record Group-59, National Archives and Records Administration, College Park, Md.
Records of the United States Information Agency, National Archives and Records Administration, College Park, Md.

Published U.S. Government Documents

Foreign Relations of the United States

Africa
    1961–1963 (Washington, D.C.: USGPO, 1995)
    1964–1968 (Washington, D.C.: USGPO, 1999)
Eastern Europe
    1964–1968 (Washington, D.C.: USGPO, 1996)
Eastern Europe Region; Soviet Union; Cyprus
    1958–1960 (Washington, D.C.: USGPO, 1993)
Kennedy-Khrushchev Exchanges
    1961–1963 (Washington, D.C.: USGPO, 1998)
Soviet Union
    1961–1963 (Washington, D.C.: USGPO, 1998)
    1964–1968 (Washington, D.C.: USGPO, 2001)
Soviet Union, Eastern Mediterranean
    1955–1957 (Washington, D.C.: USGPO, 1989)

Public Papers of the Presidents of the United States Containing the Public Messages, Speeches, and Statements of the President

Lyndon B. Johnson
> Book I. January 1–May 31, 1965 (Washington, D.C.: USGPO, 1966)
> Book II. June 1–December 31, 1965 (Washington, D.C.: USGPO, 1966)

John F. Kennedy
> January–December 1962 (Washington, D.C.: USGPO, 1963)
> January 1–November 22, 1963 (Washington, D.C.: USGPO, 1964)

JAZZ ARCHIVES

Louis Armstrong Archive. Rosenthal Library, Queens College, Flushing, N.Y.

Duke Ellington. Smithsonian Institution, Washington, D.C.

Benny Goodman Archive. Irving S. Gilmore Music Library, Yale University, New Haven, Conn.

Institute of Jazz Studies. Rutgers University, Newark, N.J.

Red Nichols Archive. Special Collections, University of Oregon Library, Eugene.

MANUSCRIPT COLLECTIONS/SPECIAL COLLECTIONS

Louis Armstrong Correspondence. Performing Arts Reading Room, Library of Congress, Washington, D.C.

National Association for the Advancement of Colored People (NAACP). Manuscript Division, Library of Congress, Washington, D.C.

INTERVIEWS

Avakian, George, jazz producer, manager, and author. Interview by author, July 3, 1993, Riverdale, N.Y. Transcript of tape recording.

Feuertag, Vladimir, Soviet jazz lecturer, scholar, producer, and author. Interview by author in Russian, July 27, 1994, St. Petersburg. Tape recording.

Saulskii, Yuri, president of the Moscow Jazz Association. Interview by author in Russian, July 25, 1994, Moscow. Tape recording, Goskontsert, Moscow.

Wein, George, president, Festival Productions. Interview by author, January 17, 1999, New York. Tape recording, Festival Productions, New York.

NEWSPAPERS AND MAGAZINES

Chicago Defender
Christian Science Monitor
Daily Listener
Down Beat
Evening Star
Izvestia
Metronome
Nairibi Sunday News
National Observer
New York Times
Pittsburgh Courier
Pravda
Reporter
Saturday Review
Sovetskaia Kultura
Sovetskaia Muzyka
Vanity Star
Variety
Washington Post

SECONDARY SOURCES

Journal Articles

Berger, Morroe. "Jazz: Resistance to the Diffusion of a Culture Pattern." *Journal of Negro History* 32 (1947): 461–494.

Culture, Gender and Foreign Policy: A Symposium. *Diplomatic History* 18 (Winter 1994): 47–142.

Davis, Nigel Gould. "The Logic of Soviet Cultural Diplomacy." *Diplomatic History* 27 (April 2003): 193–214.

"Diskussiia o dzhaze." *Sovetskaia Muzyka* 2 (February 1934): 67.

Dudziak, Mary L. "Desegregation as a Cold War Imperative." *Stanford Law Review* 41 (November 1988): 61–120.

———. "Josephine Baker, Racial Protest and the Cold War." *Journal of American History* 81, no. 2 (September 1994): 543–570.

Ellington, Duke. "Ellington: The Race for Space." In *The Duke Ellington Reader*, ed. Mark Tucker, 293–296. New York: Oxford University Press, 1993.

Gorky, Maxim. "The Music of the Degenerate." Trans. Marie Budberg. *Dial* 85 (December 1928): 480–484.

Iriye, Akira. "The Americanized Century." *Reviews in American History* (March 1983): 124–128.

———. "Culture and International History." In *Explaining the History of American Foreign Relations*, ed. Michael Hogan and Thomas G. Paterson, 214–225. New York: Cambridge University Press, 1991.

Konen, Vladimir. "Legenda i pravda o dzhaze." *Sovetskaia Muzyka* 9 (September 1955): 22–31.

Medvedev, A. "Chto vy dumaete o dzhaze i legkoi muzyke?" *Sovetskaia Muzyka* 11 (November 1956): 98–108.

Medvedev, A., and Yuri Saulskii. "Dzhaz-65." *Muzykalnaia Zhizn* 2 (January 1966): 18–19, 24.

Minkh, N. "Razmyshleniia o dzhaze." *Sovetskaia Muzyka* 2 (February 1958): 42–46.

Ninkovich, Frank. "The Currents of Cultural Diplomacy." *Diplomatic History* 1 (Summer 1977): 135–162.

———. "Interests and Discourse in Diplomatic History." *Diplomatic History* 13 (Spring 1989): 135–162.

Pereverzev, Leonid. "Iz Istorii Dzhaza." *Muzykalnaia Zhizn* 3 (February 1966): 20–21; 5 (March 1966): 22–23; 9 (May 1966): 22–23; 12 (June 1966): 22–23.

———. "Molodozhniie Dzhaze Moskvii." *Muzykalnaia Zhizn* 14 (July 1965): 22–23

Porter, Lewis. "Some Problems in Jazz Research." *Black Music Research Journal* 8 (Fall 1988): 195–206.

Robeson, Paul. "Pesni Moego Naroda." *Sovetskaia Muzyka* 7 (July 1949): 100–104.

Rosenberg, Emily. "Walking the Borders." *Diplomatic History* 13 (Fall 1989): 565–573.

Ryan, Henry Butterfield. "What Does a Cultural Attaché Really Do?" *SHAFR Newsletter* (September 1989): 2–9.

Rydell, Robert. "Cultural Complexities: The Architecture of American Foreign Policy." *Diplomatic History* 4 (Fall 1994): 565–569.

Symposium: African Americans and U.S. Foreign Relations. *Diplomatic History* 20 (Fall 1996): 532–650.

Tucker, Mark. Review of *Duke Ellington*, by James Lincoln Collier. *Notes* (March 1989): 501–502.

Wagnleitner, Reinhold. "The Empire of Fun, or Talkin' Soviet Blues: The Sound of Freedom and U.S. Cultural Hegemony in Europe." *Diplomatic History* 23 (Summer 1999): 499–524.

———. "The Irony of American Culture Abroad: Austria and the Cold War." In *Recasting America: Culture and Politics in the Age of Cold War*, ed. Larry May. Chicago: University of Chicago Press, 1989.

Books

Aksenov, Vasily. *In Search of Melancholy Baby*. Trans. Michael Henry Heim and Antonina W. Bouis. New York: Random House, 1987.

Angelou, Maya. *All God's Children Need Traveling Shoes*. New York: Random House, 1986.

Aptheker, Herbert, ed. *The Correspondence of W. E. B. DuBois*. Vol. 3, *1944–1963*. Amherst: University of Massachusetts Press, 1978.

Applebaum, Herbert. *Perspectives in Cultural Anthropology*. Albany: State University of New York Press, 1987.

Appy, Christian G., ed. *Cold War Constructions: The Political Culture of United States Imperialism, 1945-1966*. Amherst: University of Massachusetts Press, 2000.

Arensberg, Conrad, and Arthur Niehoff. *Introducing Social Change: A Manual for Community Development*. 2nd ed. New York: Aldine Atherton, 1971.

Barghoorn, Frederick Charles. *The Soviet Cultural Offensive: The Role of Cultural Diplomacy in Soviet Foreign Policy*. Princeton, N.J.: Princeton University Press, 1960.

Barkan, Elazar. *The Retreat of Scientific Racism: Changing Concepts of Race in Britain and the United States between the World Wars*. Cambridge: Cambridge University Press, 1992.

Belmonte, Laura. *Selling the American Way: U.S. Propaganda and the Cold War*. Philadelphia: University of Pennsylvania Press, 2008.

Bergreen, Laurence. *Louis Armstrong: An Extravagant Life*. New York: Broadway Books, 1997.

Beschloss, Michael R., ed. *Taking Charge: The Johnson White House Tapes, 1963–1964*. New York: Simon and Schuster, 1997.

Bichet, Sidney. *Treat It Gentle: An Autobiography*. New York: Da Capo Press, 1978.

Blakely, Allison. *Russia and the Negro: Blacks in Russian History and Thought*. Washington, D.C.: Howard University Press, 1986.

Borstelmann, Thomas. *Apartheid's Reluctant Uncle: The United States and Southern Africa in the Early Cold War*. New York: Oxford University Press, 1993.

———. *The Cold War and the Color Line: American Race Relations in the Global Arena*. Cambridge, Mass.: Harvard University Press, 2001.

Boyer, Paul. *By the Bomb's Early Light: American Thought and Culture and the Dawn of the Atomic Age*. Chapel Hill: University of North Carolina Press, 1985.

Boyer, Paul, and Sterling Stuckey. *American Nation in the Twentieth Century*. Austin, Tx.: Holt, Rinehart and Winston, 1996.

Brackett, Virginia. *Jazz Odyssey: The Life of Oscar Peterson*. London: Continuum, 2002.

Brewin, Michael. *Soul Jazz: The Heat of the Music*. Portland, Ore.: USA, 2002.

Brothers, Thomas, ed. *Louis Armstrong, In His Own Words: Selected Writings*. New York: Oxford University Press, 1999.

Buell, Frederick. *National Culture and the New Global System.* Baltimore: Johns Hopkins University Press, 1994.

Carmichael, Stokely, and Charles V. Hamilton. *Black Power: The Politics of Liberation in America.* New York: Vintage Books, 1967.

Carson, Clayborne. *In Struggle: SNCC and the Black Awakening of the 1960s.* Cambridge, Mass.: Harvard University Press, 1994.

Caute, David. *The Dancer Defects: The Struggle for Cultural Supremacy during the Cold War.* Oxford: Oxford University Press, 2005.

Cogswell, Michael. *Louis Armstrong: The Offstage Story of Satchmo.* Portland, Ore.: Collectors Press, 2003.

Cohen, Warren I., and Nancy Bernkopf Tucker, eds. *Lyndon Johnson Confronts the World: American Foreign Policy, 1963–1968.* Cambridge: Cambridge University Press, 1994.

Cooke, Mervyn. *Jazz.* New York: Thames and Hudson, 1998.

Cooke, Mervyn, and David Horn, eds. *Cambridge Companion to Jazz.* New York: Cambridge, 2002.

Crockatt, Richard. *The Fifty Years War: The United States and the Soviet Union in World Politics, 1941–1991.* London: Routledge, 1995.

Cull, Nicholas J. *The Cold War and the United States Information Agency: American Propaganda and Public Diplomacy, 1945-1989.* Cambridge: Cambridge University Press, 2008.

DeConde, Alexander. *Ethnicity, Race and American Foreign Policy: A History.* Boston: Northeastern University Press, 1992.

Denning, Michael. *The Cultural Front: The Laboring of American Culture in the 20th Century.* New York: Verso, 1996.

Doerschuk, Robert L. *88: The Giants of Jazz Piano.* San Francisco: Backbeat Books, and Toronto: Hal Leonard, 2001.

Dorfman, Ariel, and Armand Mattelart. *How to Read Donald Duck: Imperialist Ideology in the Disney Comic.* Trans. David Kunzle. New York: International General, 1971.

Duberman, Martin Bauml. *Paul Robeson.* New York: Alfred A. Knopf, 1989.

DuBois, W. E. B. *The Souls of Black Folk.* Ed. Brent Hayes Edward. New York: Oxford, 2007.

———. *The World and Africa: An Inquiry into the Part Which Africa Has Played in World History.* New York: Viking Press, 1947.

Dudziak, Mary L. *Cold War Civil Rights: Race and the Image of American Democracy.* Princeton, N.J.: Princeton University Press, 2000.

Early, Gerald. *One Nation Under a Groove: Motown and American Culture.* Hopewell, N.J.: Ecco Press, 1995.

———. *This Is Where I Came In: Black America in the 1960s.* Lincoln: University of Nebraska Press, 2003.

———, ed. *Miles Davis and American Culture*. St. Louis: Missouri Historical Society Press, 2001.

Edwards, Brent. *The Practice of Diaspora: Literature, Translation and the Rise of Black Internationalism*. Cambridge, Mass.: Harvard University Press, 2003.

Ellington, Duke. *Music Is My Mistress*. Garden City, N.Y.: Doubleday, 1973.

Ellington, Mercer, and Stanley Dance. *Duke Ellington in Person: An Intimate Portrait*. New York: Da Capo Press, 1979.

Etzold, Thomas H., and John Lewis Gaddis, eds. *Containment: Documents on American Policy and Strategy, 1945–1950*. New York: Columbia University Press, 1978.

Feigin, Leo. *Russian Jazz: New Identity*. London: Quartet Books, 1985.

Firestone, Ross. *Swing, Swing, Swing: The Life and Times of Benny Goodman*. New York: W. W. Norton, 1993.

Frankel, Charles. *The Neglected Aspect of Foreign Affairs: American Educational and Cultural Policy Abroad*. Washington, D.C.: Brookings Institution, 1965.

Franklin, John Hope. *The Color Line: Legacy for the Twenty-first Century*. Columbia: University of Missouri Press, 1993.

———. *Race and History: Selected Essays, 1938–1988*. Baton Rouge: Louisiana State University Press, 1989.

Franklin, John Hope, and Alfred A. Moss Jr. *From Slavery to Freedom: A History of Afro-Americans*. 7th ed. New York: McGraw Hill, 1993.

Gaddis, John Lewis. *Strategies of Containment*. Oxford: Oxford University Press, 2005.

———. *We Now Know: Rethinking Cold War History*. New York: Oxford University Press, 1997.

Galambos, Louis, and Duan Van Ee, eds. *The Papers of Dwight David Eisenhower*. Vol. 17. Baltimore: Johns Hopkins University Press, 1996.

Ganz, Herbert J. *Popular Culture and High Culture: An Analysis and Evaluation of Taste*. New York: Basic Books, 1975.

Garner, Gary, ed. *Jazz Performers: An Annotated Bibliography of Biographical Materials*. New York: Greenwood Press, 1990.

Garrow, David J. *Bearing the Cross: Martin Luther King, Jr., and the Southern Christian Leadership Conference*. New York: Vintage Books, 1986.

Garthoff, Raymond. *Détente and Confrontation: American-Soviet Relations from Nixon to Reagan*. Rev. ed. Washington, D.C.: Brookings Institution, 1994.

Gates, Henry Louis. *America Behind the Color Line*. New York: Warner Books, 2004.

Gates, Henry Louis, and Evelyn Higginbotham. *African American Lives*. New York: Oxford University Press, 2004.

Gates, Henry Louis, and Cornel West. *The Future of the Race*. New York: Alfred A. Knopf, 1996.

Gati, Charles. *The Bloc That Failed: Soviet-Eastern European Relations in Transition*. Bloomington: Indiana University Press, 1990.

Gayle, Addison. *The Black Aesthetic*. Garden City, N.Y.: Doubleday, 1971.

Geertz, Clifford. *The Interpretation of Cultures*. New York: Basic Books, 1973.

Gerard, Charley. *Jazz in Black and White: Race, Culture, and Identity in the Jazz Community*. Westport, Conn.: Greenwood Press, 1998.

Gibbs, Terry. *Good Vibes: A Life in Jazz*. Lanham, Md.: Scarecrow Press, 2003.

Giddins, Gary. *Riding on a Blue Note: Jazz and American Pop*. New York: Da Capo Press, 2000.

———. *Visions of Jazz: The First Century*. New York: Oxford University Press, 1998.

Gillespie, Dizzy. *To Be or Not to Bop: Memoirs*. Garden City, N.Y.: Doubleday, 1978.

Gioia, Ted. *The History of Jazz*. New York: Oxford University Press, 1997.

Goldfield, David. *Black, White and Southern: Race Relations and Southern Culture, 1940 to the Present*. Baton Rouge: Louisiana State University Press, 1990.

Haddow, Robert A. *Pavilions of Plenty: Exhibiting American Culture Abroad in the 1950s*. Washington, D.C.: Smithsonian Institution Press, 1997.

Hampton, Henry, and Steve Fayer, eds. *Voices of Freedom: An Oral History of the Civil Rights Movement from the 1950s through the 1980s*. New York: Bantam Books, 1990.

Harbutt, Fraser, J. *The Iron Curtain: Churchill, America, and the Origins of the Cold War*. New York: Oxford University Press, 1985.

Harris, Joseph E. *Africans and Their History*. Rev. ed. New York: Penguin Books, 1987.

———. *Perspectives on the Changing Relationship between Afro-Americans and Africans*. Khartoum, Sudan: Institute of African and Asian Studies, University of Khartoum, 1976.

Heald, Morell, and Lawrence S. Kaplan. *Culture and Diplomacy: The American Experience*. Westport, Conn.: Greenwood Press, 1977.

Hentoff, Nat. *Speaking Freely: A Memoir*. New York: Alfred A. Knopf, 1997.

Herring, George C. *America's Longest War: The United States and Vietnam, 1950–1975*. 3rd ed. New York: McGraw Hill, 1996.

Herskovitz, Melville. *The Myth of the Negro Past*. Boston: Beacon Press, 1990.

Hine, Darlene Clark, and Jacqueline McLeod, eds. *Crossing Boundaries: Comparative History of Black People in Diaspora*. Bloomington: Indiana University Press, 1999.

Hixson, Walter L. *The Myth of American Diplomacy: Identity and U.S. Foreign Policy*. New Haven, Conn.: Yale University Press, 2008.

———. *Parting the Curtain: Propaganda, Culture, and the Cold War, 1945–1961*. New York: St. Martin's Press, 1997.

Hogan, Michael, ed. *The End of the Cold War: Its Meaning and Implications*. New York: Cambridge University Press, 1992.

Holland, Gini. *Louis Armstrong*. Milwaukee, Wis.: World Almanac, 2003.

Holt, Thomas C. *The Problem of Race in the Twenty-first Century*. Cambridge, Mass.: Harvard University Press, 2000.

hooks, bell, and Cornel West. *Breaking Bread: Insurgent Black Intellectual Life*. Boston: South End Press, 1991.

Hunt, Michael. *Ideology and U.S. Foreign Policy*. New Haven, Conn.: Yale University Press, 1983.

Hutchinson, George. *The Harlem Renaissance in Black and White*. Cambridge, Mass.: Harvard University Press, 1995.

Iriye, Akira. *Cultural Internationalism and World Order*. Baltimore: Johns Hopkins University Press, 1997.

Johnson, Lyndon B. *The Vantage Point: Perspectives of the Presidency, 1963–1969*. New York: Holt, Rinehart and Winston, 1971.

Jones, Leroi [Amiri Baraka]. *Blues People: Negro Music in White America*. Westport, Conn.: Greenwood Press, 1980.

Jost, Ekkehard. *Free Jazz*. New York: Da Capo Press, 1981.

Kalb, Madelaine. *The Congo Cables: The Cold War in Africa–From Eisenhower to Kennedy*. New York: Macmillan, 1982.

Katzenstein, Peter J., and Robert Koehane. *Anti-Americanisms in World Politics*. Ithaca, N.Y.: Cornell University Press, 2007.

Keiler, Allan. *Marian Anderson: A Singer's Journey*. New York: Scribner, 2000.

Kelley, Robin D. G. *Race Rebels: Culture, Politics, and the Black Working Class*. New York: Free Press, 1994.

Kissinger, Henry. *Diplomacy*. New York: Simon and Schuster, 1994.

Kluger, Richard. *Simple Justice: The History of* Brown v. Board of Education *and Black America's Struggle for Equality*. New York: Vintage Books, 1977.

Kofsky, Frank. *Black Nationalism and the Revolution in Music*. New York: Pathfinder, 1970.

———. *John Coltrane and the Jazz Revolution of the 1960s*. Rev. ed. New York: Pathfinder, 1998.

Koppes, Clayton R., and Gregory D. Black. *Hollywood Goes to War: How Politics, Profits and Propaganda Shaped World War II Movies*. New York: Free Press, 1987.

Krenn, Michael. *The Color of Empire: Race and American Foreign Relations*. Washington, D.C.: Potomac Books, 2006.

LaFeber, Walter. *America, Russia, and the Cold War*. Boston: McGraw Hill, 2008.

———. *The American Age: U.S. Foreign Policy at Home and Abroad*. Vol. 2. 2nd ed. New York: W. W. Norton, 1994.

Lauren, Paul Gordon. *Power and Prejudice: The Politics and Diplomacy of Racial Discrimination*. 1988. Reprint, Boulder, Colo.: Westview Press, 1996.

Lawrence, A. H. *Duke Ellington and His World: A Biography*. New York: Routledge, 2001.

Lees, Gene. *Cats of Any Color: Jazz, Black and White*. New York: Oxford University Press, 1995.

————. *Oscar Peterson: The Will to Swing*. Rocklin, Calif.: Prima Publishing and Communications, 1990.

————. *Waitin' for Dizzy*. New York: Oxford University Press, 1991.

Leffler, Melvyn P. *A Preponderance of Power: National Security, the Truman Administration, and the Cold War*. Stanford, Calif.: Stanford University Press, 1992.

Levine, Lawrence. *Black Culture and Black Consciousness: Afro-American Folk Thought from Slavery to Freedom*. Oxford: Oxford University Press, 1977.

Lewis, David Levering. *W. E. B. DuBois: The Fight for Equality and the American Century, 1919–1963*. New York: Henry Holt, 2000.

————. *W. E. B. DuBois: A Reader*. New York: Henry Holt, 1995.

Litweiler, John. *Ornette Coleman: A Harmolodic Life*. New York: William Morrow, 1992.

Locke, Alain L. *The Negro and His Music*. Port Washington, N.Y.: Kennikat Press, 1968.

————. *Race Contacts and Interracial Relations: Lectures on the Theory and Practice of Race*. Reprint, Washington, D.C.: Howard University Press, 1992.

Loury, Glenn C. *The Anatomy of Racial Inequality*. Cambridge, Mass.: Harvard University Press, 2002.

Maga, Timothy P. *John F. Kennedy and the New Frontier Diplomacy, 1961–1963*. Malabar, Fla.: Krieger, 1994.

Marable, Manning. *The Great Wells of Democracy: The Meaning of Race in American Life*. New York: Basic Civitas Books, 2002.

————. *Race, Reform and Rebellion: The Second Reconstruction and Beyond in Black America, 1945-2006*. Jackson: University Press of Mississippi, 2007.

————. *Speaking Truth to Power: Essays on Race, Resistance, and Radicalism*. Boulder, Colo.: Westview Press, 1996.

Margolick, David. *Strange Fruit: Billie Holiday, Café Society, and an Early Cry for Civil Rights*. Philadelphia: Running Press, 2000.

May, Elaine Tyler. *Homeward Bound: American Families in the Cold War Era*. New York: Basic Books, 1988.

McCauley, Martin. *Russia, America and the Cold War, 1949-1991*. New York: Pearson Longman, 2008.

McConnel, William S. *The Harlem Renaissance*. San Diego, Calif.: Greenhaven Press, 2003.

McCormick, Thomas, J. *America's Half Century: United States Foreign Policy in the Cold War and After*. 2nd ed. Baltimore: Johns Hopkins University Press, 1995.

Merelman, Richard. *Representing Black Culture: Racial Conflict and Cultural Politics in the United States*. New York: Routledge, 1995.

Mikell, Gwen. *Cocoa and Chaos in Ghana*. Washington, D.C.: Howard University Press, 1992.

Monson, Ingrid T. *Freedom Sounds: Civil Rights Call Out to Jazz and Africa*. New York: Oxford University Press, 2007.

Moody, Bill. *The Jazz Exiles: American Musicians Abroad*. Reno: University of Nevada Press, 1993.

Myrdal, Gunnar. *An American Dilemma: The Negro Problem and Modern Democracy*. New York: Harper and Brothers, 1944.

Mysovskii, Valerii Semenovich, and Vladimir Feuertag. *Dzhaz; Kratkii Ocherk*. Leningrad: Gosydarstvennoe Muzykalnoe Izdatelstvo, 1960.

Nation, R. Craig. *Black Earth, Red Star: A History of Soviet Security Policy*. Ithaca, N.Y.: Cornell University Press, 1992.

Nicholson, Stuart. *Reminiscing in Tempo: A Portrait of Duke Ellington*. Boston: Northeastern University Press, 1999.

Ninkovich, Frank. *The Diplomacy of Ideas: U.S. Foreign Policy and Cultural Relations, 1938–1950*. New York: Cambridge University Press, 1981.

———. *Modernity and Power: A History of the Domino Theory in the Twentieth Century*. Chicago: University of Chicago Press, 1994.

Noer, Thomas J. *The Cold War and Black Liberation: The United States and White Rule in Africa, 1948–1968*. Columbia: University of Missouri Press, 1985.

O'Meally, Robert G., ed. *The Jazz Cadence of American Culture*. New York: Columbia University Press, 1998.

Panish, Jon. *The Color of Jazz: Race and Representation in Postwar American Culture*. Jackson: University Press of Mississippi, 1997.

Paterson, Thomas, ed. *Kennedy's Quest for Victory: American Foreign Policy, 1961–1963*. New York: Oxford University Press, 1989.

Peretti, Burton. *The Creation of Jazz: Music, Race and Culture in Urban America*. Urbana: University of Illinois Press, 1993.

———. *Jazz in American Culture*. Chicago: Ivan R. Dee, 1997.

Plummer, Brenda Gayle. *Rising Wind: Black Americans and U.S. Foreign Affairs, 1935–1960*. Chapel Hill: University of North Carolina Press, 1997.

———, ed. *Window on Freedom*. Chapel Hill: University of North Carolina Press, 2003.

Porter, Eric. *What Is This Thing Called Jazz: African American Musicians as Artists, Critics, and Activists*. Berkeley: University of California Press, 2002.

Porter, Lewis. *John Coltrane: His Life and Music*. Ann Arbor: University of Michigan Press, 1998.

Powell, Richard. *Black Art and Culture in the Twentieth Century*. New York: Thames and Hudson, 1997.

Radano, Ron M. *New Musical Figurations: Anthony Braxton's Cultural Critique*. Chicago: University of Chicago Press, 1993.

Ramsey, Guthrie P., Jr. *Race Music: Black Cultures from Bebop to Hip-Hop*. Berkeley: University of California Press, 2003.

Rawnsley, Gary D., ed. *Cold War Propaganda in the 1950s*. New York: St. Martin's Press, 1999.

Record, Wilson. *The Negro and the Communist Party*. New York: Antheneum, 1971.

Reid, Margaret. *Black Protest Poetry: Polemics from the Harlem Renaissance and the Sixties*. New York: P. Lang, 2001.

Richmond, Yale. *Practicing Public Diplomacy: A Cold War Odyssey*. New York: Berghahn Books, 2008.

Ripmaster, Terrence. *Willis Conover: Broadcasting Jazz to the World: A Biography*. New York: Universe, 2007.

Robin, Ron. *Enclaves of America: The Rhetoric of American Political Architecture Abroad, 1900–1965*. Princeton, N.J.: Princeton University Press, 1993.

Robinson, Harlow. *The Last Impresario: The Life, Times, and Legacy of Sol Hurok*. New York: Viking, 1994.

Rose, Phyllis. *Jazz Cleopatra: Josephine Baker in Her Time*. New York: Doubleday, 1989.

Rosenberg, Emily. *Spreading the American Dream: American Economic and Cultural Expansion, 1890–1945*. New York: Hill and Wang, 1982.

Rosenthal, David. *Hard Bop: Jazz and Black Music, 1955–1965*. New York: Oxford University Press, 1992.

Rusk, Dean. *As I Saw It*. Ed. Donald S. Papp. New York: W. W. Norton, 1990.

Said, Edward. *Culture and Imperialism*. New York: Vintage Books, 1993.

———. *Orientalism*. New York: Vintage Books, 1978.

Sales, Grover. *Jazz: America's Classical Music*. New York: Da Capo Press, 1992.

Saul, Scott. *Freedom Is, Freedom Ain't: Jazz and the Making of the Sixties*. Cambridge, Mass.: Harvard University Press, 2003.

Saulskii, Y., and Y. Chugunov. *Melodii Sovetskogo Dzhaza*. Moscow: Muzyka, 1988.

Savage, Barbara. *Broadcasting Freedom: Radio, War, and the Politics of Race, 1938–1948*. Chapel Hill: University of North Carolina Press, 1999.

Schneider, Mark R. *We Return Fighting: The Civil Rights Movement in the Jazz Age*. Boston: Northeastern University Press, 2002.

Schuller, Gunther. *Early Jazz: Its Roots and Musical Development*. New York: Oxford University Press, 1968.

Schwarz, Boris. *Music and Musical Life in Soviet Russia: 1917–1981*. Enl. ed. Bloomington: Indiana University Press, 1989.

Skinner, Elliott P. *African Americans and U.S. Policy toward Africa, 1850–1924: In Defense of Black Nationality*. Washington, D.C.: Howard University Press, 1992.

Smith, Suzanne. *Dancing in the Streets: Motown and the Cultural Politics of Detroit*. Cambridge, Mass.: Harvard University Press, 1999.

Sorensen, Theodore, ed. *Let the Word Go Forth: The Speeches, Statements and Writings of John F. Kennedy*. New York: Delacorte Press, 1988.

Southern, Eileen. *The Music of Black Americans: A History*. 2nd ed. New York: W. W. Norton, 1983.

Sowell, Thomas. *Race and Culture: A World View*. New York: Basic Books, 1994.

Starr, S. Frederick. *Red and Hot: The Fate of Jazz in the Soviet Union*. New York: Oxford University Press, 1983.

Stearns, Marshall. *The Story of Jazz*. New York: Sidgwick and Jackson, 1957.

Steinberg, Stephen. *Turning Back: The Retreat from Racial Justice in American Thought and Policy*. Boston: Beacon Press, 1995.

Stites, Richard S. *Russian Popular Culture: Entertainment and Society since 1900*. Cambridge: Cambridge University Press, 1992.

Stites, Richard S., and James von Geldern. *Mass Culture in Soviet Russia*. Bloomington: Indiana University Press, 1995.

Stovall, Tyler. *Paris Noir: African Americans in the City of Light*. Boston: Houghton Mifflin, 1996.

Stowe, David. *Swing Changes: Big Band Jazz in New Deal America*. Cambridge, Mass.: Harvard University Press, 1994.

Street, Joe. *The Culture War in the Civil Rights Movement*. Gainesville: University Press of Florida, 2007.

Sugiyama, Yasushi, ed. *Between Understanding and Misunderstanding: Problems and Prospects for International Cultural Exchange*. 2nd ed. Cambridge: Cambridge University Press, 1990.

Suri, Jeremi. *Power and Protest: Global Revolution and the Rise of Détente*. Cambridge, Mass.: Harvard University Press, 2003.

Swed, John. *So What: The Life of Miles Davis*. New York: Simon and Schuster, 2002.

Talbott, Strobe, ed. *Khrushchev Remembers*. Boston: Little Brown, 1970.

Thomas, Charles H., and Walter H. C. Laves. *Cultural Relations and U.S. Foreign Policy*. Bloomington: Indiana University Press, 1963.

Thomas, J. C. *Chasin' the Trane: The Music and Mystique of John Coltrane*. 1975. Reprint, New York: Da Capo Press, 1976.

Troupe, Quincy. *Miles and Me*. Berkeley: University of California Press, 2000.

Troupe, Quincy, and Miles Davis. *Miles: The Autobiography*. New York: Simon and Schuster, 1989.

Ulam, Adam. *Expansion and Coexistence*. 1968. Reprint, New York: Praeger Press, 1974.

Volkogonov, D. A. *Psikhologicheskaia Voina*. Moscow: Voennoe Izdatelstvo, 1984.

Von Eschen, Penny M. *Race against Empire: Black Americans and Anti-Colonialism, 1937–1957*. Ithaca, N.Y.: Cornell University Press, 1997.

———. *Satchmo Blows Up the World: Jazz Ambassadors Play the Cold War*. Cambridge, Mass.: Harvard University Press, 2004.

Wagnleitner, Reinhold. *Coca-Colonization and the Cold War: The Cultural Mission of the United States in Austria after the Second World War*. Chapel Hill: University of North Carolina Press, 1994.

Wagnleitner, Reinhold, and Elaine Tyler May, eds. *Here, There, and Everywhere: The Foreign Politics of American Popular Culture*. Hanover, N.H.: University Press of New England, 2000.

Ward, Geoffrey C., and Ken Burns. *Jazz: A History of America's Music*. New York: Alfred A. Knopf, 2000.

Webster, J. B., and A. A. Boahen. *The Revolutionary Years: West Africa since 1800*. Essex, England: Longman Group, 1980.

West, Cornel. *Race Matters*. 2nd ed. New York: Vintage Books, 2001.

West, Cornel, and Henry Louis Gates. *Future of the Race*. New York: Vintage Books, 1997.

Whitfield, Steven J. *The Culture of the Cold War*. 2nd ed. Baltimore: Johns Hopkins University Press, 1996.

Williams, William Appleman. *The Tragedy of American Diplomacy*. 1959. Reprint, New York: W. W. Norton, 1972.

Zubok, Vladislav. *The Soviet Union in the Cold War: From Stalin to Gorbachev*. Chapell Hill: University of North Carolina Press, 2007.

Zubok, Vladislav, and Constantine Pleshakov. *Inside the Kremlin's Cold War: From Stalin to Khrushchev*. Cambridge, Mass.: Harvard University Press, 1996.

Zubok, Vladislav, and Eric Shiraev. *Anti-Americanism in Russia From Stalin to Putin*. New York: Palgrave, 2000.

Index